Magic and Mysticism

Magic and Mysticism

An Introduction to Western Esotericism

Arthur Versluis

ROWMAN & LITTLEFIELD PUBLISHERS, INC.
Lanham • Boulder • New York • Toronto • Plymouth, UK

ROWMAN & LITTLEFIELD PUBLISHERS, INC.

Published in the United States of America
by Rowman & Littlefield Publishers, Inc.
A wholly owned subsidiary of The Rowman & Littlefield Publishing Group, Inc.
4501 Forbes Boulevard, Suite 200, Lanham, Maryland 20706
www.rowmanlittlefield.com

Estover Road
Plymouth PL6 7PY
United Kingdom

British Library Cataloguing in Publication Information Available

Library of Congress Cataloging-in-Publication Data:
Versluis, Arthur, 1959-
 Magic and mysticism : an introduction to Western esotericism / Arthur Versluis.
  p. cm.
 Includes bibliographical references and index.
 ISBN-13: 978-0-7425-5835-9 (cloth : alk. paper)
 ISBN-10: 0-7425-5835-5 (cloth : alk. paper)
 ISBN-13: 978-0-7425-5836-6 (paper : alk. paper)
 ISBN-10: 0-7425-5836-3 (paper : alk. paper)
 1. Occultism. I. Title.

 BF1411.V46 2007
 130—dc22   2007000378

Printed in the United States of America

∞™ The paper used in this publication meets the minimum requirements of American
National Standard for Information Sciences—Permanence of Paper for Printed Library
Materials, ANSI/NISO Z39.48-1992.

To those who were there at the very beginning, Antoine Faivre, Jean-Pierre Brach, H. T. Hakl, Wouter Hanegraaff, Claire Fanger, Joscelyn Godwin, Nicholas and Clare Goodrick-Clarke, Christopher McIntosh, Marco Pasi, Kocku von Stuckrad, and Karen-Claire Voss to the founding members of the Association for the Study of Esotericism, true colleagues every one, and to all who share the spirit of exploration.

Contents

Chapter One

Introduction

WHAT IS ESOTERICISM?

Strictly speaking, the term *esoteric* refers to knowledge reserved for a small group; it derives from the Greek word *esotero,* meaning "within," or "inner." In our context, the word *esoteric* implies inner or spiritual knowledge held by a limited circle, as opposed to *exoteric,* publicly known or "outer" knowledge. The term *Western esotericism,* then, refers to inner or hidden spiritual knowledge transmitted through Western European historical currents that in turn feed into North American and other non-European settings. Defined in this simple way, esoteric knowledge can be traced throughout Western history from antiquity to the present, even if it is richly varied in kind, ranging from the Mysteries of ancient Greece and Rome to Gnostic groups to Hermetic and alchemical practitioners, all the way to contemporary esoteric groups or new religious movements.

Characteristic of esotericism is a claim to gnosis, or direct spiritual insight into cosmology or metaphysics.[1] This characteristic has the advantage of being broad enough to include the full range of esoteric traditions, but narrow enough to exclude exoteric figures or movements. Furthermore, such a traditional term preserves the distinction between conventional or mostly rationally obtained knowledge on the one hand, and gnosis on the other. Alchemists search for direct spiritual insight into nature and seek to transmute certain substances thereby; astrologers seek direct spiritual insight into the cosmos and use it to analyze events; magicians seek direct spiritual insight and use it to affect the course of events; theosophers seek direct spiritual insight in order to realize their own "angelical nature." But in all cases, aspirants seek direct spiritual insight into the hidden nature of the cosmos and of themselves — they seek gnosis.

1

Esotericism refers, then, to the various traditions that emerge around these various approaches to gnosis, and one could as accurately refer to "Western gnostic" as "Western esoteric" traditions. Western esoteric traditions broadly speaking are, of course, widely varied in form and nature, but as we see below, they all have in common:

1. gnosis or gnostic insight, i.e., knowledge of hidden or invisible realms or aspects of existence (including both cosmological and metaphysical gnosis) and
2. esotericism, meaning that this hidden knowledge is either explicitly restricted to a relatively small group of people, or implicitly self-restricted by virtue of its complexity or subtlety.

In other words, Western esoteric traditions, generally speaking, entail secret or semisecret knowledge about humanity, the cosmos, and the divine.

MAGIC AND MYSTICISM

Both the words *magic* and *mysticism* remain somewhat nebulous. Scholars continue to disagree about what magic is, and for that matter, about what mysticism is. Commonly, of course, magic is held to do with achieving worldly aims through supernatural means; and mysticism is seen as a term describing those who seek and who claim to realize union with the divine. Yet these are problematic distinctions—many magicians seem rather mystical in inclination; and conversely, some mystics seem rather close to magic in what they espouse or claim. To give two examples: the well-known *Book of Abramelin the Mage* edited by S. L. MacGregor Mathers includes a ritual of seclusion and of a kind of mysticism (seeking union with one's guardian angel) that on the face of it does not seem to belong to "magic" so much as to mysticism. And one might also note the assertion of John Pordage (1608–1681) at the end of his *Letter on the Philosophic Stone* that one who followed his path of spiritual alchemy will become a magus. This is the expected achievement of one who follows the counsel of Pordage, arguably the greatest mystic of the theosophic tradition after Jacob Böhme![2] Clearly it is not as easy as it might seem to divide mysticism and magic into two discrete categories.

Still, we may broadly say that esoteric traditions tend to belong to one of two general currents: outward, toward cosmological mysteries, or inward, toward spiritual knowledge or knowledge of the divine. Of course, these two tendencies should not be too strictly interpreted, since they often overlap or merge. But one can distinguish roughly between magical traditions whose primary aims are essentially cosmological in nature—that is, more or less "worldly" in the sense of garnering wealth or power—and mystical traditions that explicitly reject worldly aims in favor of inner or spiritual illumination. This distinction is a fundamental one in the West, and we can see it recurring again and again. A mystic like Eckhart and a medieval magus or necromancer do belong to different currents, not least because whereas Eckhart seeks divine wisdom, the magus seeks cosmological knowledge or power. Magic has to do with power over others or over nature; often, the magician seeks to command. Mysticism, on the other hand, has to do with the surrender and transcendence of self and of power; the mystic's primary interest is not in worldly command but in realization of the divine.

Both magic and mysticism belong under the broad rubric of "esotericism" because both magicians and mystics pursue or claim esoteric knowledge that belongs only to them or to their tradition. They themselves exclude the hoi polloi and lay claim to inner or secret knowledge. Indeed, we can go further than that: for we may also say that magic and mysticism form the twin currents that, like the intertwined serpents of Hermes's caduceus, together make up much of the stream of Western esotericism. On the one hand, we have the current of cosmological gnosis to which belongs not only magic, but also alchemy, astrology, the various "mancies" like geomancy or chiromancy, and all those other forms of secret or semisecret knowledge of the cosmos. And on the other hand we have the current of metaphysical gnosis, the most lucid form of which is the negative mysticism of Dionysius the Areopagite or Meister Eckhart. Together, these two currents, which intertwine and separate, form the larger field of Western esotericism.

Put another way, magic and mysticism represent the ends of a spectrum that we may term Western esotericism, and most esoteric figures and groups are to be found in the middle, that is, incorporating aspects of both (see figure 1.1). Thus we may refer to "mystico-magical" or "magico-mystical" currents, along the lines of recent scholarship in Jewish esotericism. Moshe Idel refers to a "theosophical-theurgical" model—dealing with "the map of the divine realm (theosophy) and the way in which human deeds affect it (theurgy)"—as the most common in kabbalistic tradition.[3] But he also refers to a "mystico-magical model" that represents not the "escape of the soul from this world into the spiritual universe" so much as "the induction" or "even the compulsion of the divine powers within the material world." Thus divine annihilation may be a means of reaching "magical, energetic attainments."[4] While we can find examples of a "theosophical-theurgical" model in Western esotericism, especially in the lineage of Jacob Böhme, examples of "mystico-magical" or "magico-mystical" models are much more widespread. Understood in this way, alchemical writings, for instance, may be neither a mystical code nor a magical protochemistry, but partake of both currents at once.

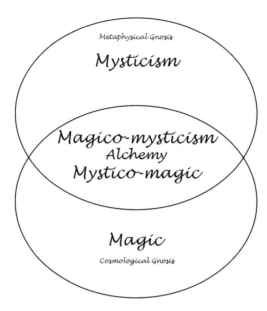

Metaphysical Gnosis
Mysticism

Magico-mysticism
Alchemy
Mystico-magic

Magic
Cosmological Gnosis

Figure 1.1.

Whether under the rubrics of magic or mysticism, *gnosis* refers to direct insight into what is largely hidden from rationalistic modes of knowledge. A primary difference is in intention: the mystic seeks direct insight for its own sake, whereas the magus seeks to have effects in the world. But as the scholar of Jewish esotericism Elliot Wolfson reminds us, "ecstasy and theurgy can be seen as two manifestations of the same phenomenon." Driven by "extraneous taxonomic concerns," he continues, contemporary scholars indeed may "artificially separate" what in fact are "concurrent" or closely related processes.[5] Just so. I am not suggesting that magic and mysticism are the same thing, but rather that they both, as cosmological and metaphysical forms of gnosis, belong to and indeed help to define the larger spectrum of the esoteric.

DYNAMIC MODES OF THE ESOTERIC

Of course, the Christian West has a long history of heretic hunting that goes back to the foundational period of late antiquity, and that later was institutionalized in the Inquisitions during the medieval period. As I show in *The New Inquisitions*, we still are influenced by the legacy of heretic hunting, which continues to inform religion, politics, and even scholarship right up to the present.[6] What Wouter Hanegraaff calls the "grand polemical narrative" of antioccultism and heresiophobia remains a shaping force in scholarship, even in scholarship on esoteric religious traditions.[7] As a result, there are almost uncharted areas of Western religious and cultural history, mainly because these areas were often dismissed with terms like *heresy*, or *occultism*, or *superstition*. The history of esotericism has to be seen in light of this antiesoteric dynamic, which continues to manifest itself .

An implicit antiesotericism sometimes appears in a rigorously externalist approach that by its very nature remains outside and even hostile to the esotericism that it apparently studies. In the sphere of the esoteric, this is potentially far more disastrous than a "religionist" approach that at least seeks to understand an esoteric tradition, figure, or group on its own terms. Externalism is visible in a variety of reductionisms, including deconstructionism. As Moshe Idel puts it, whereas "traditional radicalism in Kabbalah was ready to deconstruct the text in order to find God by a more direct experience," "modern deconstruction had first to kill God or transcendental meaning in order to divinize the text."[8] Magic and mysticism as subjects of academic study are still marginalized, in part because of the long-standing antiesoteric bias in the West, and by the related desire to turn both subjects into objects of rationalist discourse and manipulation.

What I am suggesting, in other words, is that in magic and mysticism we see areas of study that by their very nature are not entirely reducible to objects of rationalist discourse and manipulation, but instead border on and open into dimensions of life that remain partially veiled to us unless we enter into them for ourselves. Better than alternative terms, the word *gnosis* helps convey some sense of these other dimensions of consciousness. Esotericism, in other words, borders on consciousness studies, and its experiential center also results in its inherent and definitive syncretism (mingling disparate religious beliefs) or syncrasis (mingling practices). From antiquity to the present, esoteric practitioners have consistently mingled together disparate beliefs, traditions, and practices in order to create new esoteric syntheses. As the study of esotericism continues, it will have to develop more sophisticated phenomenological ways of approaching and understanding what is esoteric.

Such approaches may be in terms of dynamic social relationships. These relationships can be characterized in terms of polarities, for instance, (1) insider/outsider, or esoteric/exoteric, closely related to a heretic/orthodox dynamic—a recurrent refrain throughout the history of Western esotericism; (2) experiential gnostic/rationalist. Esoteric currents like alchemy, magic, or mysticism inherently include experiential dimensions that can be described as gnostic, that is, direct experiential knowledge of invisible or transcendent realms; and (3) synthetic flexibility/rigid doctrinalism or heretic/orthodox.

Esotericism tends toward fluid joining of disparate religious traditions or practices but is often defined from the outside by heresiophobic rhetoric. All of these represent social vectors that help shape esotericism as a dynamic phenomenon. Although this book is an introduction to the twin esoteric themes of magic and mysticism, it is also informed by awareness of how esotericism is shaped by social dynamics, and of the potential benefits of remaining open rather than closed or self-consciously external, let alone hostile to one's subjects.

ESOTERICISM AS A FIELD FOR ACADEMIC INQUIRY

Until relatively recently, the field of "esotericism" or "esoteric studies" remained more or less ignored in academia. There were, of course, major individual works devoted to the field in the mid- to late twentieth century—one thinks, for instance, of the books of historian Frances Yates, and of course of the many books and articles by Antoine Faivre, on his own a major force in the development of Western esotericism as a domain of inquiry. But throughout most of the nineteenth and twentieth centuries, there had remained almost no acknowledgment in academia that "esotericism" or "Western esoteric traditions" could be seen as constituting a whole area of study, that such diverse traditions or movements as alchemy, astrology, magic, Rosicrucianism, and theosophy all bear certain defining elements in common and should be considered in the larger historical context of Western esoteric traditions from antiquity onward. This situation, however, most emphatically has begun to change.

There are a number of reasons for the new scholarly interest in Western esotericism. From the seventeenth through the twentieth centuries, academic institutions and scholars tended to more or less assiduously ignore those fields or topics that might be seen as calling into question the premises of scientific materialism, or that had historically been censured by the Christian church. Additionally, a field like Western esotericism cuts across numerous academic disciplinary boundaries and cannot easily be pigeonholed, especially since study of such traditions entails work in disciplines ranging from history and religious studies to literature and art history, to name only a few. In many respects, Western esoteric traditions have remained closed areas of scholarly inquiry, shut off by a variety of artificial barriers.

But by the late twentieth century, many scholars had recognized the concept of "transdisciplinarity," meaning the possibility of scholarly exploration beyond or in the interstices between particular disciplinary limitations. A major figure in this movement is the French physicist Basarab Nicolescu, who founded an international association devoted to transdisciplinarity, and who himself published a book on the potential relationships between the Christian theosophy of Jacob Böhme and the contemporary sciences, in particular physics. This new openness to interdisciplinary and transdisciplinary scholarly research reflects what may be a fundamental shift in modern academia away from strict disciplinary boundaries and into new fields of research.

It seems no coincidence that at precisely the same time that transdisciplinarity emerged in academia, so too the investigation of Western esoteric traditions began to flourish. Antoine Faivre held the first academic chair, in the Sorbonne, devoted specifically to this field (a position now occupied by Jean-Pierre Brach); and Wouter Hanegraaff holds a specially endowed chair, at the University of Amsterdam. Nicholas Goodrick-Clarke is professor of Western Esotericism and director of the Exeter Center for the Study of Esotericism at the University of Exeter in England. In addition, the number of scholarly publications devoted to this field began to multiply; the State University of New York Press and Peeters Publishing both developed publications series in the field, and a number of international journals emerged, including *ARIES* and *Esoterica* (www.esoteric.msu.edu). What is more, the International Association for the History of Religion (IAHR) and the American Academy of Religion (AAR) have begun to include whole sections devoted to Western esotericism. In North America, the Association for the Study of Esotericism (ASE) was founded in 2001 and held its first international conference (see www.aseweb.org) in 2004; shortly thereafter, the European Society for the Study of Western Esotericism (ESSWE) was founded.

The contemporary academic study of esotericism began with Antoine Faivre, author of *Access to Western Esotericism*, who works historically and typologically. He defines six basic characteristics of modern Western esoteric thought (i.e., from the seventeenth century to the present), these being:

1. *Correspondences.* As the Hermetic dictum has it, "as above, so below," meaning that there are precise correspondences between all aspects of the universe, including between the human microcosm and the macrocosm.
2. *Living Nature.* Nature is not a collection of objects to be manipulated, but alive and connected via hidden, subtle forces that can be awakened and drawn upon through *magia naturalis*, natural magic.
3. *Imagination and Mediations.* Here imagination refers not to wild fantasy, but to a means of spiritual perception, insight into the *mundus imaginalis* or spiritual realm(s) that can be seen only by those with purified vision.
4. *Experience of Transmutation.* Transmutation here refers to metamorphosis, sometimes of natural substances (as of lead into gold via alchemical work) and sometimes of the individual (from ignorance to illumination).

5. *Praxis of the Concordance.* Essentially, Faivre refers here to the tendency of esotericists to see the parallels between various traditions, as when in antiquity one finds Hermetists who are also Gnostic Christians. It is very close to syncretism or syncrasis—the joining of various traditions in practice.

6. *Transmission.* An emphasis on the importance of the initiatic chain—the transmission of secret knowledge from master to disciple—a tendency found in traditions as disparate as alchemy and magic.[9]

Faivre's typology emphasizes the cosmological dimensions of esotericism and focuses on the early modern and modern periods, whereas other scholars have sought to widen the scope of the field. Dutch scholar Wouter Hanegraaff argues, in a whole series of articles, for an empiricohistorical approach to a field that de facto ranges from antiquity to the New Age.[10] A German scholar, Kocku von Stuckrad, argues even more broadly from a perspective of discourse analysis that Western esotericism has two primary characteristics: claims to higher knowledge, and means of access to that higher knowledge. "Higher knowledge" is "a vision of truth as a master key for answering all questions of humankind," and the means to higher knowledge include primarily the mediation of revelatory beings like Hermes, and direct individual experience.[11] My own approach here is a new, inclusive one that incorporates many aspects of these other perspectives and draws from a range of disciplines while remaining historically grounded.

One of the most striking future areas for investigation lies in comparative religious studies. Many Western esoteric traditions parallel Asian religious traditions in various ways—there are, for instance, Asian alchemical traditions that correspond strikingly to some forms of European alchemy; just as there are some interesting parallels between Vajrayana Buddhism and Christian theosophy, or between Asian and European astrological or magical traditions. These are all comparative fields that remain largely unexamined and that could shed much light on the traditions concerned. But investigations of this nature require great sophistication of knowledge in a range of fields and languages, as well as extensive general knowledge of various eras. In many respects, only now are such comparisons even possible.

In short, it appears we stand on the brink of a new era for scholarship in esotericism. The aim of this book is to orient readers and potential scholars to this particular field and to its possibilities, but also to provide a new, more integrative approach. Some authors have warned against bringing esotericism into the academy, and there are indeed dangers in doing so.[12] However, by approaching these esoteric figures and traditions historically and empirically, working integratively rather than by approaching them with any particular ideological axe to grind, we may well discover much of value that had too hastily been jettisoned or ignored in the past several centuries. What follows is a new, historically grounded approach to esotericism that focuses on the twin themes of magic and mysticism, of cosmological and metaphysical gnosis. One enters into the field with a sense of adventure, and I hope that this sense of adventure both pervades this work and will continue in the future, for that above all is the sign under which investigation in this field necessarily proceeds.[13]

NOTES

1. Some might object to the term *cosmological gnosis* to describe, say, a magical ritual, but if we consider that the practice of magic, including erotic or other kinds of mundane magic, entails an effort at union with or effects upon others or on the cosmos through union with (or partial union through control of) unseen forces or principles, then the word *gnosis* modified in this way becomes appropriate. The kind of knowing implied in magical or mystical gnoses is not identical with rationally obtained knowledge, and hence another term than *knowledge* is preferable.

2. See, for example, *The Book of the Sacred Magic of Abramelin the Mage,* ed. S. L. Macgregor Mathers (London: Watkins, 1900), which includes a ritual of seclusion and of a kind of mysticism (seeking union with one's guardian angel) that on the face of it does not seem to belong to "magic." See also William Bloom, *The Sacred Magician: A Ceremonial Diary* (Glastonbury, UK: Gothic Image, 1992). Bloom sought to pursue the ritual magical tradition that is said to lead to union with one's guardian angel. For Pordage's assertion, see Arthur Versluis, ed., *Wisdom's Book: The Sophia Anthology* (St. Paul, MN: Paragon House, 2000), 76. The specific sociological and anthropological controversies over *magic* and *mysticism* are simply too extensive to delve into here. Various books that address these controversies include Bruce Kapferer, *Beyond Rationalism: Rethinking Magic, Witchcraft, and Sorcery* (New York: Berghahn, 2003); Owen Davies, *Cunning-folk: Popular Magic in English History* (London: Hambledon, 2003); and Paul Mirecki and Marvin Meyer, *Magic and Ritual in the Ancient World* (Leiden: Brill, 2002), to cite only a handful of the most recent. Likewise, one could cite the various books and articles belonging to the controversies over mysticism, especially the works of, on the one side, Stephen Katz, and on the other, Robert K. C. Forman.

3. See Moshe Idel, *Kabbalah and Eros* (New Haven, CT: Yale University Press, 2005), 214.

4. Idel, *Kabbalah and Eros,* 86–87.

5. See Elliot Wolfson, *Language, Eros, Being: Kabbalistic Hermeneutics and Poetic Imagination* (New York: Fordham University Press, 2005), 209–10.

6. See Arthur Versluis, *The New Inquisitions: Heretic-hunting and the Origins of Modern Totalitarianism* (New York: Oxford University Press, 2006).

7. Wouter J. Hanegraaff, "Forbidden Knowledge: Anti-Esoteric Polemics and Academic Research," *Aries* 5 (2005) 2: 225–54.

8. See Moshe Idel, *Absorbing Perfections: Kabbalah and Interpretation* (New Haven, CT: Yale University Press, 2002), 419.

9. Antoine Faivre, *Access to Western Esotericism* (Albany: SUNY Press, 1994), 10–15.

10. See Wouter Hanegraaff, "Empirical Method in the Study of Esotericism," in *Method and Theory in the Study of Religion* 7 (1995) 2: 99–129; Hanegraaff, "On the Construction of 'Esoteric Traditions,'" in A. Faivre and W. Hanegraaff, eds., *Western Esotericism and the Science of Religion* (Leuven: Peeters, 1998), 11–61; Hanegraaff, "Beyond the Yates Paradigm: The Study of Western Esotericism between Counter-culture and New Complexity," *Aries* 1 (2001) 1: 5–37; and Hanegraaff, "The Study of Western Esotericism: New Approaches to Christian and Secular Culture," in Peter Antes, Armin Geertz, and Randi Warne, eds., *New Approaches to the Study of Religion* (Berlin: DeGruyter, 2004).

11. See Kocku von Stuckrad, "Western Esotericism: Towards an Integrative Model of Interpretation," in *Religion* 35 (2005) 78–97, in particular, 88–89, 92–93. To these two, he adds a third, which is "ontological monism," that is, "their cosmology derives from world views that constitute a unity of material and non-material realms of reality." And he concludes by noting that just as it is not necessary to define "religion" too specifically in order to conduct research in religious studies—there is a generally agreed-upon area of research—so too there is a rough agreement on the domain of esotericism. This is, in general, true. See also Kocku von Stuckrad, *Western Esotericism: A Brief History of Secret Knowledge* (London: Equinox, 2005).

12. See Richard Smoley and Jay Kinney, *Hidden Wisdom: A Guide to the Western Inner Traditions* (Wheaton, IL: Quest, 2006), xi.

13. A note regarding documentation: when possible, I cite from section and chapter or other general headings in primary sources so that they can be referenced easily in different editions. My guiding principle is to rely on primary works when possible, and to suggest some secondary works that may be useful if readers wish to pursue a given topic further.

Chapter Two

Antiquity

The roots of Western esoteric traditions are manifold, but there are a number of specific sources that we consider here. Among these are (1) ancient mystery traditions, (2) ancient Greek and Roman magical traditions, (3) Plato and Platonism, followed by (4) Hermetism, (5) Gnosticism, (6) Jewish mysticism, and (7) Christian gnosis, exemplified by such figures as Origen, Clement of Alexandria, and Dionysius the Areopagite. To these, we could also add more extraneous currents like Manichaeism, although the precise influences of the religion of light, for example, are not quite so clear or enduring as these others. We discuss each of these sources in turn, but begin where the word *esoteric* itself derives from—with the Mystery traditions of antiquity.

However, for thematic reasons, I would like to begin with a fundamental distinction proposed by Christian gnostic Dionysius the Areopagite between what he termed the *via positiva*, or the path of symbols, and the *via negativa*, or the path of negation or absolute transcendence. We discuss Dionysius's work in detail in the next section, but here I would like to remark on the apparent predominance, in the ancient Egyptian tradition, of hieroglyphic symbolism. As we look at what remains to us of antiquity, the various steles and wall carvings, we certainly could conclude that both in the Egyptian tradition and in the subsequent Greco-Roman Mystery traditions, the *via positiva* or path of symbols predominates. In antiquity, initiatory truths were conveyed primarily through myths and symbols and affiliated rites, and not so much through the kinds of sheer negation that one finds in what Dionysius calls the *via negativa*. This is an important general remark to make because so much of the subsequent Western esoteric traditions also were to correspond to the *via positiva* rather than to the *via negativa*. One might attribute this tendency toward the symbolic in part to the Egyptian origins of Greco-Roman Mystery and Hermetic traditions.

Western esoteric traditions exist in a continuum, the beginnings of which may be traceable as much to ancient Egypt as to any other source. Recent scholarship has at least demonstrated that Greco-Roman Hermetism did indeed draw upon Egyptian sources, as did the Mystery traditions of antiquity. The Mysteries were certainly esoteric traditions, in that those who were initiated into the various Mystery traditions were forbidden to disclose them to noninitiates, and as a result, we have relatively little knowledge of what actually went on in the ancient Mysteries. Still, as Garth Fowden points out in his book *The Egyptian Hermes*, "the intellectual origins and context of Hermetism, viewed in ever closer relationship to traditional Egyptian thought and to gnosticism, are the subject of a fast-increasing number of scholarly studies."[1]

Prominent among these studies are Fowden's own, and those of Jean-Pierre Mahé, both of whom have shown conclusively the links between Egyptian traditions and the Greco-Roman Mystery and magical traditions. Up to and through the twentieth century, it was conventional to dismiss many of the Greek or Roman claims of direct connections to Egyptian traditions. But by the end of the twentieth century, the tide had turned, so that for instance the prophecies about the fall of Egypt and Egyptian tradition found in the *Perfect Discourse (Asclepius)*, read variously as prophesying the fall of paganism before Christianity [the view of Lactantius and Augustine], or as mere insertions into the *Hermetica*, in fact can now be read as genuinely reflecting much earlier Egyptian traditional views concerning the loss of Egyptian religious culture. "Egypt will be abandoned," we read in the *Hermetica*; in the coming dark age, Egypt will become merely a desert; the wicked will be regarded as good; the temples will be abandoned; only evil spirits will remain, to goad men into war and crime; and the earth will become barren. Only after such prophecies are fulfilled will the Golden Age come, and a renewed Egypt. These prophecies, Fowden argues, reflect a genuinely Egyptian viewpoint, as do the warnings in the *Hermetica* concerning the importance of maintaining traditional Egyptian instead of translating Egyptian into Greek.[2]

Why would the Greeks and Romans have drawn on Egyptian traditions so extensively, as Fowden, Mahé, and others have argued? There are a number of reasons. One is the immense antiquity of Egyptian culture, and its consequent mystique. By drawing on Egyptian culture, Greeks and Romans could lay claim to a power and authority that Greek or Roman cultures on their own did not have. Thus, for instance, Greco-Roman cultures had a tendency to regard fate as implacable (as evidenced by Stoic philosophy); whereas a Greek could turn to Egyptian gods like Isis or Serapis or Hermes-Thoth because they were believed to have power that went beyond the implacability of fate.[3] Egyptian tradition was regarded by the Greco-Romans as synonymous with magic and ancient wisdom as well as divinatory power, so it is not surprising that the Mystery traditions and the *Hermetica* reflected this.

THE MYSTERIES

The Greco-Roman Mystery traditions were often closely tied to Egypt even if the traditions themselves, like the Bacchic or Dionysiac Mysteries, were not themselves necessarily Egyptian in origin. In part, this linkage derived from the presence in Egypt of many Greeks, especially in the area of Alexandria. In fact, the Ptolemaic kings themselves "favoured the cult of Dionysius;" "the devotion of Ptolemy Philopator to Dionysius is well known."[4] But the Mysteries, whether celebrated by kings or ordinary country folk, were celebrated with copious symbolism and imagery; they most emphatically belonged more to the *via positiva* (broadly speaking) and might well be seen as a central reason that the later Western esoteric traditions also tended toward cosmological mysteries.

In the Eleusinian Mysteries, an initiate was called an *epoptes*, or one who beholds, while a priest was called a *hierophant*, or one who reveals the sacred. Visual symbolism, obviously, was important, and the Mystery traditions, particularly when celebrated under the auspices of a king, were quite striking in pageantry. Typically in such a pageant, the statue of Dionysius would be carried on a car decorated with vines and fruits of every kind, and followed by a great train of Satyrs and Bacchants, as well as many women wreathed with ivy. Behind would follow a giant phallus on a car, and a wine press, much wine, and drinking vessels, as Dionysius was the god of wine. Similar pageants were held for the other Mystery traditions at the appropriate times of the year, many held only at night and some traditionally celebrated chiefly or exclusively by women.

The Mysteries are most well known, of course, for their orgiastic celebrations, or *orgia*. While it seems likely that some lurid Roman accounts of drunkenness, orgies, and even ritual murder and cannibalism in the celebration of the Bacchic Mysteries were exaggerated in the manner of tabloid journalism, the fact remains that there are so many allusions to or accusations of orgiastic celebrations among the initiates in antiquity that it becomes impossible to deny that something of the sort went on. As is well known, the Roman historian Livy tells how the Bacchanalia entailed "not one form of vice alone," but many, including drunkenness, promiscuity, even poisoning and murder concealed by clashing cymbals and drums.[5] Those who were privy to the Mysteries had passwords by which they could know one another, all of which led to scandalous accusations among the Romans that the *Bacchantes* were a threat to Roman security, and eventually to persecutions and the execution of thousands of people.[6]

This said, it is important to consider why orgiastic celebrations might have taken place in antiquity. Here, we may leave aside questions concerning the possible or even likely later degeneration of the Mystery traditions, and simply look at the religious symbolism involved. The Mystery traditions were often indivisible from nature and the seasons: they brought together the powers of nature and the human world, and infused both with divine power. To hold a celebration of Demeter at night is at once to invoke the divine power of the goddess in the blessing of nature or the earth in order that human society might also flourish. But to invoke divine power is not necessarily a mild affair: divine power is vast and not subject to human constructs. To invoke the power of Dionysius is to let loose sheer wildness; orgiastic behavior is both an invocation and a manifestation of Dionysian force whose effect is to renovate both the natural and the human realms. The theme of orgiastic celebration is a recurring one in subsequent esoteric traditions, even if only as an accusation against this or that medieval or modern group.

APULEIUS, *THE GOLDEN ASS*

If the Mysteries' best-known aspect is orgiastic celebration, this is perhaps because so little is known about the origins or the nature of the Mysteries as they were practiced. One of the only surviving accounts from the viewpoint of an initiate is that found in the second century A.D. account of Apuleius in his delightful novel *The Golden Ass*.[7] In this novel, we follow the comical and often bawdy fortunes of Lucius, who early on in the book is turned into an ass—literally. In this form, he undergoes many adventures, and then in the eleventh book, he finds himself on the shore of the ocean under a full moon. Desperate, he dips his head in the ocean water seven times and cries out a prayer to Isis, the goddess of the moon, who then appears to him in her full splendor. This revelation is perhaps the only account we have from antiquity that gives us a sense of the initiate's devotion.

Lucius falls asleep and in sleep he sees Isis herself, who has an abundance of hair crowned by many wreaths and flowers. Her garments are many colored, but wrapped with a pitch-black cloak sprinkled with stars, in the center a full moon, its border garlanded with fruits and flowers. She carries a brass sistrum, a three-stringed instrument, as well as a golden vessel containing a serpent, and her shoes are woven of palm. Breathing forth with breath spiced with Arabian scents she tells Lucius that she is the mother of all life, the supreme divinity, queen of all in Hades, first of all in heaven, she whose name is venerated over all the earth in many forms. Her true name is Isis, and she comes to tell him that when the Mystery pageant takes place the following day, he must eat of the priest's roses, and he will be freed of his asinine form. Her only requirement: that he serve her until his death as one of her initiates.

The following day, Lucius does as she says and is indeed returned from asinine to human form. The priest then remarks that Lucius is freed from the bonds of misery and is victorious over his fate by the providential power of the mighty Isis. This, of course, is not the initiation, which takes place later. This Lucius describes as taking place in a temple where the priest reveals secret books written in hieroglyphic characters. Lucius fasts for ten days and is brought into the temple where—he cannot divulge what happens. Yet he tells us that he approached death, the realm of Proserpine, and saw the sun shining at midnight; he approached the gods and stood among them. This, he says, was his experience, but it makes sense only to other initiates, and more he cannot tell us. There is a slightly sardonic quality to Apuleius's narration, but at the very least, his novel does offer some narrative sense of what the Mysteries must have been like.

PLATO AND PLATONISM

Without doubt, the Mysteries do remain one of the foundational influences on the later Western esoteric traditions. Another major such influence, itself at least in part a reflection of the Mystery traditions, is Platonism. Here, of course, we do not have space to discuss Platonism in detail, but only to outline esoteric aspects of Plato's writings as well as of the subsequent Platonic philosophic tradition. Plato (427–347 B.C.) is best known for having written down the dialogues of Socrates, his teacher, who was sentenced to death by his fellow Athenians for having "corrupted" youth with his philosophic questioning. The Platonic dialogues are often depicted as emphasizing rational inquiry as the basis for philosophic knowledge, a depiction that belies the more esoteric aspects to be found therein, particularly those elements that directly reflect the Mysteries' more esoteric forms of knowledge.

Probably the most famous of Plato's dialogues is known as the *Republic*, a work in which Socrates discusses the ideal polity and related topics. While *Republic* certainly includes discussion of more or less exoteric matters like the best forms of government, there are also clearly esoteric themes in the work as well. The best-known of these is of course the allegory of the Cave of Book VII, in which Socrates offers a parable about human existence. Imagine, he says, human beings living in an underground den, where they have been chained. Above and behind them is a fire, so that the prisoners see the

shadows of those who walk near them. Imagine further that one of the prisoners is liberated and is allowed to step into the light: he is blinded at first,
but then he has clearer vision and sees not shadows but the actual objects.
Suppose further he then is brought into the upper world, where he sees the
dazzling light of the sun. This too is painful, but eventually his eyes adjust.
When he returns to the Cave, he is at first unfamiliar with the darkness, and
the dwellers there do not want to hear about the world above, in which they
disbelieve.[8]

In brief: the one liberated from the Cave is privy to esoteric knowledge,
while those within the Cave probably do not wish to hear what he has to say.
Socrates concludes that the Cave-prison is the world of sight, and the journey
upward is the ascent of the soul into the intellectual world. It is no surprise,
he continues, that those who attain to the beatific vision of the upper world
are not inclined to descend into the lower one of mankind again. But they
must do so, for only they will be able to discern what is true, and act for the
best interests of all, rather than chasing shadows as the majority of humanity
does now. That state in which rulers are most reluctant to govern is always the
best and most quietly governed, and the state in which they are most eager,
the worst. It is a sacrifice for those with esoteric knowledge of the upper
world to return to the darkness of the Cave, yet it is their duty, even if those
in the Cave do not wish to see the truth but only to chase shadows.

This famous allegory of the Cave reveals themes that reappear throughout
the subsequent history of Western esoteric traditions, above all, the conflict
between the uninitiated and those who have eyes to see. The entire allegory
plays on the idea of spiritual vision—indeed, the esoteric knowledge in question is gained by *sight*—and this in turn directly reflects the Mystery traditions in which the initiates were known as *epoptes*: those who have seen. Now
there are cultures in the world that center on and support those who are spiritual visionaries—Tibetan Buddhism comes to mind—but it certainly is the
case in the West that from the death of Socrates to the death of Christ to the
death of Giordano Bruno onward, there has been a marked tendency for those
who are not initiates to oppose or attack those who see themselves as or are
perceived as initiates or spiritual visionaries. The *Republic* also resonates
with the recurrent idea of creating a spiritual utopia governed by an enlightened elite, a concept found much later, for example, in the Rosicrucian movement of the seventeenth century.

The second aspect of *Republic* that we might remark upon is found in the
tale of Er the Pamphylian, found in Book X, 614. Er was slain in battle, but
ten days afterward his body was found to be undecayed, and on the twelfth
day he awoke and told of what he saw in the next world. Er had gone on an
otherworldly journey out of his body, where he saw those who had died ei-

ther ascending by a heavenly path to an Elysian field, or descending to a place of punishment. After eight days, those in the field were then sent to a place where they beheld a column of colored light like an axis of heaven and earth, on which turned the "spindle of Fate," along which spun the various planets. The souls there must choose their new lives, and so they do, eventually being driven to their new births like shooting stars. Shortly after seeing this, Er came to on the funeral pyre and could tell his story because he had not (as the other souls did) drunk of the river of Lethe or forgetfulness. Socrates concludes the tale, and *Republic*, by admonishing Glaucon to pass safely over the river of forgetfulness so that his soul is not defiled, and so that it will be well for him (and us) in this "pilgrimage of a thousand years."[9]

Here again we have esoteric themes recurrent in the West as in cultures around the world: first, that of the individual who has seen into the secrets of nonphysical existence; and second, that of the corresponding secrets of the cosmos. In the vision of Er, we are introduced not only to the concept of reincarnation, but also to the idea that there is a hidden structure in the cosmos to which only those with spiritual vision are privy. Important in this hidden structure are the planetary spheres, again a theme that we see repeated not only among the Gnostics in late antiquity, but also in the medieval and into the modern era. Here, as in the allegory of the Cave, we find in Plato what is clearly an esoteric tradition that is transmitted orally from Socrates to Glaucon. By knowing this tradition, one becomes able to free oneself from Fate or necessity, and thus it reflects the ancient Mysteries. It also inaugurates a common and perhaps paradoxical tendency in Western esotericism: that esoteric ideas are written down and thus conveyed in a more or less public form, one available to those who can read it.[10]

The final Platonic theme we must mention is that found in *Phaedrus*—the theme of art, specifically poetry, as closely allied to spiritual illumination. In *Phaedrus*, Socrates discusses various kinds of "divine madness" and eventually comes to the fourth, that of one who recalls the beauty and delight shining in brightness of the other world. One whose initiation into these mysteries is recent is close to these kinds of beauty, seeing them even in this world, and as it were "grows" a pair of wings in order to fly upward again. Others might think such a one mad, but in fact this is a holy state like that of a lover drawn to a beloved. The language here is clearly initiatory, as is that of the second major theme—writing. Socrates remarks that writing, attributed in origin to the Egyptian god Thoth, is a kind of falsification: what is written down is not real but only a facsimile. Initiatory secrets are conveyed orally, not in writing.

These two themes form the final ways that Plato's dialogues correspond to later esoteric traditions. Throughout the history of Western esoteric traditions, one finds that esoteric knowledge is transmitted chiefly through works of art, hieroglyphically, if you will, and through writing. It is no accident that Plato's *Phaedrus* ends with a discussion of the Egyptian mysteries of Thoth and their relation to writing—precisely the same theme is found in the *Hermetica* of late antiquity, where the author laments the loss of oral secret knowledge when it is written down and translated. Throughout the Western esoteric traditions, one finds this paradox reiterated: from Plato's dialogues to Gnosticism right up to the modern period, esoteric knowledge is conveyed in symbolic and written form even as the various authors acknowledge that writing and the symbols do not truly convey the esoteric knowledge. This paradox may well have its origin in Egyptian hieroglyphics, which after all are simultaneously symbolic images and writing at once.

Subsequent major Platonic figures include Plotinus (205–270 A.D.), Porphyry (233–305), Iamblichus (260–330), author of *De Mysteriis [On the Mysteries]*, and Proclus (412–485). Of these, the most influential is of course the first, Plotinus, whose *Enneads* continue to attract many readers and ongoing philosophical analysis. In the *Enneads* are without doubt some of the most sublime passages in all of ancient philosophy, as when he writes of the ascent to sheer transcendence and the ineffability of the One. That there is an esoteric cast to Plotinus's writings is visible near the end of *Enneads*, where he writes of "that rule of our Mysteries: 'Nothing divulged to the non-initiate'"[11] Holy things, he continues, are not to be revealed to strangers or to any "who has not himself attained to see." Yet even those who have never found entry into this Transcendence must admit the existence of the Invisible, and those who are instructed or initiated may read the signs aright, enter the holy place itself, and actually see what now is Invisible. This, Plotinus concludes, is the aim of human life: liberation from the sufferings of earthly existence, the ascent of the Alone to the Alone.

But Plato and the Platonic tradition have long been criticized for their focus on transcendence and their rejection of matter and of earthly life. As is well known, Plotinus was reported to have said that he at times felt ashamed of having a body, this even though in *Enneads* he inveighs against those (evidently Christian Gnostics) who vilify the corporeal. While Plotinus defends the beauty and divinity of the cosmos, he acknowledges that Plato himself indicts the body as a hindrance to the soul (II.9.17). The difference, in the end, Plotinus tells us, is that the Gnostics and the Platonists are like two people in a stately house: one of them inveighs against its architect, while the other cheerfully resides there and looks forward to the day when he may leave it (II.9.18). At any rate, in Plotinus and the other Platonists one does see a kind of middle-way approach to the body that has more in common with Hindu and Buddhist perspectives than with the kind of extreme anticosmism sometimes attributed to groups under the heading of "Gnostic."[12]

Regardless of how one interprets the various Platonic views of the body and the cosmos, Platonism remains quite influential in subsequent esoteric traditions for two primary reasons: first, because throughout it has explicitly esoteric dimensions, and second, because it provides a clear philosophic framework not only for the Mystery traditions upon which it draws for its symbolism and language but also for its theurgic or ritual magical aspects. The theurgic or magical side of Platonism, represented especially by Iamblichus and Proclus, has largely been shunted aside in favor of those works and figures more amenable to a modern rationalist perspective, but when one looks at subsequent Western esoteric traditions and particularly Renaissance "white magic," it is not the rational so much as the theurgic aspect of Platonism that predominates. But this we discuss later.

GRECO-ROMAN MAGIC

When we delve into the sphere of Greco-Roman magical practices, we are entering into the realm of folk magic, of practices meant to accomplish particular ends, like attracting a certain man or woman, or like vanquishing one's enemies. The more one studies magical practices from, say, the fifth century B.C. to the fifth century A.D., the more matter-of-fact and seemingly ubiquitous one finds them to be. Archaeologists continue to unearth *defixiones*, tablets or images meant for cursing or controlling others; and there remain a number of magical papyri, collections of magical spells from antiquity that draw on a wide array of divinities or supernatural powers or beings. These spells or *defixiones* for the most part reflect the very mundane or prosaic goals of ordinary folk magic: they represent supernatural means of making one's way in the world.

Magical spells in antiquity tend to work in one of three ways: first, by simply asking a deity or power to accomplish some end; second, by giving the deity something, like incense, and then "billing" the deity by saying "I have done X for you, and now it's your turn to accomplish Y"; and third, by outright threatening and commanding a deity by saying "you must accomplish X for me or you will get no rest." In his collection entitled *Arcana Mundi*, Georg Luck includes quite a number of spells that fall into one or two of these categories. A fairly typical example of the first category is to be found in the *Papyri Graecae Magicae*, in a love charm that entails making wax or clay figures of the man and the woman, into the latter of which the magician is to stick thirteen iron needles in various parts of her body. Then, after writing on a lead plate, the magus or the customer is to recite "I deposit this binding spell with you, gods of the underworld," "Kore, Persephone . . . Hermes . . . Anubis" to "bring me A, the daughter of B, and make her love me." She is to have no peace until she is with whoever is ordering this ritual.[13]

Spells like these—that simply invoke the power of an often very heterodox series of divinities from numerous traditions—are most common in Greco-Roman antiquity. Naming Greek, Roman, Egyptian, Jewish, and Christian divine powers in rapid succession in a spell might seem a kind of overkill, but if the magician's central goal is that the magic be effective, one can understand why he would hedge his bets by including every deity likely to help in the endeavor. One also finds spells that refer to very specific deities, like a repulsive spell from the *Papyri Graecae Magicae* in which the magician drowns a cat by "making it" the Egyptian God Osiris, in this way hoping to attract the attention and power of the God by in effect insulting and brutalizing him in drowning the cat, then stuffing magical messages in the cat's orifices.[14]

Many of the remaining incantations from this period are aimed at others and thus represent various kinds or levels of black magic. Charioteers make *defixiones* to make other charioteers fail; spurned lovers curse their spurners; enemies make curses against one another, and so forth. Actually, we even find such black magic going on against great philosophers, notably Plotinus. In his *Life of Plotinus*, Porphyry tells of how Plotinus was magically attacked by an enemy, Olympius of Alexandria, but Plotinus was so strong psychically that these attacks rebounded on his attacker. Plotinus himself wrote about magical spells and witchcraft in his *Enneads*, concluding that those caught up in a life of events and action are certainly subject to magical influence, and that only a contemplative remains free from such influences.[15]

It may well be that one of the reasons for the triumph of Christianity in late antiquity has to do precisely with this ubiquity of magical spells in Greece, Rome, and elsewhere. Christianity in its various forms represented the transcendence of the pagan gods and thus may have conferred a kind of magical invincibility in many of its adherents' minds. Christopher Faraone and Dirk Obbink offer a discussion in *Magika Hiera* of protection amulets belonging to Greeks, Jews, and Christians, but they note elsewhere the well-known general disdain for magic among the church fathers.[16] This disdain is itself a kind of protection: it places Christians in their own view as being beyond magic, thus freeing them from the cycle of magical attack / response or retaliation that was not uncommon in antiquity. Even so, the kinds of folk magic we find in Greco-Roman antiquity did not disappear entirely with the advent of Christianity but continued on in an "underground" fashion, not only in Italy and Greece but throughout Western Europe, carried on by ordinary folk whose worldly desires and petty vindictiveness by no means ceased with the ascent of Christianity and its clerisy into a place of authority.

CONCLUSION: FOUNDATIONS OF WESTERN
ESOTERIC TRADITIONS IN ANTIQUITY

Virtually all the main aspects of Western esoteric traditions have their foundations in antiquity and, in fact, make direct or indirect reference to their origins there. Alchemy, astrology, philosophy, the conveying of esoteric truths through images and parables, as in the ancient Mysteries, concepts of initiation and initiatory transmission, the various forms of magic and theurgy, all of these and more can be traced to antiquity. Greece, Rome, and their links to ancient Egypt certainly form the mythical and to a considerable degree the literal origins of the later esoteric traditions. This is by no means to assert a stasis, as though Western esotericism were a single thing that emerged in antiquity and simply was preserved subsequently—that would be ridiculously simplistic. But in order to understand later Western esoteric traditions, one must understand what came before them. And with that, let us turn to the emergence, in this Greco-Roman ambience, of Hermetic, Gnostic, and Christian forms of esotericism in late antiquity.

NOTES

1. See Garth Fowden, *The Egyptian Hermes: A Historical Approach to the Late Pagan Mind* (Princeton, NJ: Princeton University Press, 1986), xxiii.

2. See Fowden, *Egyptian Hermes*, 46–50.

3. Fowden, *Egyptian Hermes*, 94.

4. See Martin Nillson, *The Dionysiac Mysteries* (Lund: Svenska Institute, 1957), 11.

5. Livy, *Livy* (Cambridge, MA: Harvard University Press, 1919–1959), viii; xxxix.8 ff.

6. See Nillson, *Dionysiac Mysteries*, 18–19.

7. This wonderful novel exists in a number of translations. Personally, I've enjoyed Apuleius, Jack Lindsay, trs., *The Golden Ass* (Bloomington: Indiana University Press, 1962).

8. See Plato, *Republic*, Book VII, 514A–517A; for instance, in Plato, *Republic*, R. E. Allen, ed. (New Haven, CT: Yale University Press, 2006), 227–32.

9. See Plato, *Republic*, Book X, 613E–621D; for instance, in Allen, ed., 350–58.

10. See, in this regard, Arthur Versluis, *Restoring Paradise: Western Esotericism, Literature, and Consciousness* (Albany: SUNY Press, 2004), which is a lengthy treatment of the relationships between literature and esotericism in the West.

11. See Plotinus, *Enneads*, VI.9.11. See, for instance, Plotinus, *Enneads*, Stephen McKenna, trs. (Burdette, NY: Larson, 1992), 708–9.

12. See R. Baine Harris, ed., *Neoplatonism and Indian Thought* (Albany: SUNY Press, 1982).

13. See Georg Luck, *Arcana Mundi: Magic and the Occult in the Greek and Roman Worlds* (Baltimore: Johns Hopkins University Press, 1985), 92–93.

14. Luck, *Arcana Mundi*, 97.

15. See Plotinus, *Enneads* IV.4.40–44; for instance, see Plotinus, *Enneads*, Stephen McKenna, trs., 369–74.

16. See Christopher Faraone and Dirk Obbink, *Magika Hiera: Ancient Greek Magic and Religion* (New York: Oxford University Press, 1991), 118–20, 181–82.

Chapter Three

Late Antiquity: Hermetism, Gnosticism, Jewish Mysticism and Christian Gnosis

There are in late antiquity (from the first through the fifth centuries A.D.) three central religious currents that we must examine here: Hermetism, Gnosticism and Jewish mysticism, and Christian gnosis. Hermetism, as the name implies, represents the traditions surrounding the figure of the revealer-divinity Hermes; Gnosticism is a somewhat contested term applying to a whole range of groups within the ambience of early Christianity; and Christian gnosis refers to such figures as Origen, Clement of Alexandria, and Dionysius the Areopagite, who insisted on the existence of an authentic Christian gnosis or inner spiritual knowledge as the hidden center of orthodox Christianity. While such a series of brief definitions would seem to imply clear demarcations between such seemingly different traditions, in fact these various currents often run together not only in the period of late antiquity but even more so as they influence much later figures and movements.

It was only in the twentieth century that scholars began to develop a much clearer image of this period and of these various currents, not least because in the early Christian era the struggle between Gnostic and what came to be known as orthodox Christianity was so definitively decided in favor of the latter. Subsequent Christian history was written almost exclusively by those who denigrated various Gnostic groups and individuals. An emphasis on historicist Christianity took precedence over the mythological and ahistoricist Gnostic perspectives, and one had to discern what Gnostics believed largely through the writings of their opponents, Church Father "heresiologists" like Irenaeus and Tertullian. As a result, by the medieval period all three of our primary currents went more or less underground or, in the case of Gnosticism, were virtually eliminated.

This is a very important, indeed, critical point. Clearly what became orthodox Western or Eastern Christianity emerged in an atmosphere conducive
to esotericism, but particularly hierarchic Roman Catholicism became relatively hostile to even the *concept* of esotericism. In his book *Hidden Wisdom:
Esoteric Traditions and the Roots of Christian Mysticism*, Guy Stroumsa remarks on this fundamental shift in Christian history.[1] All of the traditions of
antiquity and late antiquity that we are discussing were at least to some degree esoteric and initiatory, closed to outsiders; yet as Stroumsa notes, the
emergence of mainstream Western Christianity in such figures as Augustine
and his successors entailed the rejection of esotericism. The truth of Christianity, so the consensus became, was open to all and thus there were no esoteric aspects within the tradition. Baptism, which in early Christianity was
initiatory, in later Christianity was not regarded in this way. Belief in a historical Christ was sufficient for salvation.

This tension between historicist Christianity on the one hand and esotericism on the other continued from late antiquity all the way to the present day,
manifesting itself in a frequent Christian hostility toward those individuals
who insisted on the possibility or necessity of an esoteric process of spiritual
awakening. Certainly there were figures who stood midway between the two
poles of exotericism and esotericism, like Dionysius the Areopagite, Clement
of Alexandria, and Origen, all of whom endorsed the possibility of an au-
thentically Christian esotericism. What is more, the existence of Neoplatonism, Hermetism, and esoteric traditions of alchemy, astrology, and magic in
the West insured the subterranean continuation of esotericism. But the advent
of historicist Christianity inaugurated a long tradition of mainstream suspicion of anyone who appeared to resemble the heretical Gnostics who flourished between the first and fourth centuries A.D.

HERMETISM

The figure of Hermes is a fascinating one whose history and influence, as Antoine Faivre has shown in his book *The Eternal Hermes*, is far from limited
to antiquity. Hermes, of course, is the fleet-footed messenger-god of the
Greeks, but the Hermes under discussion here is an amalgam of that figure
with the Egyptian god Thoth, whom Greeks since the time of Herodotus were
inclined to call *Hermes,* with the addition of *Trismegistus,* meaning "Thrice-
greatest." Hermes Trismegistus is an hieratic figure who reveals spiritual
truth to the initiate in visionary or dream experience, and whose revelations
and teachings are found in the collection of writings in both Greek and Latin
known as the *Corpus Hermeticum*, or the *Hermetica*.

The *Hermetica* do not represent a single viewpoint, but rather a collection of treatises from a number of somewhat different perspectives with common features. As Garth Fowden and others have shown, some of the Hermetic treatises arguably do have their origin in Egyptian tradition, but Walter Scott's observation is also accurate that the *Hermetica* represent the written records of existing oral master-disciple transmissions commonplace during the period and by no means limited to Hermetism. One finds a similar oral and initiatory tradition in Platonism, as when Plotinus sought out and remained with his master Ammonius Saccas, and for that matter in Christian Gnosticism as well. The *Hermetica* are distinguished from these, however, by their cosmological focus and their emphasis on dialogic, sometimes visionary revelation by the figure of Hermes Trismegistus. Taken as a whole, the *Hermetica* probably represent different aspects of a common Hermetic spiritual tradition realized by a range of people whose differences are reflected in the works themselves.

Undoubtedly the most famous and influential of the Hermetic treatises is the *Poemandres*, which begins with a visionary revelation narrated in the first person. The narrator recalls how he had been thinking lofty thoughts and went into a reverie in which

> there came to me a Being of vast and boundless magnitude, who called me by my name and said to me: "What do you wish to hear, see, learn, and come to know by thought?" "Who are you?" I said. "I am Poemandres, Mind of the Sovereignty," he replied. "I wish to learn the things that are, and understand their nature, and gain knowledge of God," I said. He answered: "I know what you wish, for I am with you everywhere; keep in mind all that you desire to learn, and I will teach you." Suddenly everything changed and opened out into a boundless view, a light, mild, and joyous light pervading all. Then within the light appeared a roiling darkness that smoked, out of which came forth a Word within the Light.[2]

From this beginning of the narrative account, we can see that the language could be read by Christians as consonant with Christianity, and indeed it was read in precisely that way by many later Christians, including such major historical figures as Marsilio Ficino, Cornelius Agrippa, and others in the Renaissance who sought to look back to antiquity and see a harmony between Hermetism, Platonism, and Christianity. Some of the *Hermetica* seems to manifest a real antipathy toward the advent of historicist Christianity, but one cannot deny the parallels between the beginning of the *Poemandres* and the beginning of the Gospel of John.[3] One can also see in this account that it is a direct spiritual revelation by the mysterious Poemandres to Hermes Trismegistus himself—and it is a revelation of the nature of things as well as a knowledge of God. The revelation of this secret knowledge of the cosmos and of God is accompanied, in *Poemandres*, by exhilaration: it is an initiatory knowledge that fills the narrator with delight.

Much of the *Hermetica* is concerned with cosmological revelation conjoined with spiritual illumination, and virtually all of it is suffused with an awareness that these are revelations for the few and not for the many. *Asclepius I*, for instance, begins with the admonition of Hermes Trismegistus that his revelations are fit only for Asclepius himself and Ammon, and not for a crowd of listeners, "for it would be impiety to make public . . . a discussion so full of God in all his majesty" (1b). Later, Trismegistus reiterates that his are doctrines that the masses do not believe, but that are accepted by the wise (10). What are his doctrines? In *Asclepius I and II*, the doctrines of Trismegistus concern the nature of the cosmos and of humanity, of the various beings possessing soul, of the daemons and the elements, of the nature of evil and of the eternity of God. So far as the cosmos as a whole is concerned, Trismegistus insists that it is good, not fundamentally flawed (27a). Further, in *Asclepius III*, he turns his attention to the nature of God, who cannot be named and who is bisexual in nature, just as are all beings (21). The cosmos is in God's image, and therefore both are good.[4]

Here in the *Hermetica*, then, begin a number of themes that repeat themselves throughout the subsequent Western esoteric traditions. First, we find here a written dialogic revelatory tradition: there is a revealer, and one to whom truths are revealed. Second, the truths revealed are considered to be esoteric. Third, the revelations concern the cosmos and the relationships between humanity, the cosmos, and an apparently monotheistic deity. Fourth, there is a syzygic relationship between the deity and the cosmos that the deity has created. It is not only that both are said to be good, it is that the cosmos reflects and manifests the spiritual qualities of the deity. The deity is bisexual, and so too are all creatures, who are the outward manifestation of that inner spiritual bisexuality of the deity. To cite the famous dictum of the *Tabula Smaragdina*, or *Emerald Tablet*: as above, so below.

These themes reemerge again in the period of the Renaissance in what now goes under the general rubric *Hermeticism* and flourish as never before during the early modern period, when appeared the various modern forms of Western esotericism—alchemy, Christian Kabbalah, magical traditions, Christian theosophy under the aegis of Jacob Böhme, Rosicrucianism and Freemasonry, the various secret and semisecret orders of the seventeenth and eighteenth centuries. All of these various individuals and groups bear some indebtedness to the Hermetism of the early modern period, not least in their continuation in one form or another of the four themes mentioned. While the diversity of Western esoteric traditions is striking, they share not only common origins but also a focus on cosmological revelations that derives at least in part from Hermetism in antiquity.

GNOSTICISM

While Hermetism is one of the primary currents in Western esotericism, another is certainly what goes under the general rubric of Gnosticism. Of course, the precise nature of Gnosticism—or, for that matter, whether there is any coherent movement or current in antiquity that can be called "Gnostic"—remains a matter for debate. Gnosticism is a hybrid category that, although it belongs broadly to Christianity, emerged in a Jewish and pagan ambience and incorporated elements of all these currents. Even those who argue that there is a specific current that we can call "Gnostic" in antiquity must acknowledge a congeries of figures and sects within it, many of which disagreed with one another on significant and even major concepts. But such debates about the precise nature and import of Gnosticism are by no means exclusively modern, for in antiquity, too, there was extensive disagreement about the nature of what we now call Gnosticism.

Much of what was known of Gnosticism up to the twentieth century in fact came from its most bitter opponents, the ante-Nicene Church Fathers Irenaeus, Tertullian, and Epiphanius. Admittedly, not all the Church Fathers were hostile to the concept of gnosis—indeed, as we see in more detail below, Origen and Clement of Alexandria were included among the Ante-Nicene orthodox authors, and they explicitly embraced the concept of an orthodox Christian gnosis. But more influential in the history of Christianity were anti-Gnostic figures like Irenaeus and Tertullian, who mercilessly ridiculed and denigrated those they labeled Gnostics.

Before delving further into this contested area, however, we should begin by recognizing various important terms and their meanings. The word *Gnostic* refers, of course, to those groups or individuals in antiquity who have been labeled "heretical" Christians according to the "orthodox" perspectives of Ireneus and others. *Gnosticism* refers to the kinds of religious thought characteristic of Gnostics, but the word *gnosis* has a broader meaning not limited to heretical Gnosticism. *Gnosis* refers to direct spiritual insight or knowledge; and the lowercase word *gnostic* refers, not to a heretical Gnostic but simply to someone who had or has such direct inner spiritual knowledge, as opposed to someone who simply has religious belief or faith in various religious concepts. Thus the word *gnostic* can be applied to medieval or early modern figures like Meister Eckhart or Jacob Böhme, whereas the words *Gnostic* or *Gnosticism* are, strictly speaking, reserved for "heretical" figures in antiquity.

Here, our focus is on those figures generally regarded by the Church Fathers as heretical and grouped under the general rubric of "Gnosticism." Michael Williams, in his book *Rethinking "Gnosticism"* (1997), argues forcefully that in fact there is no such thing as a coherent Gnostic movement, and he makes some persuasive points. Certainly many scholars now question the perspective embodied in arguably the most influential book on Gnosticism in the twentieth century—Hans Jonas's *The Gnostic Religion* (1958)—that Gnosticism represents a single body of "anticosmic" doctrines and symbols. Indeed, Jonas's title alone indicates his thesis, the precise opposite of which is Williams's argument that there is no such thing as a single "Gnostic" doctrine.

In his best-known book, Jonas argues that Gnosticism as a kind of thought can be identified by the following themes: a cosmic dualism and a sense of human alienation from this world, combined with a sense of the "otherness" of the divine. The human individual is a stranger cast down in an alien and hostile place, this world, a "fallen being" caught in a state of intoxication or sleep, who hears a call from beyond the worldly din, a call from his distant homeland, the world of light.[5] According to Jonas, the Gnostics launched a full-fledged attack on the classical Greek view of the cosmos as a beneficent and harmonious place, seeing it instead as "the opposite of divine," a place subject to the "tyrannical and evil law" of the demiurge (the ignorant creator of and tyrant over this botched realm), a kind of cosmic trap from which only the Gnostic or knower of the divine can escape.[6]

Jonas's view of Gnosticism as an anticosmic form of dualism (as he himself later acknowledged) bore a strong resemblance to and undoubtedly owed much to the spirit of his own age and in particular to existentialist philosophy that saw humanity as adrift in a meaningless cosmos. In an interview in 1975, remarking on the popularity and influence of his depiction of Gnosticism, Jonas acknowledged that "I think that I had touched the sensitive nerve of an epoch. This is not an argument—and I must stress it—that my interpretation of Gnosticism was correct: it simply fitted to the moods provoked by historical circumstances. It is very possible that the next historical attempt, based on the newly discovered materials, will make the book obsolete."[7] While Jonas's book presents a coherent and therefore attractive view of his subject, it does not acknowledge the varieties of Gnosticism.

In *Gnosis and Literature* (1996) I proposed the following spectrum as a means of loosely categorizing different forms of Gnosticism in antiquity. Obviously, this spectrum is somewhat loose, but it does present a schema whereby a reader can begin to recognize the major delineations between forms of Gnosticism and historicist Christianity (see figure 3.1). I am not willing to go as far as Williams in attempting to throw out the category "Gnosticism" entirely but, rather, prefer to draw attention to the major historical figures in question and thus begin to establish an overview of the tendencies during this era.[8]

Irenaeus and Tertullian, of course, are representative of the ante-Nicene Fathers who directly and vociferously opposed heretical and antinomian Gnostics. They upheld what has come to be known loosely as "orthodoxy," meaning an emphasis on belief in a historical Christ, and a tendency toward both

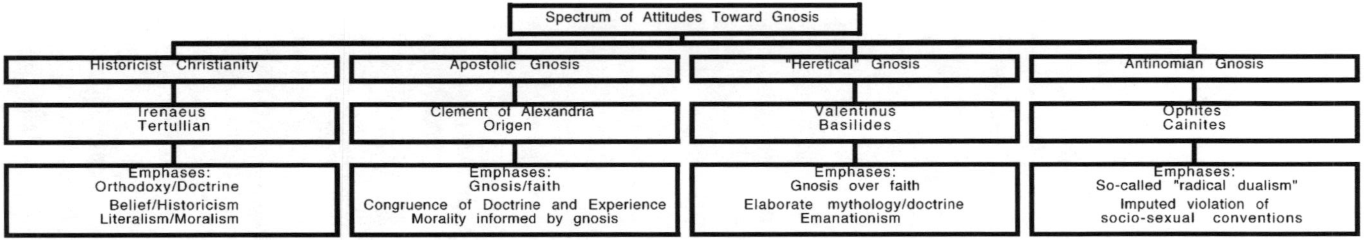

Spectrum of Attitudes Toward Gnosis			
Historicist Christianity	Apostolic Gnosis	"Heretical" Gnosis	Antinomian Gnosis
Irenaeus Tertullian	Clement of Alexandria Origen	Valentinus Basilides	Ophites Cainites
Emphases: Orthodoxy/Doctrine Belief/Historicism Literalism/Moralism	Emphases: Gnosis/faith Congruence of Doctrine and Experience Morality informed by gnosis	Emphases: Gnosis over faith Elaborate mythology/doctrine Emanationism	Emphases: So-called "radical dualism" Imputed violation of socio-sexual conventions

Figure 3.1.

literalism and moralism. They laid emphasis on the importance of church doctrine as opposed to what they saw as fanciful mythologies created by the Gnostics.

Valentinus and Basilides, on the other hand, represent the best-known of the historical Gnostics, sometimes termed "heresiarchs." They emphasized the primacy of gnosis over faith and elaborate mythological and cosmological traditions; Basilides is well known for a description of divine transcendence that much resembles the Prajñaparamita Sutra in Buddhism, while Valentinus is remembered as creator of an extensive theosophic tradition. Little remains of their writings, and thus scholars have been compelled to reconstruct their systems of thought from fragments or accounts by their opponents, but it is clear that both were remarkable, highly intellectual men.

On the far end of the spectrum are the antinomian Gnostics, the so-called radical dualists who supposedly saw this world as the botched creation of an evil, ignorant demiurge and who believed that gnosis set them free to do as they will, to violate conventional mores, to enter into orgies or to sin in order to break beyond their confinement in this world. Exemplary of this category are such figures as the "Cainites" and the "Ophites" attacked by the apparently breathless Epiphanius, their orgiastic behavior revealed in his exposé. Whether or not such behavior ever took place in antiquity, indeed, whether there really were any Cainites or Ophites at all, is a matter open to some debate. But it is certainly true that antinomianism is a kind of thought and behavior that does recur in later Western history in such figures as the Ranters of seventeenth-century England, and that therefore it is indeed a reasonable category to posit in antiquity as well.

When we look at the depictions of the Gnostics included among the ante-Nicene Fathers, notably the writings of Irenaeus and Tertullian, we find two approaches: first, a kind of reportage, and second, denigration. Often these two are combined. Irenaeus, in his "Against Heresies," writes at length about the doctrines of major Gnostic figures, and while his condemnatory attitude is obvious, he does offer a great deal of information about the Gnostics. Tertullian, on the other hand, while he too includes some perhaps valuable observations on such figures as Valentinus, compromises himself with the extravagant violence of his rhetoric. For instance, in a section of "Against the Valentinians" entitled "Other Turgid and Ridiculous Theories about the Origin of the Aeons, Stated and Condemned," Tertullian writes about the "buffooneries of a master who is a great swell among them" and pronounces the whole of Valentinian mythology "tiresome," and "utterly poor and weak."[9] It is not hard to sense here a certain prejudice.

In fact, it is often difficult to discern exactly what in various ante-Nicene Fathers's accounts is reasonably accurate and what is sarcastic bombast or outright confabulation. Irenaeus frequently insists that the Gnostics engaged in magic, alleging of Basilides's circle that they "practice magic, and use images, incantations, invocations, and every other kind of curious art. Coining also certain names as if they were those of the angels, they proclaim some of these as belonging to the first, and others to the second heaven" (xxiv.5).[10] Of Carpocrates's circle, Irenaeus insists that they "practice also magical arts and incantations; philters, also, and love-potions; and have recourse to familiar spirits, dream-sending demons, and other abominations, declaring that they possess power to rule over, even now, the princes and formers of this world" (xxv.3).[11] There are indeed strings of vowels in some of the Gnostic writings discovered in the Nag Hammadi Library collection in 1945. But there is little evidence in the actual Gnostic writings of magical practices like those alleged by Irenaeus, and little or no chance of definitively verifying what he writes.

On the other hand, even though Tertullian writes with great virulence against Valentinus and his followers, one can discern the outlines of Valentinian thought despite the bombast. It is clear from Tertullian's survey that Valentinian thought is extraordinarily complex, with a mythological superstructure that requires considerable explanation. Tertullian outlines the Valentinian system, beginning with the *Ogdoad*, or eight aeonic emanations that emerged from the *Bythos*, or depths of the divine. The first four of these eight are said to be Bythos and Sige (Silence), Nous (Mind), and Veritas (Truth), out of which emerged the Word and Life, and Homo (Man) and Ecclesia (the Church). He outlines the Valentinian myth of the fall of Sophia (Wisdom), and the restoration of the Pleroma (or fullness) (vii–xii).[12] Indeed, Tertullian outlines a great deal of Valentinian thought, all the while heaping heavy-handed ridicule upon it. While Tertullian's rhetoric is obnoxious, in fact his account of Valentinianism does accord in many respects with what we find in the Nag Hammadi Library.

From such accounts by Irenaeus, Tertullian, Epiphanius, and others, scholars in the nineteenth and twentieth centuries developed what we might term a stereotypic view of Gnosticism. What is the defining characteristic of this stereotypic Gnostic approach to understanding? Salvation by the world of light from this world of darkness. Giovanni Filoramo summarizes this view:

> The process of salvation, which is revealed in the very heart of the Gnostic through the acquisition of a knowledge that is certainly in itself salvific, is placed in being if, and only if, a revealing, illuminating force intervenes from outside. For Gnosis is principally a cry from above, light from the light world of the Pleroma. By himself the gnostic is incapable of salvation. Gnosis is revealed knowledge, divine *charis*, or love, charity, which springs from the compassionate heart of the Father. It therefore requires a Revealer, the Gnostic *sôtêr*.
>
> All this will become clearer if we turn briefly to the existential situation of the Gnostic. By their anthropological constitution they are prisoners of demonic powers. Equally, one can say of their cosmic *Dasein*, or existence: cast down to

live, not only in a body, but also in a cosmos dominated by hostile, clever forces continually seeking their destruction, how could they escape from this closed universe except through the intervention of an external power?[13]

Gnosticism, in short, entails from this perspective a cosmos in which humanity is trapped, beset by hostile forces, and seeking a way into the kingdom of light.

We can outline the following elements as characteristic of stereotypic Gnosticism:

1. a hostile cosmos (Gnostic antipathy to nature)
2. a demiurge, or ignorant creator responsible for botched creation and hostile to human spiritual awakening
3. dualism: opposition between the realm of light and the realm of matter
4. an elaborate mythology
5. myths concerning Sophia (Wisdom) and her fall and restoration
6. belief in a hidden God (not the demiurge)
7. difficulty of spiritual progress due to the archons or other hostile powers in the cosmos; ignorance the inherent (fallen) human condition
8. existence of the ogdoad, or eight spheres (including the seven planetary spheres) and possibility of their transcendence
9. the necessity of gnosis, or direct spiritual knowledge from the realm of light

These nine elements of stereotypic Gnosticism should not be read as actually characterizing all the various figures and works frequently grouped under the rubric "Gnostic"—rather, these represent characteristics found in a wide range of twentieth century scholarly depictions of Gnosticism, particularly in the wake of Hans Jonas's seminal *The Gnostic Religion*. And indeed, one can certainly find many and arguably all of these elements implied or outright in the remarkable collection of Gnostic writings found in the Nag Hammadi Library, discovered in a cave in Egypt in 1945 and first published in English in 1977.

The Nag Hammadi Library allows an unprecedented glimpse into the kinds of writings that various Gnostic groups and individuals produced or collected. Some of the Nag Hammadi writings are visionary accounts, like The Apocalypse of Adam, while others, like The Sentences of Sextus or The Teachings of Silvanus are moralistic aphorisms pertaining to right conduct. Still other works in the collection, like The Discourse on the Eighth and Ninth, correspond as much to the Hermetic as to the Gnostic tradition, and included also among the various treatises is a somewhat corrupted selection from Plato's *Republic*. Some works in the Nag Hammadi Library correspond to stereotypic Gnosticism, but others do not fit well at all under that rubric.

Certainly many of the elements alleged to be characteristic of heretical Gnosticism by Irenaeus and Tertullian are in fact visible in such works in the Nag Hammadi Library as The Hypostasis of the Archons and On the Origin of the World.[14] In Hypostasis of the Archons, we find a clear sense that "a veil exists between the World above and the realms that are below," that below is a "Shadow" that became matter, and in it a "blind god," "Samael," reigns. We find a complex mythology that concerns Sophia (Wisdom) as a spiritual revealer, and that posits humanity's "bondage" under the "Authorities," powers hostile to human spiritual awakening. We find reference to how the "Children of the Light" will be freed ultimately from their bondage by the illuminating Truth—in short, enough characteristics of stereotypic Gnosticism to verify much, although certainly not all, of the Church Fathers' descriptions of such movements and figures.

At the same time, the Nag Hammadi Library collection also includes works that do not correspond very much at all with what I am calling stereotypic Gnosticism. For instance, in the remarkable treatise The Thunder, Perfect Mind, spoken entirely from an oracular feminine perspective, there is no trace of dualism. Instead, the treatise emphasizes that "I am the first and the last. / I am the honored one and the scorned one. / I am the whore and the holy one"[15] It is full of paradoxes, like "You who deny me, confess me, and you who confess me, deny me" (43–44); she is unlearned, yet all learn from her; she is sinless and she is the root of sin; she is lustful and yet full of inner self-control. She is the one who alone exists, and only those who become "sober" and return to their "resting-place" will "find me there/and they will live, and they will not die again." Despite George MacRae's remark that this work presents no essentially Gnostic themes, we can at least acknowledge the fact that its revealer is feminine, and that it insists that only direct knowledge of the divine is salvific.[16] But certainly little if anything in this work corresponds to our nine elements of stereotypic Gnosticism.

Or once again, one might look closely at the well-known Gospel of Thomas, where again we find little to corroborate the stereotypic elements alleged to be so characteristic of Gnosticism. It is true that, as Helmut Koester points out, this "collection of sayings intends to be esoteric: the key to understanding is [in] the interpretation of secret meanings" . . . for "whoever finds the interpretation of these sayings will not experience death."[17] But while the Gospel of Thomas is filled with gnomic sayings of Jesus, it does not evince a sense of cosmic dualism, nor does the figure of a demiurge appear, nor are there archons, and indeed, it often suggests the same kind of divine unity that one finds in Thunder, Perfect Mind. For instance, in saying 51, Jesus's disciples ask when the new world will come, and Jesus replies that "What you look forward to has already come, but you do not see it." Jesus tells the disciples to "Become passersby" (42) and advises them to "Split a

piece of wood, and I am there. Lift up the stone, and you will find me there"
(77). This kind of advice does not seem very closely related to stereotypic
Gnosticism.

What can we conclude from these discrepancies? One could argue that
there are multiple Gnosticisms of various kinds, and that they simply do not
agree with one another. Or one could argue that there is in fact an overarching unity among these various works and that even if the specific elements of
stereotypic Gnosticism are not visible in some treatises, still there is little in
such works as the Gospel of Thomas or Thunder, Perfect Mind that stands in
opposition to stereotypic Gnosticism, either. The fact is that Gnosticism remains an enigma, and although the Nag Hammadi Library has offered us numerous new clues to that enigma's solutions, it is difficult to definitively argue which of the various possible interpretations is correct.

The Gnostic Legacy

It is an open question to what extent Gnosticism continued to exist historically after the early Christian era and the establishment of a Roman Catholic
orthodoxy. Some more or less popular authors have claimed that Gnosticism
did continue in an underground fashion in the West, reemerging in such later
heretical movements as the Bogomils and Cathars during the medieval period, disappearing after Church persecution, only to reappear in the modern
era. This is, of course, a romanticized view of history.[18]

More likely is the proposal of Ioan Culianu that one look, not for hypo-
thetical secret lineages, but for central ideas that exist as possibilities within
a tradition and that recur again and again within it.[19] Thus, for instance, the
concept of a feminine Sophia or Wisdom recurs within the Jewish and Christian traditions in various forms; it is a natural possibility in a Judeo-Christian
context, and thus it can reappear in the seventeenth century in Böhmean
theosophy without any direct link to ancient Gnosticism.

Certainly it is the case that the various elements of stereotypic Gnosticism
did not vanish with the disappearance of the Gnostic sects themselves. One
does find among the Cathari, for instance, an antiworldly asceticism quite
reminiscent of what we find much earlier in the Gnostic "Sentences of Sextus." And one can see similarities between the sheer transcendence represented in the sermons of Meister Eckhart and the sheer transcendence discussed in a famous passage by the Gnostic Basilides. But this is not to say that
such parallels represent any kind of historical continuity; if anything, they
represent an ahistorical continuity, since there is no demonstrable historical
linkage between these disparate figures, movements, and works.

Yet least of all did the concept of secret spiritual knowledge vanish—
rather, it was continued on in numerous forms throughout the history of West-

ern esotericism. Indeed, for this very reason, we may speak of "gnosis" as a common characteristic of countless esoteric traditions (according to some, including non-Western esoteric traditions, in particular Buddhist Tantrism) with or without positing any linkage to ancient Gnosticism.[20] One can unquestionably argue for the existence of gnosis within Hermetic and alchemical traditions, as within the works of figures like Meister Eckhart and Johannes Tauler (14th c.) (who indeed might better be termed gnostics than mystics), not to mention in the work of figures like Jacob Böhme (17th c.) or Franklin Merrell-Wolff (20th c.), or in various magical traditions like that of the Golden Dawn (19th c.).

What is more, the latter half of the twentieth century saw the emergence of neo-Gnostic figures and groups like the self-styled California Gnostic Bishop Stephen Hoeller, and thus the reappearance of Gnosticism as a religious tradition more or less in its own right. Even if one discounts to some extent the twentieth-century Gnostic churches as a "New Age" phenomenon, it remains the case that whether in popular culture like the novels of Philip K. Dick, in various popular films, or in the scholarship of authors like Elaine Pagels, as well as in the philosophical musings of such figures as Emile Cioran, heretical Gnosticism continues to have an impact more than fifteen hundred years after its reported demise.

JEWISH MYSTICISM

Gnosticism, in its variety of sects and lineages, emerged in an ambience not only of Greco-Roman and Hermetic religion and philosophy, but also, importantly, of Judaism. Jewish mysticism during the period of late antiquity was profoundly influenced by what is termed *Merkabah*, or Throne mysticism. This term derives from the vision of the prophet Ezekiel, who saw in a vision a cloud of fire, within which was a roaring chariot accompanied by mysterious creatures, and on the chariot was a throne, seated on which was a fiery anthropos-figure that Ezekiel saw as God.[21] From this strange and frightening vision emerged the tradition of chariot mysticism—the chariot representing movement or transport between the divine and the human worlds. *Merkabah* mystics saw Ezekiel's chariot as the prototype for ascending into the world above and for glimpsing the divine Temple of Jerusalem there.

The period before and after the destruction of the earthly Temple of Jerusalem in 70 B.C. saw the emergence of various Jewish sects or groups of mystical practitioners who were deeply influenced by the experience of Ezekiel and by the possibility of mystical knowledge or gnosis. One such mystic was Rabbi Akiva ben Yosef (50–135 A.D.), whose circle practiced a mysticism of ascent that apparently entailed considerable dangers, and that is discussed in the Talmud. But there were numerous groups and sects during the period of late antiquity. Among them were the producers of the Dead Sea Scrolls at Qumran, the Essenes, and numerous others who practiced ascetic disciplines, some of whom also underwent visionary experiences. Not only Gnosticism, but also the Christian New Testament, and in particular the Book of Revelation, should be seen in this larger context of Jewish visionary mysticism.

We should note here that mysticism is not necessarily to be identified only with exotic visionary experiences. Some scholars also write of what they term "normal mysticism," meaning that "the average Jewish layperson living a life imbued with observance of Jewish law and liturgy can achieve a variety of mystical experiences." In other words, mystical experience (defined as "conscious awareness of and a relationship with God") is not necessarily the province of ascetics or esoteric practitioners but may be attained or experienced by anyone who is an observant Jew. This, Max Kadushin termed "normal mysticism," and it provides the basis for other, more esoteric forms of Jewish mysticism, many of which combine magic and mysticism (or theurgy and theosophy) and ecstasy in a variety of ways.[22]

There is, of course, already a vast literature on the history of Jewish mysticism, and even more on the development of Kabbalism during the medieval and modern periods. But there are certain areas that remain less charted, and those are arguably the ones most important for our subject. These less charted areas are what we might term realms of synthesis or religious cross-fertilization. Scholars have tended to concentrate, understandably, on mapping the lines of demarcated religious traditions or territories, and they have spent less time on the points of transfer or border areas where these traditions meet and intermingle. What were the relationships between Jewish mysticism and Gnosticism? What were the relationships between Jewish and Islamic mysticism in Persia, for instance, during the strong Jewish presence there up to the emergence of Kabbalah in Western Europe in the twelfth and thirteenth centuries? How precisely did Jewish magic and mysticism emerge in Christian magical or mystical traditions? Esotericism often flourishes in periods and areas when apparently disparate religious traditions meet and mingle, and esotericism is also very often synthetic in nature, so some of the most valuable research to come may well focus on answering exactly such questions, which belong more broadly to esotericism.

The study of Jewish mysticism, magic, and Kabbalah is, of course, its own domain, with numerous great scholars devoted to it. Here, I must primarily point readers toward that large and growing body of literature, while continuing to point out major juncture points with the stream that we are calling "Western esotericism."[23]

CHRISTIAN GNOSIS

If heretical Gnosticism in its various forms died out relatively early, the concept of gnosis did not disappear from the Christian world. While heresiarchs like Valentinus and Basilides were remembered in the context of diatribes against them, still the concept of an orthodox Christian gnosis did continue into the medieval period through the works of those we might call "orthodox gnostics:" chiefly Origen, Clement of Alexandria, and most of all, Dionysius the Areopagite. These figures, and particularly the latter two, were immensely influential in later Christianity, and they insisted on the possibility, indeed, the necessity for direct experiential spiritual knowledge.

Of these three seminal Christian writers, Origen discusses gnosis the least, and largely by implication. For instance, in his *Commentary on John*, Origen distinguishes between "The Somatic [Bodily] and the Spiritual Gospel" and insists on the importance of both.[24] He affirms the bodily coming of Christ but also affirms the immense importance of John's "eternal Gospel," properly called the "spiritual Gospel," which concerns the "mysteries" and "enigmas" of Christ's life and words. We must, Origen concludes, be Christians "both somatically and spiritually" and partake in the Word (Christ) (I.9). And in his *De Principiis*, Origen alludes to the celestial "ordering and arrangement of the world," to the "holy and blessed orders" through which humanity can ascend back to the condition of happiness from which many have fallen (VI.2). Here Origen is referring to the hierarchic orders of thrones, principalities, and dominions, of angelic hierarchies that, by implication, are realms through which humans can ascend to return to their divine condition.

But whereas Origen is somewhat oblique about gnosis—it exists as a concept implicit in his work—Clement of Alexandria is much more explicit. In his *Stromata*, or *Miscellanies*, Clement writes at length about how "the gnostic alone is truly pious" (VII.1) and affirms that gnostic souls "surpass in the grandeur of contemplation" even the "holy ranks," for the gnostic who is perfected in virtue and contemplation attains to the "nearest likeness possible to God and his son."[25] Clement is not at all endorsing heretical Gnosticism but rather is insisting on how gnosis is "a perfecting of man as man, [which is] consummated by acquaintance with divine things," for by gnosis is faith perfected" (VII.10). In brief, the "gnostic soul, adorned with perfect virtue, is the earthly image of the divine power" (VII.11). The "life of the gnostic," in Clement's own view, is "nothing but deeds and words corresponding to the tradition of the Lord" (VII.16).

Hence Clement of Alexandria placed gnosis at the very heart of the Christian tradition, clearly distinguishing between heretical Gnostics who despised matter and creation, and his own understanding of gnosis as the true purpose and crowning glory of the Christian faith. To be a gnostic, in Clement's view, is to enter more and more deeply into the spiritual knowledge and mysteries revealed by Jesus Christ. Faith is crowned by gnosis, but gnosis is not opposed to faith, and it requires a chaste way of life. One must, Clement insists, lead a moral life, a life of virtue, and only then can one penetrate into the deeper mysteries of Christianity. It is interesting to consider the orthodox gnosticism of Clement in relation to the ascetic works in the Nag Hammadi Library—Clement clearly places himself on the side of orthodoxy, but what he writes certainly corresponds in some respects with Nag Hammadi ascetic gnosticism. Here one sees, once again, a spectrum of gnostic views in antiquity rather than the rigidly opposed camps delineated by heresiologues like Tertullian.

In the works of Dionysius the Areopagite we find the most influential discussions in the history of orthodox Christian gnosis. It is not so much that Dionysius explicitly affirmed gnosis per se as Clement of Alexandria did, but rather that he laid the foundations for a gnostic understanding within Christianity. Dionysius is not at all concerned with defending gnosis within the Church or with differentiating orthodox from heretical gnosis, but rather focuses entirely on paths to and the nature of gnostic understanding itself within an orthodox Christian perspective. It is for this reason primarily that Dionysius remained so profoundly influential: his explication of celestial hierarchy and of gnostic understanding of scriptural analogy, as well as his affirmation of divine transcendence, were immensely appealing to later medieval Christian gnostics like the anonymous author of the English *Cloud of Unknowing* treatises. If Western Christianity was to retain or develop inner spiritual practices, a larger framework for understanding such practices was necessary, and that was precisely what Dionysius's work provided.

VIA POSITIVA AND *VIA NEGATIVA*

Central to Dionysius's thought—and for that matter, to understanding the whole of Western esoteric traditions—is the Dionysian distinction between the *via positiva* and the *via negativa*. *Via,* of course, means "way," and the *via positiva* is the way of positing or affirming—it is the path that goes through symbols and images, through analogies and visions. The *via positiva*, then, naturally leads through the realm of the imagination conceived not as fantasy but as an organ of perception: through symbols and images one can perceive aspects of the divine. The *via positiva* corresponds, then, by extension, to what Henry Corbin termed the "active imagination," which allows one to perceive something akin to Plato's realm of forms—the divine celestial archetypes or images that exist behind or above the physical realm. The *via positiva* is allied with the arts, with poetry, with all that has to do with the imagination.

By contrast, the *via negativa* consists in the negation of all that one might posit of the divine. If the *via positiva* consists in affirmation, the *via negativa* consists in denying that anything created or imagined in fact corresponds to the divine. Not concepts of above, not below, not right, not left, not yes, not no, not a lion, not a tiger, not hands, not feet, not sense consciousness, not mental consciousness, nothing that one can posit corresponds in actuality to the divine. Indeed, one has to be struck by how closely Dionysius's string of negations in his "Mystical Theology" corresponds not only to the similar negations attributed to the Gnostic Basilides, but also to the negations found in the Prajñaparamita Sutra in Buddhism. Yet the *via negativa* is not nihilism—it is not positing that ultimately nothing exists, but rather affirming the divine by way of negation. Nothing in existence can be said to be "it"—no concept, no idea, no image, nothing. Yet for all that it is not nothing, even if it is also not something. Here we are not too far from the paradoxes of Gnostic treatises like Thunder, Perfect Mind.

But Dionysius remains steadfastly orthodox, and indeed, his works can be seen to exist within and affirm the orthodox church. Exemplary of this unity between the outward church and the divine or spiritual hierarchy is Dionysius's work "Ecclesiastical Hierarchy," which corresponds to his "Celestial Hierarchy" in that both affirm the principle of the greater initiating the lesser. Dionysius's cosmos is an hierarchic one, organized from the absolute divine transcendence at the top and extending downward through the descending ranks of the angels to humanity and other beings. Dionysius does not discuss infernal hierarchies but restrains his discussion to the angelic and its relationships to the human. Human beings can *act* as angels inasmuch as they can initiate others into the divine mysteries, and thus just as the angels exist in a celestial hierarchy, so too the visible church correspondingly represents the human forms of that hierarchy. Of course, this means that the true ecclesiastical hierarchy is based on greater initiatory knowledge of the divine—those who are bishops are so because they have a correspondingly greater direct spiritual knowledge than those beneath them on whom they bestow illumination.

It is obvious, then, that although Dionysius affirms an ecclesiastical hierarchy, it is a hierarchy based on degrees of illumination or gnosis and thus distinctly different from any ecclesiastical hierarchy based on political or social appointment. Dionysius referred with great love to his own initiator, Hierotheus, whose work Dionysius himself saw as "too magisterial" and too profound even for those who were "teachers of the newly initiated."[26] Hierotheus "excelled all other sacred initiates," and thus in Dionysius's works one can see the existence of an initiatory lineage that descends from Hierotheus's initiator to Hierotheus to Dionysius to Timothy, and onward in an initiatory, hierarchic tradition. This is the true inner hierarchy, with the initiate's master at its head (analogous in some ways to lineages in Sufism or in

Vajrayana Buddhism). Still, Dionysius's affirmation of ecclesiastical hierarchy, even if fundamentally different from the hierarchy of the Roman
Catholic Church as it later developed, represented a kind of protection and
sanction for the works of Dionysius.

For Dionysius, the concept of *via positiva* is intimately linked to that of celestial hierarchy, for it is through the symbolic that we receive understanding
of the higher degrees of illumination than our own. In the first section of "Celestial Hierarchy," Dionysius exhorts us to raise our thought

> according to our power, to the illumination of the most sacred doctrines handed
> down by the Fathers, and also as far as we may let us contemplate the Hierar-
> chies of the Celestial Intelligences revealed to us by them in symbols for our up-
> liftment: and admitting through the spiritual and unwavering eyes of the mind
> the original and super-original gift of Light of the Father who is the Source of
> Divinity, which shows to us images of the all-blessed Hierarchies of the Angels
> in figurative symbols, let us through them again strive upwards toward Its pri-
> mal ray.[27]

We ascend upward through the celestial hierarchies by way of images that reveal the nature of the next hierarchic degree to us, for human comprehension
works through symbol and imagination. In short, through the forms of poetic
symbolism the formless transcendent is revealed to us.

Thus the *via positiva* is also esoteric, in that the meanings of the sacred
symbols are, Dionysius writes, not available or comprehensible to the masses.
Holy symbols remain self-secret, so to speak, whether they operate through
likeness (as when one speaks of God as light) or through unlikeness, as in
both cases only those with eyes to see can see what is represented through
analogy or discordant symbolism. There are hierarchic levels of understanding that are successively more hidden and profound, and that naturally protect what Dionysius calls "intelligible pearls" from being thrown before
swine. But each level or degree has an obligation to illuminate those beneath
it who are capable of receiving illumination. Hence Dionysius also writes that

> those who purify should bestow upon others from their abundance of purity their
> own holiness: those who illuminate, as possessing more luminous intelligence,
> duly receiving and again shedding forth the light, and joyously filled with holy
> brightness, should impart their own overflowing light to those worthy of it; fi-
> nally, those who make perfect, being skilled in the mystical participations,
> should lead to that consummation those who are perfected by the most holy ini-
> tiation of the knowledge of holy things which they have contemplated.[28]

If on the one hand the meaning of the sacred symbolism is inaccessible to the
hoi polloi, on the other hand those with higher knowledge are obliged to re-

veal it to those worthy of it, so that each level of initiate perfects the level beneath it.

And so we can begin to see how the ordered cosmos of Dionysius the Areopagite, which inherited so much from Platonism, itself forms a foundation for understanding much of Western esotericism that was to follow. For it is at best only a small exaggeration to say that Dionysius allows esotericism to exist in a Christian context; his work synthesizes Platonism and Christianity in a fusion that allows for, indeed, depends upon the existence of Christian gnosis and insists upon the importance of sacred symbolism in revealing that gnosis. Although the concept of a fusion between the ecclesiastical and the gnostic hierarchies was not one that continued within mainstream Christianity, it was Dionysius's work that developed the possibility of spiritual revelation through sacred symbol and provided the foundation for the hierarchic view of the cosmos that was to inform Western esotericism from antiquity onward.

Yet if on the one hand Dionysius affirmed the *via positiva* that remains so central for understanding the much later efflorescence of complex and even baroque symbolism in the Hermetic, alchemical, and theosophic Western esotericism of the seventeenth through the nineteenth centuries, on the other hand it is also to Dionysius that we can trace the *via negativa*, or way of negation that is so central for what is often called the Western mystical tradition represented by such figures as Meister Eckhart, John Tauler, and the author of the *Cloud of Unknowing*. Absolutely central for the *via negativa* tradition is Dionysius's influential treatise entitled *Mystical Theology*, in which he outlines the most secret mysteries of his initiatory Christian tradition—the mysteries of sheer transcendence. Whereas the *via positiva* represents ascent through the support of symbols, the *via negativa* represents the ascent entirely beyond symbolism into the divine darkness.

Dionysius refers to the *via negativa* as holding even greater mysteries than those of the *via positiva*. He advises his disciple in this way:

> do, dear Timothy, in the diligent exercise of mystical contemplation, leave behind the senses and the operations of the intellect, and all things sensible and intellectual, and all things in the world of being and nonbeing, that you may arise by unknowing towards the union, as far as is attainable, with it that transcends all being and all knowledge. For by the unceasing and absolute renunciation of yourself and of all things you may be borne on high, through pure and entire self-abnegation, into the superessential Radiance of the Divine Darkness.[29]

This sublime contemplation, Dionysius admonishes Timothy, is not to be revealed to the uninitiated, by which he means "those who are attached to the objects of their thought." Such a definition is quite revealing, not least because it implies an opposition between those who embrace the way of symbols on the one hand, and those who go beyond them on the other. It is possible to mistakenly cling to symbols as the reality, but the *via negativa* is the corrective for this error because it requires the transcendence of all symbols.

Just how far Dionysius is willing to go in the exercise of this principle we can see in the striking conclusion to *Mystical Theology*. In it, he soars to the heights of negation, writing of this dazzling gnostic darkness that

> ascending yet higher, we maintain that it is neither soul nor intellect; nor has it imagination, opinion, reason, or understanding; nor can it be expressed or conceived, since it is neither number nor order; nor greatness nor smallness; nor equality nor inequality; nor similarity nor dissimilarity; neither is it standing, nor moving, nor at rest; neither has it power nor is power, nor is light; neither does it live nor is it life; neither is it essence, nor eternity nor time; nor is it subject to intelligible contact; nor is it science nor truth, nor kingship nor wisdom; neither one nor oneness, nor godhead nor goodness; nor is it spirit according to our understanding, nor filiation, nor paternity; nor anything else known to us or to any other beings of the things that are or the things that are not; neither does anything that is known as it is; nor does it know existing things according to existing knowledge; neither can the reason attain to it, nor name it, nor know it; neither is it darkness nor light, nor the false nor the true; nor can any affirmation or negation be applied to it, for although we may affirm or deny the things below it, we can neither affirm nor deny it, inasmuch as the all-perfect and unique Cause of all things transcends all affirmation, and the simple preëminence of Its absolute nature is outside of every negation—free from every limitation and beyond them all.[30]

This transcendence is not godhead nor goodness, not darkness nor light—here Dionysius's negations become daring in their sublimity. But such daring is intrinsic in the exercise of this principle: the principle of absolute negation of concepts requires negating even orthodox concepts of the divine. Absolute transcendence means transcendence even of that which is good. This is a paradox that has informed much of the Western mystical tradition, both heretical and orthodox, and one can certainly trace it in its origins to the works of Dionysius.

CONCLUSION

Without question, Dionysius the Areopagite stands as a central figure in the history of Western esotericism. His importance is twofold: he was influential in the history of Christianity because he represents a synthesis of Platonic and gnostic currents under the aegis of orthodox Christianity, thus creating a conduit for an orthodox Christian esotericism; but he is also vital to understanding subsequent magical and gnostic currents because of his concepts of *via positiva* and *via negativa*. Dionysius's concept of the *via positiva* helps illuminate the path of imagination, the visionary and imaginative traditions of the West that certainly include magical practices and alchemy as well as the visionary mystical traditions represented by figures like Hildegard of Bingen. And his concept of the *via negativa* represents a vital source for understanding subsequent gnostics like Meister Eckhart (d. 1327).

But Dionysius also had a powerful and more general influence in Western Christianity. Indeed, Jaroslav Pelikan remarks that "it has become a widely accepted view that Dionysian spirituality may have been more influential in the West than in the East," not least through its adoption or absorption by such pivotal figures as Augustine, Boethius, Bonaventure, and Aquinas (to name only a few).[31] The construction of medieval cathedrals, laden with imaginative symbolic beauty, reflect the Dionysian angelic hierarchies and the *via positiva*, and so do bear some debt to Dionysian spirituality. Medieval Christianity was certainly shaped by the Dionysius corpus and cosmology, and even if the influence is not always direct, the Dionysian tradition is immensely helpful in understanding the various forms of Christian esotericism that were to come.

NOTES

1. Guy Stroumsa, *Hidden Wisdom: Esoteric Traditions and the Roots of Christian Mysticism* (Leiden: Brill, 1996).

2. See Walter Scott, ed., *Hermetica: The Ancient Greek and Latin Writings*, (Boston: Shambhala, 1985), I.115.

3. An antipathy toward Christianity, or what one presumes is Christianity, can be seen in *Ascl. Lat.* III.25 ff., in particular the famous "O Egypt, Egypt" lamentation over the destruction of sacred traditions and the degenerate era then appearing.

4. See Scott, ed., *Hermetica*, I.333–334.

5. See Hans Jonas, *The Gnostic Religion* (Boston: Beacon, 1963), 48–95.

6. Jonas, *Gnostic Religion,* 250–54.

7. Ioan Petru Culianu, *Gnosticismo e Pensiero Modern: Hans Jonas* (Rome: L'Erma, 1985), 138.

8. See Arthur Versluis, *Gnosis and Literature* (St. Paul, MN: Grail, 1996).

9. See Tertullian, "Against the Valentinians," xxxvii; xxxvi, in Allan Menzies, ed., *The Ante-Nicene Fathers* (Grand Rapids, MI: Eerdmans, 1990 ed.), III.519–20.

10. See *The Ante-Nicene Fathers*, I.348–351.

11. See *The Ante-Nicene Fathers*, I.350–351.

12. See *The Ante-Nicene Fathers*, III.506–510.

13. Giovanni Filoramo, *A History of Gnosticism* (London: Basil Blackwell, 1990), 104–5.

14. See Hypostasis of the Archons II.4 and On the Origin of the World II.5 in James Robinson, ed., *The Nag Hammadi Library* (San Francisco: Harper, 1977), 152–79.

15. See The Thunder, Perfect Mind, VI.2, lines 11–13, in *Nag Hammadi Library*, 271–77.

16. *Nag Hammadi Library,* 271.

17. See *Nag Hammadi Library*, 117.

18. See Jacques LaCarriere, *The Gnostics* (New York: Dutton, 1977). This pseudonymous work is very poetically written and should be seen as an interesting essay explicating a twentieth-century existentialist perspective rather than a work explicating Gnosticism in a reliable historical sense.

19. See Ioan P. Culianu, *The Tree of Gnosis: Gnostic Mythology from Early Christianity to Modern Nihilism* (New York: HarperCollins, 1994).

20. Several Buddhist scholars have argued in favor of much closer historical connections between Christian Gnosticism and Buddhism than has hitherto been alleged. See, in particular, Keith Dowman, *Sky Dancer* (London: Routledge, 1984), and John Reynolds, *The Golden Letters* (Ithaca, NY: Snow Lion, 1996). Reynolds especially uses an explicitly "gnostic" vocabulary in a Buddhist context and believes that Gnosticism represents the best vocabulary in a Western context for understanding highly esoteric Buddhist teachings like Dzogchen.

21. See Ezekiel I.

22. See Byron Sherwin, *Kabbalah: An Introduction to Jewish Mysticism* (Lanham, MD: Rowman & Littlefield, 2006), 14–16.

23. For introductions to Kabbalah, see Byron Sherwin, *Kabbalah,* as well as David Ariel, *Kabbalah: The Mystic Quest in Judaism* (Lanham, MD: Rowman & Littlefield, 2006). See also Moshe Hallamish, *An Introduction to the Kabbalah* (Albany: SUNY Press, 1998), and Moshe Idel, *Kabbalah: New Perspectives* (New Haven, CT: Yale University Press, 1988).

24. See Origen, *Commentary on John*, I.9, in Allan Menzies, ed., *The Ante-Nicene Fathers* (Grand Rapids, MI: Eerdmans, 1990 ed.), X.297–322.

25. See Clement of Alexandria, *Stromata*, VII.1-3, in *The Ante-Nicene Fathers*, II: 523–24.

26. See Dionysius the Areopagite, "Divine Names," 681A,B, Colm Luibheid, trs., *Pseudo-Dionysius: The Complete Works* (New York: Paulist Press, 1987), 69–70.

27. Dionysius the Areopagite, "Celestial Hierarchy," I/121B, in Luibheid, trs., *Pseudo-Dionysius: The Complete Works*, 145–46.

28. See Dionysius the Areopagite, "Celestial Hierarchy," III/168A, Luibheid, trs., *Pseudo-Dionysius: The Complete Works*, 155.

29. See Dionysius the Areopagite, *Mystical Theology*, MT I/999–1000A, in Luibheid, trs., *The Complete Works*, 135–36. Cp. John Jones, trs., *The Divine Names and Mystical Theology* (Milwaukee, WI: Marquette University Press, 1999), 211–12.

30. See Dionysius the Areopagite, *Mystical Theology*, MT V.1048A, B, in Luibheid, trs. *The Complete Works*, 135–36. Cp. John Jones, trs., *The Divine Names and Mystical Theology* (Milwaukee, WI: Marquette University Press, 1999), 221.

31. See Jaroslav Pelikan, "Introduction" in *Pseudo-Dionysius: The Complete Works*, 24.

Chapter Four

The Medieval Era

MAGIC

In order to understand the two primary medieval traditions of magic and mysticism, we must consider the foundations of medieval Western Christianity, and thus it is important to note here the importance of theurgy as magical practice in the Neoplatonism of late antiquity. Theurgic practice derives in part from Julian the Chaldean, who lived during the reign of Marcus Aurelius (161–180 A.D.) and who developed the concept of drawing down divine powers for the purpose of purifying the operator and bringing him closer to the divine. The pivotal text here is the complex and enigmatic *Chaldean Oracles* collection of theurgic sayings. Iamblichus and other Neoplatonic theurgists differentiated their theurgic practices from sorcery precisely because whereas a sorcerer seeks to control supernatural powers, the theurgist seeks to purify himself and unite with divine powers. According to this distinction, the sorcerer compels, while the religious magician or theurgist submits to divine power and seeks to channel it.

Of particular importance in the theurgic tradition is Iamblichus (d. 330), who in *De mysteriis* wrote at length about various kinds of theurgic practices meant to invoke the gods by way of ritual. As is well known, Iamblichus argued in favor of theurgic practice and held that invoking the power of gods and daimones (spiritual beings) is a natural part of the Platonic traditions. According to Iamblichus, daimones are divine messengers who translate divine energies into forms that human beings can contact and use (I.5).[1] There are evil daimones, he writes, but the theurgist works with the good ones (I.10). One invokes these good daimones by, as Iamblichus writes, "employing a material mode of worship" (V.14), by invoking their powers into earthly vehicles. By contrast, Porphyry (d. 303) was skeptical about theurgy and argued that theurgic practice was not only unnecessary for religious practice but also made practitioners potentially subject to the deceptions of evil daimones.

This division concerning theurgy within Neoplatonism in turn was taken up by Augustine of Hippo (d. 430) in his *City of God*, who sided with Porphyry, citing approvingly his skepticism about deception of theurgists by evil daimones (X.11).[2] It is also through Augustine that we possess remnants of Porphyry's lost *Letter to Anebo*, where he apparently also detailed his doubts about theurgic praxis. Clearly Augustine, like Porphyry, believes in the existence of daimones, but—and this is a critically important shift for the history of magic in Christianity—Augustine regards the daimones as fraudulent spirits who play tricks on gullible souls in order to lead them astray. Apuleius, the author of the extraordinary novel *The Golden Ass*, wrote an account of daimons in his *De daimon socratis*, but Augustine in his *City of God* drew upon that account in order to argue that daimones were not merely airy or ethereal messengers between the gods and man as Apuleius had written, but instead are "spirits fanatically bent on doing harm, completely at odds with justice, swollen with pride," "well practiced in deceit," who live in the air because they were cast down from heaven (VIII.22). Thus in Augustine's works we see a pivotal shift taking place, which can be summed up as the consigning of all daimones to the realm of demons, that is, evil spirits.

This shift, it is true, is not merely a matter of the Christians of late antiquity regarding everything that preceded them as demonic in inspiration and thus discarding it. For as Peter Brown and other historians have noted, late antiquity was riddled with trials of sorcerers, and in fact the penalties for sorcery imposed by some of the Roman emperors and by the Roman legal system were actually much harsher than the penalties exacted by Christians.[3] Interestingly, Ankarloo and Clark argue that "one of the objects of the demonisation of magic in late antiquity seems indeed to have been the offering of a means of escape, for some of the different practitioners of magic . . . and the proferring of asylum in the Christian Church."[4] By making all daimones into demons and presenting itself as utterly superior to any magical tradition, Christianity could offer conversion as an escape route from a society beset by magical attacks and counterattacks as well as persecutions. And this shift corresponded also to the Christian concept of the previous era as that of the Law, while the Christian era is one of mercy that extended also to converted magicians.

What is more, Western Christianity did not wholly jettison non-Christian magical practices or beliefs, which this shift from daimones to demons might imply. Rather, Christianity drew on prior traditions in order to better overcome them and to vanquish the fear of magical or demonic attack upon Christians. If Augustine attacked Neoplatonic theurgy, he also in the *City of God* included recourse to the Christian "good angels," be they thrones, dominions, principalities, or powers, whose mercy we enjoy by resembling them in spirit and by worshipping with them the God they worship (VIII.24–25). Thus the place held by the good daimones of Neoplatonism was now held by the good angels, and the Greco-Roman concept of an individual daimon or genius was transformed into the Christian guardian angel. In other words, Christianity tended to incorporate and thus assert its superiority over the prior non-Christian religiomagical traditions of antiquity.

JEWISH SOURCES

The relationships between Jewish and Christian forms of magic and mysticism has always been not only close, but complicatedly so. Christian Gnosticism was not far from Jewish Gnosticism during the first half of late antiquity, and even if Christian Gnosticism later (mostly) disappeared, Jewish magicians and gnostics certainly continued to exist and to influence Christianity. From late antiquity onward through the medieval period, Christian magicians were to draw on Jewish magical traditions. Certainly one also cannot overlook the complex relationship between Christians and the Old Testament, for Old Testament attitudes toward sorcerers were to inform the harsh penalties against sorcery imposed during the early medieval period in Christian Europe. But most important is that much of Christian gnostic and magical traditions—and opposition to the practice of magic—can be shown to bear some relation to their Jewish origins or parallels.

Of course, Jewish monotheism is an influential element in the formation of a monotheistic Christianity that regards the majority of discarnate entities as demonic. A monotheistic God does not leave room for competitors, and this attitude is intensified in the Jewish apocalyptic literature belonging to the centuries around the year 0 A.D., in which demonic or destructive powers often abound. According to the Book of Enoch, for instance, in great antiquity various fallen angels, led by Azazel and Semjaza, lusted after earthly women, teaching them charms, enchantments, and herbalism (6:1–3). Their offspring became the evil spirits that torment mankind. Some of these noncanonical sources correspond in various respects to the canonical Old Testament—in which the book of Leviticus also discusses Azazel (16:1–28)—and in general, both clearly tend toward the definition of all demons or fallen angels as evil.

As a result, all sorcerers are condemned, as is visible in Deuteronomy 18:10–13 and Exodus 22:18, where sorcery is proscribed and sorcerers are to be given the death penalty, or in Exodus 7: 8–13, where Moses is confronted with and overcomes Pharaoh's sorcerers. Of course, Augustine points out in

The City of God, Moses's victory is itself a magical triumph, but one based upon the superior power of the angels over the pharaoh's magicians' demons (X:8). And this argument, which of course existed in Judaism as well, inaugurates a long tradition in both Judaism and Christianity of attempting to clearly differentiate between legitimate angelic Jewish or Christian magic drawing on the power of God, and illegitimate non-Jewish or non-Christian magic that relies upon demons. However, there are a wide range of responses to such attempts, ranging from on one end of the spectrum, those who in late antiquity insist on the falsehood of all forms of magic and sorcery, to those on the other end of the spectrum who insist that it is lawful for those who are within the tradition and in divine service to command the demons. Since God can command demons, why cannot the holy individual in service to God?

Thus Jewish and Christian magical traditions tend toward what we might call a complicated monotheism—complicated or modified by an emphasis on the necessity of drawing upon intermediate beings, be they angels or demons, to achieve various ends. It is no accident that later forms of Christian magic rely upon angels with Hebrew names and roots; the various Christian angelic names have their origins almost totally in Jewish magical traditions. Scholem lists the following examples of Jewish magical texts from the late Talmudic period: *Sefer ha-Malbush*, *Sefer ha-Yashar*, and the *Sefer ha-Razim*, the latter including incantations drawn in part from Greek sources.[5] From the circles whence these books came, later associated with *Merkabah* mysticism, also emerged the magical uses of the Torah and the Psalms that became a well-known feature of Jewish life. Magical practices remained a controversial area not only in Christianity but also within Judaism itself, yet they continued to flourish in both traditions during the medieval era.

Moshe Idel has discussed at length the complex relationships between mysticism and magic in Jewish Kabbalah, with special attention to the fifteenth century, when what he terms a magico-Kabbalistic model emerged. Magico-Kabbalism held that the advent of the Messiah is to be accomplished "by magical procedures enacted by a group of Kabbalists which will disrupt the continuum of history and cause radical change in the natural order."[6] This magical mode of Kabbalah developed especially in Spain, when Jews were under great political pressure, and it resulted also in a body of literature detailing the revelations of angels who were unveiling the secrets of an imminent apocalypse. During this era, Kabbalah also developed an extensive demonology and, among some practitioners, a belief that it was necessary to battle, to contain, or to demolish demonic powers in order to establish Jewish freedom from Christian persecution and, ultimately, to bring about the advent of the Messiah and redemption.[7]

While magico-Kabbalism or practical Kabbalah did emerge in an environment of Christian anti-Semitism, and in the context of a reciprocal Jewish hostility toward Christianity, Christian magicians nonetheless were subsequently to draw on this same magico-Kabbalistic tradition in order to develop Christian forms of magic that relied upon Hebrew names, words, and letters as well as Kabbalistic tradition. In short, one cannot deny the deeply interwoven interconnections between Jewish and Christian forms of magic that continue in the medieval period and last all the way into the modern era. But there is a range of medieval esoteric traditions, not only magical ones, and we must also consider these, beginning with cosmological and metaphysical forms of gnosis.

MEDIEVAL GNOSIS

The Via Positiva and Nature

While magical traditions in the medieval period can be divided very roughly into two camps—folk, and scholarly—medieval gnosis, as one might expect, belongs almost exclusively to the scholastic category. To trace medieval gnosis along the lines suggested by the work of Dionysius the Areopagite is to discuss the great figures and works of the period, following two primary courses: the visionary and the transcendent, or the affirmative and the negative. Of course, it is not quite so simple as to separate these two courses completely, for both exist in the works of Dionysius himself, and both also exist or are implied in many later works as well. Still, it is not difficult to separate a gnostic figure like Meister Eckhart from a visionary like Hildegard of Bingen, in part because the visionary tradition does not derive nearly as much as the gnostic from a scholarly lineage. But let us begin with the historical movement of Dionysian spirituality through the medieval period.

Without doubt, one of the medieval figures most profoundly influenced by the Areopagite is John Scotus Eriugena, sometimes called Erigena (fl. 850 A.D.). Eriugena is without question a central figure not only because in his master work *Periphyseon: De divisione naturæ* he drew explicitly and at length upon the Dionysian corpus while adding to and developing it along the lines of Platonic dialogue, but also because he translated Dionysius's works and thus made them more available to medieval Europe. Eriugena was clearly a major conduit for the transmission of Dionysian spirituality into Western Christianity and was especially important because he also drew upon the works of Maximus the Confessor and Gregory of Nyssa for his views drawn from Dionysius, thus incorporating into the Western current several major figures of Eastern Christianity.

Eriugena's views are complex and very developed, owing a considerable debt to Neoplatonism as well as to Dionysius. Eriugena wrote at length about what he called the divine "Nothing" that precedes and transcends all being, in this theme following Dionysius but also anticipating such prominent figures as Eckhart, Tauler, Böhme, and much later, Berdyaev and others (*Periphyseon* 687A, B).[8] Eriugena saw a grand order in the cosmos, which is arranged hierarchically both upward and downward. If human beings have fallen into ignorance, it is certainly possible for them to rise again progressively toward transcendent knowledge. Like Origen before him, and Jane Leade after, Eriugena held that hell was not a permanent but a temporary place of punishment, a controversial view underscoring his insistence on the fluidity of consciousness in the cosmos, and the potential for universal restoration.[9]

Eriugena also represents a preoccupation with nature to be found throughout much of the subsequent Western esoteric traditions. He is very much concerned, as the title *Periphyseon [The Division of Nature]* would suggest, with the relationships between the transcendent and nature. Hence, while Eriugena does discuss the "Divine Goodness that is called 'Nothing,'" much of the work is concerned more with the manifest theophanies of nature, with the descent "from the negation of all essences into the affirmation of the essence of the whole universe," with the emergence of the Divine "from itself into itself," from formlessness into "innumerable forms and species" (Book III, 681C). Eriugena is not what we might call a nature philosopher in the sense that one could apply the term to authors of, say, eighteenth-century Europe—he is deeply and primarily concerned with Dionysian and Augustinian theosophic and theological issues—but the place (or the nature) of nature nonetheless plays a central role in his thought.

This preoccupation with nature was to continue into and flourish in the twelfth century, where we find a number of major European figures continuing to focus on the relationship between nature and the divine, or the earthly and the heavenly. Among such figures are Bernardus Sylvestris, who belonged to the school of Chartres, and who wrote *De mundi universitate* (1147), and Alain of Lille (1128–1203), who wrote *De planctu naturae*. These works continue to reflect the Platonic emanationist cosmology that we saw in Eriugena, and they have implications both for gnosis on the one hand (it is not dualistic) and for magic.

Indeed, Bernardus Sylvestris's work has clear magical implications. In *Cosmographia*, he outlines his Platonic cosmologic schema, discussing the hierarchic structures of the macrocosmos and the microcosmos. And in chapter 7, he discusses the various kinds of discarnate spirits, beginning with the highest of the angelic host, those near the godhead itself and dwelling in the "eighth sphere" in the absolute serenity of divine contemplation. His outline descends from level to level of angelic spirits associated with each of the planets, down to the sublunary discarnate beings.[10] Those at the top are serene, but as one descends in the sublunary realm, one encounters below the midpoint evil spirits who have been "only slightly cleansed of the ancient evil of matter" and persist in wickedness, often also punishing criminals. These are the "renegade angels," and below them are the earthly spirits, the sylvans, pans, and naiads, whose bodies are of elemental purity.[11] While Bernardus Sylvestris does not discuss magic at this point, his schema certainly presents a framework in which both pagan and Christian magical practices could be understood. It is more than a little interesting that his *Cosmographia* was read before and commended by Pope Eugene III in 1147.

During the same period we find the remarkable Hildegard of Bingen (1099–1180), author of a number of works and several hundred letters as well as her most famous work, *Scivias*, an illustrated record of her visionary experiences. *Scivias* is a work in the line of Dionysius's *via positiva*: it records and explicates Hildegard's visionary experiences, which began in her forty-third year with a waking vision of a great iron mountain enthroned upon which was the blinding Holy One. At the foot of the mountain stood an image full of eyes on all sides, before which stood a child wearing a tunic and white shoes; and in the mountain itself were many windows in which human heads appeared, some of which were white. Hildegard explicates each line of her own account of such visions, explaining along the way the nature of the wind and the stars, the sandy globe of earth and, in passing, the falsehood of the magical arts (Vision III.1–15, 22).

While one might think that links and perhaps even a grand synthesis might easily be made between the *via positiva*, nature theology, visionary experiences, and magic, in fact this does not seem to be the case. Although the *via positiva* is the path through symbols and visionary experiences—hence seeing what is above through images that resemble what is below—and although the medieval natural theology of Bernardus Sylvestris, Alain of Lille, and to a lesser extent Hildegard could be seen as providing a framework for a magical worldview, in fact one does not find here a coherent union of all of these; there is, it seems, no single grand medieval synthesis that joins together magic, nature theology, and visionary mysticism into a single overarching perspective, although there are a number of efforts in this direction by such figures as Ramon Lull (1235–1316), who leans rather heavily in the direction of the *via positiva* and whose work is affiliated with magic and alchemy. Still, one can trace themes or modes of thought that reappear in various forms and traditions that have much in common but that do not often directly overlap. In fact, what in Dionysius's work is joined—the *via positiva* and *via negativa*—in the medieval period begins to bifurcate or, to be more precise, to trifurcate.

Certainly one can argue that the *via negativa* and the *via positiva* begin to separate during this period. On the one hand one sees the visionary mysticism of a Hildegard of Bingen, clearly an extension or manifestation of the *via positiva*. And on the other hand one sees the emergence, only a century later, of the greatest *via negativa* gnostics of Christian history, Meister Eckhart (1260–1327), Johannes Tauler (1300–1361), Heinrich Suso (1296–1366), and Jan van Ruysbroeck (1293–1381) along with the anonymous English author of the *Cloud of Unknowing* and related treatises. While all of these were influenced by Dionysian spirituality, the most powerful and influential of the *via negativa* gnostics are Eckhart and the anonymous author of the *Cloud of Unknowing* and the *Pursuit of Wisdom*. These represent the sheer transcendence of gnostic negation more purely and clearly than any other works.

On the other hand, one also sees during this period the emergence of a *via positiva* cosmological gnosis in the work of Ramon Lull (1233–1316), who is best known for having developed a complex symbolic method called the "art of memory." This art of memory or the "Lullian art" represented a complicated use of symbols in visualized "wheels" that opened insight into the archetypal forms or Platonic ideas above physical existence. Thus the Lullian art proposed itself as a potential key to all the sciences, including not only theological but also medical, astrological, magical, biological, psychological, and other kinds of knowledge. Human knowledge here opens into divine knowledge, as demarcated by the qualities of God himself: eternity, power, wisdom, and so forth, each in turn with their analogical affiliations that ramify throughout creation.

While the Lullian art of memory could certainly be applied to magical and alchemical purposes and was the forerunner and direct source for similar complex systems of thought in the Renaissance, the *via negativa* of Eckhart and Tauler is not concerned with the symbolism and meaning of nature so much as with the sheer transcendence of gnosis. Eckhart's and Tauler's works have cosmological implications, but they are not concerned with cosmology as such. By contrast, what we see emerging in the line that runs, roughly, from Bernardus Sylvestris through Ramon Lull and into the Renaissance via such a figure as Henry Cornelius Agrippa in his *De occulta philosophia* is a focus on cosmology and therefore on magic, that is, on the manipulation of the cosmos.

This is a critically important division, and one that has been overlooked far too often. Here is the trifurcation to which I earlier alluded. It seems self-evident, but bears pointing out, that scientific rationalism did not emerge *ex nihilo* in the seventeenth and eighteenth centuries in Europe, but came out of a longer current to which the medieval *via positiva* tradition (loosely speaking) and much of the Renaissance unquestionably belongs. Thus the *via positiva* leads into two parallel currents: one is the more subterranean current of magical traditions, alchemy, and related symbolically based ways of seeing and manipulating the world; and the other is what became the more mainstream current of scientific rationalism. But these two currents remain closely intertwined because they have the same predecessors, whereas the *via negativa* becomes the "third way," one that is almost totally excluded from subsequent Western European traditions. I cannot think of a single influential figure representing *via negativa* gnosis after the fifteenth century—certainly there is no one in the seventeenth through the nineteenth centuries who corresponds to an Eckhart or whose work corresponds to a *Cloud of Unknowing*, with the possible and complex exception of Jacob Böhme.

The *Via Negativa* in the Medieval Era

It is true that the *De divisione naturae* of Eriugena was condemned by Pope Honorius II in 1225, and all copies called to Rome to be burnt, but obviously some were preserved, as were Eriugena's translations of Dionysius. Nonetheless, within a quarter century, Albertus Magnus was lecturing in Paris on the Dionysian works, and a scant ten years later, Thomas Aquinas was lecturing on the *Divine Names*. And it was at roughly the same time that Hugh of St. Victor and Richard of St. Victor flourished, whose Dionysian school became known as that of the Victorines and was noted for its strong opposition to the Aristotelianism that had begun to dominate in the academy.[12] What is more, it is precisely at this same time that we find the appearance of Meister Eckhart (1260–1327/8) and Johannes Tauler, who both certainly belong to the camp of the *via negativa*. It is in these authors' works, and in the later works of the author of the *Cloud of Unknowing*, that this tradition reaches its zenith.

The works of Eckhart are, of course, renowned since their rediscovery by the great nineteenth century German theosopher Franz von Baader. Eckhart's works are sermons on various topics, mostly traditional scriptural exegeses, but within those exegeses are dazzling and paradoxical revelations of sheer transcendence. For instance, in his sermon 14a (Quint edition 16a) Eckhart remarks that spiritually speaking, one is always in the other: that which embraces, embraces itself, a point that if understood, means that one has heard enough preaching.[13] In sermon 1 (Quint 57), he quotes Dionysius the Areopagite several times and points out that the freer one is from images, the more receptive one is to God, for God himself is utterly free from all images. You must, Eckhart exhorts his hearers and readers, withdraw from all things, for God scorns working with images; indeed, were the soul not free to transcend images, it would be unable to be blessed. The soul must enter into the essential ground of all things, totally beyond all images, and there it will find divine peace.[14] While Eckhart was censured posthumously as heretical, he remains squarely within and one of the most subtle exponents of *via negativa* gnosis.

Johannes Tauler, a bit younger than Eckhart, was also somewhat more cautious in expression, and as a result had a greater subsequent impact on German and European spirituality. His sermons, as well as spurious writings attributed to him, spread over much of Europe and were quite influential. In his sermon 1, Tauler writes about how we may achieve an elevation above ourselves by renouncing our own will and worldly activity, orienting ourselves wholly toward God. For, he continues, we can meet God only in a complete abandonment of ourselves. If one's eye were to perceive an image on the wall, it must give up all other images in order to perceive that one. To perceive God, then, one must give up all images and be inwardly empty and free. For the more we give up or empty ourselves, the more the Divine may fill us. Likewise, in sermon 24, Tauler cites Augustine as saying that the soul has a hidden abyss in it, and into this secret realm descends the divine bliss, but only when the soul is utterly removed from all things.[15] It is evident that while Tauler is more circumspect in how he expresses his Dionysian *via negativa*, it is not at heart different from that of Eckhart.

But it is in the works of the anonymous English author of the *Cloud of Unknowing* that we find the most strikingly specific descriptions of transcendent gnosis. In chapter 65 of the *Cloud*, the author does discuss imagination, but only insofar as it generates various unseemly images or fanciful pictures that are "always" false and deceptive. In chapter 68, the author advises us to "Leave aside this everywhere and this everything in exchange for this nowhere and nothing." Our senses cannot understand the nothing, yet in fact the soul is blinded by it because of its abundance of spiritual light. And in chapter 70, the author writes that what he is discussing cannot be perceived or understood at all by the eyes, ears, nose, taste, or any other sensory means, nor even by spiritual understanding, for—and here he cites Dionysius directly—"The truly divine knowledge of God is known by unknowing." And this unknowing can be experienced during ordinary life, during standing, sitting, and walking (chapter 71).

Hence it should not be surprising that the *Cloud* author also translated Dionysius's *Mystical Theology*, where we find an even more elaborate description of how one must ascend into the hidden theology by doing away with all things other than God. One must, as Dionysius advises his disciple Timothy, ascend beyond every substance and every kind of knowledge; one must go beyond all that has existed and now exists, into the radiant divine darkness. This is exactly the same advice that we find in the author's "Letter of Privy Counsel," where he advises his disciple in turn that if "any idea of any particular thing" comes into his mind, immediately he is off course. For in this "dark contemplation" of the divine darkness, one must remain "one with God," while one eats, sleeps, walks, speaks, lies down, rides, and so forth; reason and the senses are not the way into the divine darkness, which is realized through grace and inner recollection.

If anything in the entire history of Western esotericism is truly esoteric in the strict sense—that is, meant for and understood by a relative few—it is the works belonging to the tradition of negative theology and in particular, the writings of the *Cloud* author. The author of the *Cloud* in fact begins his treatise by insisting that it is not meant for worldly "chatterboxes" or "fault-finders," nor is it even meant for clever clerics. Rather, he tells us at the outset, it is meant only for those enabled by an abundance of grace to share in the work of contemplation at the highest level.[16] His esotericism is explicit and clearly entails a direct and specific practice or path that is outlined in detail in his "Letter of Privy Counsel" and in other works. It is interesting to consider how this tradition largely disappeared in the course of centuries to follow, a subject to which we will return when discussing both Jacob Böhme and such twentieth-century figures as Nicholas Berdyaev, Bernadette Roberts, and Franklin Merrell-Wolff.

MEDIEVAL FOLK MAGIC AND WITCHCRAFT

If the *via negativa* represents the most austere form of gnostic traditions, folk magic and witchcraft or sorcery represent the most worldly of Western traditions. The aims of folk magic or witchcraft have virtually nothing to do with transcendence like that found in the *Cloud of Unknowing*; folk magic is concerned with mundane power, with controlling nature or other people. The aims of folk magic of course vary widely, ranging from revenge to enthralling a lover, from preventing hail to causing rain, from gaining wealth to thievery, from encouraging crops to grow to making sure that a neighbor's milk cow dries up. There are, of course, also a spectrum of means to such ends, ranging from the magic of simulacra to the pacts with or command over demons and spirits. But the majority of folk magic belonged to the former category—that of sympathetic magic.

We have already seen how magical practices pervaded Greco-Roman antiquity, and how relatively nascent Christianity frequently presented itself as a refuge from malevolent magical attacks. But the advent of Christianity over much of Europe did not entail the elimination of magical practices drawn from Greco-Roman or other preexisting non-Christian traditions. Rather, one often finds "pagan" magical practices continuing as a substrata of nominally Christian society. Among such practices, some of which continued throughout the medieval period, were pagan festivals celebrating the New Year, equinox or solstice celebrations, May dances, and "night riding" practices associated with Diana or some other lunar (or fertility) goddess. Orgiastic or celebratory traditions reminiscent of the ancient Mysteries did continue into the medieval period, just as did folk magical practices.

In fact, there are a great many varied magical practices or transformations that could be brought together under the umbrella rubric of folk magic (I am here eschewing use of the term *low magic*). Among these various magical terms or practices are: (1) *herbarius*, or practitioner of herbal medicine; (2) *veneficus*, or preparer of potions, love, poison, or otherwise; (3) *divinator* or diviner; (4) *tempestarius*, or storm-maker; (5) *wicca* or *wicce*, a spell caster (Anglo-Saxon); (6) *incantator*, or enchanter; (7) *hexe*, witch or sorceress (German); (8) *striga*, a kind of succubus-vampire and later a witch (Italian); (9) *lamia*, or vampire; and (10) *maleficus*, or one who does malevolent magic. Among the things witches were presumed capable of doing: shape shifting from human to animal form; blighting through the evil eye; becoming invisible; riding out through the air to orgies at night; using potions or salves; killing children or infants; and gaining powers by use of spirits or demons.[17] These are not meant as exhaustive lists but as indicative of the variety of terms and their meanings as well as of alleged powers, all of which can be seen as elements of folk magic.

It is obvious that the majority of terms, practices, or transformations here can be seen as malevolent, and that although the word *wicca* is actually masculine, to a considerable degree these terms and practices were attributed to women, stereotypically, to older women. At the same time, one should note that because the practices and abilities of folk magic practitioners were so varied, it would be a distortion to insist that folk magic, including but not limited to witchcraft, belonged exclusively to women. And it would also be a mistake to assume that all folk magical practices were malevolent or limited to only a few people. In the period prior to, roughly, 1000 A.D., non-Christian religious traditions certainly continued to exist not only in the Mediterranean region but also in the North. While these traditions were condemned by synod and canonical Christian authors, reverence for sacred springs, rocks, groves, caves, and hills continued, as did the use of charms carried on from antiquity, as well as some animal sacrifice. None of these folk traditions can, in themselves, be construed as malevolent toward other people.

But as we saw above, the spread of Christianity in Greco-Roman lands entailed the transformation (in Christian eyes) of pagan divinities into demons, and a corollary to this transformation as Christianity spread throughout Europe was the perception of Celtic, Teutonic, Norse, or other ancient gods as also demonic. This transformation naturally extended eventually to many magical practices that derived from these older, non-Christian traditions. But this does not mean that one finds universal condemnation of folk magical practices during this period—far from it. By and large, the secular condemnations one finds of witchcraft remain rather pragmatic, as can be seen in the seventh-century Salic fine of two hundred shillings for a witch's eating someone, and the subsequent denial of the edict of Rothari in 643 that witch-cannibalism was even possible.[18] It is true that some secular edicts insisted on the death penalty for malevolent witchcraft, but unquestionably only a segment of folk magical activity falls into such a category. The impetus for total demonization of magical practices and of witchcraft in particular only came later, and came from the Roman Catholic Church.

Despite the Church's tendency to see folk magical traditions largely in black and white terms, the nature spirits of the Northern folk traditions stubbornly retained their more or less neutral quality. Kobolds, fairies, gnomes, elves, leprechauns, even naiads and dryads—these were not evil spirits, and certainly not comparable to the fallen angels or demons of Christian tradition. Rather, they belong to an intermediate category that the clever individual can turn to his or her own benefit. Naturally, there are dangers for those who consort with or attempt to bargain with the "little people"—but those dangers are like the dangers of nature itself, which can be harsh or punishing. And one might very well also extract a gift from association with nature spirits, who can bestow presents just as nature can be beneficent. From the official view of the Roman Church, however, sacrifices made at sacred springs or groves were seen as sacrifices to demons; and the "little people" belonged more to the category of demonic familiars for witches than that of more or less neutral nature spirits.

Regarded as demonic superstition or not, however, one finds that folk magical practices and traditions were very popular and widespread during the medieval period in Europe, as evidenced by such works as *The Book of Secrets,* spuriously attributed to the great medieval scholastic Albertus Magnus. *The Book of Secrets* is among the most well-known of a number of medieval lapidaries, herbals, and books of marvelous recipes for folk magic, and it includes some wonderful instructions for dealing with various ordinary problems of daily life. If, for instance, one wants an animal to become pregnant, one should take the herb called *Lurumboror* by the Chaldeans, temper it with mandrake juice, give it to a female animal, and she will give birth. A beneficial side effect is that when the "gum tooth" of the pup is dipped in meat or drink, all who partake will be wild in battle fury.[19] My personal favorite, however, is the recipe from the "Marvels of the World," in which one is instructed to dry the blood of a snail in a linen cloth, make of the cloth a wick, give it to a man and when he lights it on fire, "he shall not cease to fart, until he let it depart, and it is a marvellous thing."[20] These recipes are often delightful, and many of them are intended for healing, but some, like that for flatulence generation, do edge slightly toward the malevolent. One can see in such cases that beneficent and malevolent magic derive from the same principles and are so closely related that someone with a reputation for the former might easily be also accused of the latter. If one can make an animal pregnant or induce battle valor, one also can induce a nasty farting spell.

But it is after 1000 A.D., and particularly in the twelfth century with the emergence of the gnostic heresy of the Cathars, that one finds the Church systematically going after heretics and, to some degree, witches. The Inquisition did see itself as going after those who had pledged themselves to the devil, who had made pacts with demons, who, in short, had become evil. At first fire was used as a means of trial—the theory being that God would protect the pure from being burnt—and only later did fire become a means not of testing but of purification. One can imagine that such a test produced rather few who were exonerated, and paradoxically, such a one would presumably have control over fire, thereby perhaps being a witch or sorcerer all the same! Such are the dilemmas into which persecution inevitably drags one.

The persecutions of witches derived in part from the later development of medieval Aristotelianism and the shunting aside of the Platonic tradition represented by such earlier figures as Eriugena and, before him, Dionysius the Areopagite. Aristotelianism represented a more or less materialist and rationalist worldview outside the purview of which stood magical traditions. As we have seen, the Neoplatonism of such figures as Iamblichus allowed for and even encouraged magical practices; and Platonic Christianity naturally continued this tendency. Platonic Christianity is more fluid and subtle; it allows for a range of magical traditions, some of which are acceptable, others of which are not. But Aristotelianism encouraged a comparatively simplistic dualism of rational/irrational or religious/demonic out of which emerged the persecutions of witches and heretics in the later medieval period.

Thus some of the intellectual justification for the witch hunts can be laid at the feet of Thomas Aquinas (1225–1274), who held that marvels cannot be produced through natural means but must come from demonic intervention. On the one side is the realm of ordinary causation that can be understood through logic; and on the other side is the realm of demonic intervention in human and natural affairs through which supernatural effects are produced. The logic runs along these lines: all supernatural effects that cannot be explained rationally must derive from demonic intervention; demons are by definition evil, and all supernatural effects entail implicit pacts with demons; therefore all forms of magic that cause supernatural effects are evil. It is not a great leap from this perspective to the persecution of witches or sorcerers; from this view they are all implicitly in league with the devil if they practice magic of any kind.

It seems self-evident—given the array of possibilities the term *witch* could describe—that such a perspective is rather extreme. But by the fifteenth century, this had become the official position of Roman Catholicism and of the Inquisition. By this time, too, heresy and witchcraft had been so thoroughly conflated as to be inseparable. A witch was a member of *secta strigarum* or *hæretici fascinarii*, that is to say, of an heretical sect, and thus heretics and witches were tried and punished more or less alike. Heretical groups like the Albigensians or the Cathars, and purportedly heretical groups like the Beguines, were regarded as fundamentally like the witches, practicing similar ceremonies, renouncing the Church, and thus by definition being in league with the devil. One of the most perplexing of such cases, however, is that of the Waldensians.

The Waldensians were a group akin to the Cathars and saw themselves as an apostolic circle devoted to poverty and spiritual practice—but they and their name eventually became almost inseparable from witchcraft. Indeed, finally witches were known colloquially as *Waudenses* or Waldensians, and this terminological confusion was officially recognized by Pope Eugenius IV in a papal bull dated 23 March 1440.[21] How is it that heretics and witches were so thoroughly confused? To this there is no single clear historical answer. It is possible that the development of antinomian variants of heresies during this time—groups like the Brethren of the Free Spirit, Adamites, and others, who insisted on spiritual freedom that extended to sexual license—was confused with or even actually intermingled with aspects of folk magic and witchcraft. But from the outside perspective of the Inquisitors, whether a group that met naked in the forest was Adamite or a group of witches is not as important as the fact that their doing so (or their being alleged to do so) marked them as in league with the devil either way.

In 1486, Heinrich Institoris (b. 1430) and Jacob Sprenger (b. ca. 1437) published the *Malleus Maleficarum*, colloquially known as the "Hammer of the Witches," and this marked the beginning of the witch persecutions of the next century. Prefaced by a notorious papal bull of Pope Innocent VIII, *Summis desiderantes* (widely taken as papal imprimitur for the witch hunts), *Malleus* became the manual for subsequent witch persecutions not only in Roman Catholic lands but also later in Protestant lands; it offers the intellectual rationalization for the existence of witches and outlines their destructive practices, which include not only cursing and incantations as well as shape shifting but also the blasphemous use of Christian sacraments, pacts with the devil, and—that old charge going back to the early days of the Christian church, once applied to Christians more generally—that they cooked and ate children.

One should recognize the rationalization that underlies the terminology and the practices of the witch and heretic persecutors who, as is well known, did not hesitate to torture their victims to gain confessions. The places where witches met were often termed "synagogues," and this word reveals a premise: witches, heretics, Jews, these are those who refuse or denigrate the message of Christ. The practice of magic is allied with the denial of Christ and the church; the dualism that we saw emerging earlier with the separation between angelic and demonic magic here is becoming a dualism of orthodoxy and magic-heresy conflated. Exemplary of the results of this dualism is the story of the *benandanti* (those who do well) unearthed by Italian scholar Carlo Ginzburg.[22] Ginzburg shows the existence of an organized group in Italy devoted to the cult of Diana who had fought with a local *striga* or witch cult. But when the Inquisition arrived, they tortured the benandanti, forced them to confess to witchcraft, and by 1640, had so changed the situation that the benandanti now saw themselves as diabolic *striga*! One can scarcely think of a clearer example of how the Inquisitorial witch and heresy-hunters dualistically, simplistically applied a blanket definition to all situations. In many respects, here, in the witch persecutions, we can find the origins of the later rationalist rejection of all magic or paranormal phenomena as superstition or delusion—it is the same blanket dismissal.

KABBALAH AND MAGICO-MYSTICISM

Origins

That there were historical connections between Jewish and Christian Gnostics in the early Christian era is well known—one can see these links or influences scattered throughout the Christian Gnostic literature of the period. Gershom Scholem in fact argues that some of the Gnostic groups usually listed as Christian—like the Ophites for instance—were in fact "basically Jewish rather than Christian."[23] Certainly it is the case that in late antiquity one finds very close relationships between Jewish and Christian gnosticisms, as well as many "intermediate" groups drawing on and arguably belonging to both traditions. Thus, as early and late medieval Christian traditions developed subsequently, it is not surprising that the close relationships between Jewish and Christian gnostic and magical traditions should continue to evolve.

The origins of medieval Jewish mystical and magical traditions are to be found in earlier apocalyptic literature, which is strikingly esoteric in character. Intended for an elite, literature like the Book of Enoch and various other works under the names of Biblical characters reveal to their audiences the secrets of the cosmos, aspects of the angelic and demonic powers, and revelations concerning the "Throne of God"—which in turn led to the period of

Merkabah [Chariot] mysticism that was to follow. Merkabah mysticism details the ascent to the realms of the divine and the mysteries of creation, and hence is a visionary tradition with its origins at least in part visible in the Dead Sea Scrolls where one finds reference to the "Throne of the Chariot." The ascent to the throne is a secret or semisecret initiatory tradition that corresponds in some respects to the *via positiva*.

Hence it is not surprising that in the associated *heikhalot* [divine palaces] gnostic literature of the first several centuries of the common era one finds a strongly theurgic tradition that in turn lent itself from very early on to the practice of magic. Here we find the emergence of the "measure of the body" [*Shi'ur Komah*] mysticism associated with the mysteries of creation in its more recondite aspects. The gnostics outlined the secret names and numbers or measurements of the divine body, and it is here that we also find much in the way of *gematria* or number-letter symbolism, which was to become a primary theme for much of subsequent Kabbalistic tradition during the medieval period. These traditions—combined with the concept of the visionary ascent to the divine that requires avoiding demonic obstructions and drawing on angelic powers—in turn connected rather naturally to associated magical practices. And so by the third century, one finds numerous magical treatises delineating incantations that offer protection from demons, as well as various other kinds of magical workings.

The most important work from this period is the engimatic *Sefer Yetzirah*, probably composed before the sixth century A.D., in which we find the elements of subsequent Kabbalistic tradition—that is, the notion of the ten *Sefirot* or aspects (stages) of divine creation, and the elaborate number-letter symbolism of *gematria*. In the *Sefer Yetzirah*, the first four *Sefirot* are associated with the elements of spirit [*ru'ah*], air, water, and fire; the last six *Sefirot* correspond to the six dimensions of space (above, below, and the four directions).

These associations were to become much more complex with the development of Kabbalah proper later on, and the emergence of the "Tree of Life" in all its intricate emanatory symbolism. Likewise, in the *Sefer Yetzirah* we find an extended analysis of the secret meanings of the twenty-two letters, which are broken up into patterns of three letters, seven letters, and twelve letters. The patterns of three correspond to the elements of air, fire, and water; those of seven correspond to the seven planets and the seven weekdays or stages of creation; and the patterns of twelve correspond to the Zodiac and the months of the year. Thus the *Sefer Yetzirah* has to do with the mysteries of creation, and not surprisingly, offered much in the way of magical interpretation and application.

Out of the Merkabah tradition and that represented by the *Sefer Yetzirah* emerged not only later Kabbalistic mysticism, but also the allied tradition of

Kabbalistic magic. Jewish magicians who could draw on the tradition of the secret Names of God represented a tradition to which even Christians turned and that in turn greatly influenced the emergence of medieval Christian scholarly magical or theurgic traditions. Jewish magic drew very much on the symbolism of the sacred alphabet, on the premise that all of creation is informed by the secret numbers and letters of divine creation. By manipulating the secret names or numbers of creation, one could, the theory goes, influence events, nature, or individuals, for one is working with the secret principles of existence itself. While this tradition was not necessarily associated with the practice of magic initially, it certainly became so later in the medieval period.

GNOSIS AND MAGIC IN MEDIEVAL JUDAISM

In effect, in medieval Judaism we can see the emergence of two related streams that do not necessarily conflict with one another: that of gnosis, and that of magic. Moshe Idel argues in his book *Messianic Mystics* (1998) that these two streams converged in the Jewish messianic traditions of the later medieval period (i.e., by the late fifteenth century), but prior to this time one also sees these two streams closely intertwined. The flowering of Kabbalah took place during the twelfth and thirteenth centuries in Spain, particularly in the region of Castile but also in Provençe in France. There are too many important figures during this period to trace here, so instead we focus on only a few figures or works that remain central to our argument, beginning with Abraham Abulafia.

Were one to concentrate only on figures such as Abulafia, one would be able more easily to make the argument that gnosis and magic remained relatively separate traditions during this period. The gnostic Abulafia, of course, is a remarkable figure perhaps best known for his emphasis on "writing down the Names," combining and recombining letters until he or his disciple entered into an ecstatic state. It is clear from Abulafia's writings and those of his disciples that his is an initiatory gnostic tradition and more or less separate from any magical aims. Through the combination of the names, the initiate enters into a state of transcendence, but this transcendence is an end in itself, not a means to some magical end. Such states were achieved through solitary practices that involved special postures, kinds of breathing, particular scents, singing, but above all, a form of meditative writing of sacred divine names.[24] Yet we do find similar ritual practices prescribed for rituals that are today often catalogued as "magic."

The Sefirot

Now we must remark on the appearance of the Zohar and the full-fledged doctrine of the Sefirot, which represent the union of magic and gnosis both cosmological and metaphysical. The Sefirot, or Tree of Life, has become very widely known and indeed was incorporated much later than its introduction—largely as a result of the efforts of Eliphas Lévi in the mid-nineteenth century—into the practice of Western magic. This incorporation came about because the various Sefirot represent a complex set of correspondences and images that are extremely useful in constructing a magical "system," even if that was only part of their original import.

Because the ten Sefirot are so highly symbolically charged, there are many names for each Sefira, but the following arrangement and names are the most common (see figure 4.1).

In essence, this is an emanatory pattern that corresponds in some respects to the Neoplatonic tradition of creation as emanating downward from the One into multiplicity. But there are numerous differences, not the least of which is that in the Kabbalistic schema, creation takes place entirely within the Divine via patterns of three. Above, however, is not the One but the 'Ain Sof, or primordial and hidden root or origin out of which the Sefirot or qualities of existence emanate. 'Ain Sof is the infinite and transcendent above and beyond existence itself, and about it one can ultimately say nothing.

Hence of the Tree of Emanation, the "root" is said to be above, not below, and this is what Keter represents; Keter is the crown of creation, and is also known as the "naught" or "nothing" in that it is beyond conceptualization. The second Sefira, Hokhmah, is wisdom, and corresponds to the upper body of the divine king; it represents Wisdom or being emerging from the transcendence of being. Binah, or the third Sefira, is understanding, and is the receptacle for wisdom, thus also representing limitation or contraction. Binah is considered the origination of the left side of the Tree. These three together constitute the first group; the second group as a whole is that of the bottom seven, corresponding to the "seven days of creation." The upper three correspond to transcendence; the bottom seven to the intrinsic aspects of creation. The remaining seven Sefirot are: Gedulah, or Hesed, which means abundance of light; Gevurah, the restriction of the light-giving Hesed; and Tiferet, known as the Sefira of compassion or mercy, which tempers the potentially world-destroying tension between Hesed and Gevurah. Tiferet is known as the "second Keter," as it is the origination point for the lowest Sefirot. The lower Sefirot are Nesah and Hod, which correspond to Hesed and Gevurah on a less extreme level and are the source of prophetic inspiration; Yesod, which is the intermediary between Nesah and Hod but also between all the Sefirot

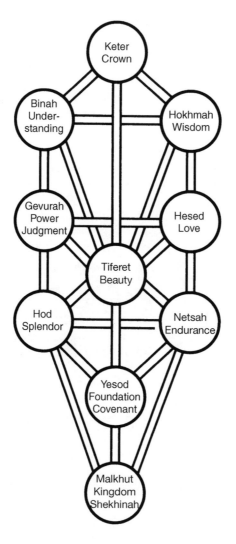

Figure 4.1.

above it (male) and that below it, Malkhut, seen as female, receptive, the mother, the queen, and the earth.[25]

The Tree of Emanation is an almost infinitely complex constellation of symbols. Each Sefira came to be associated with intricate number-letter combinations as well as wordplay, colors, elements, directions, and so forth. The Tree can be read as a kind of lightning-stroke traveling downward in a zigzag pattern, or it can be read as a series of three groups of three plus one, or it can be read as three lines traveling downward from above (i.e., two outward lines and a middle). Indeed, the Tree is perhaps best understood as a glyph for the whole of existence that bears within it countless interrelated glyphs, each of which reveals connections to others in complicated patterns. While such a system may be amenable to the practice of gnostic ascent, one should keep in mind that the Tree itself represents emanation downward or outward into existence, and is thus at least equally amenable to the practice of magic in that drawing on its symbolism naturally reverberates into the whole of creation that it represents.

We must also note the appearance, in the thirteenth century, of the "Treatise on the Left Emanation" by Isaac ha-Kohen, who with his brother Jacob traveled in Spain and Provençe in the period of 1260–1280. In the "Treatise on the Left Emanation," we see the "other side" [*sitra ahra*] of the Tree of Emanation, its demonic counterpart.[26] A new series of emanations and beings emerge in this and similar literature, a kind of new mythology that outlines the nature of the demonic forces and, indeed, an entire demonic Sefirotic pattern that in turn has all manner of correspondences not of a positive sort, like those of the conventional Sefirot, but negative correspondences. The implications of these innovations for sorcery are obvious: if one can "map" and control the demonic powers, one could harness them for beneficial purposes.

One finds a similar tendency in a primary work for the emergence of Kabbalism: the Zohar, or "Book of Splendor," which dates from the thirteenth century and is often attributed in part at least to Moses de Leon. The Zohar is an extraordinarily complex work consisting in layers or what Scholem calls "strata" of different forms and traditions; in printed versions it comprises five volumes that include commentaries, midrashic statements, stories set in both fictional and real places and featuring Simeon ben Yohai and ten companions whose discussions and monologues are often self-referential and are full of symbolism and allusion. While the Zohar certainly belongs to the realm of gnosis, it also includes references to magical traditions and in particular to sorcerers and evil spirits. As a number of scholars of Kabbalah have detailed, both the Zohar and the works of Moses de Leon feature a great deal of mythic imagery, sexual symbolism in reference to the relationships between the Sefirot, and considerable interest in demonology and sorcery.[27]

Kabbalistic Magic and Sorcery

Thus as Kabbalist tradition developed, it naturally lent itself to what has become known as "practical Kabbalah," or magic. Magical traditions in Judaism predated the emergence of the Zohar and the ever more complex elaborations of the Sefirot and continued through these later traditions, drawing on earlier works like the *Sefer ha-Razim* and including such practices as the magical uses of the Sacred Names; the angelic or archangelic alphabets sometimes called "eye writing" because the letters resemble small eyes; the creation of amulets and protective spells; the vanquishing of enemies; the gaining of powers like that of unveiling hidden treasure; various kinds of folk medicine, and so forth. These correspond more to "white" or "gray" magic; but as such treatises as that on the Left Emanation would attest, one also finds an increasing interest in "black" magic, which is to say, sorcery drawing on demonic powers in order to destroy or harm others. Traditionally, Kabbalists reject black magic, but in the Zohar, for instance, there is something of a justification for knowing about and even drawing upon destructive powers in order to convert them to the good—one can fight the *sitra ahra* with its own weapons, in other words.[28]

It is not surprising, then, that the existence of practical Kabbalah gave credence to the general medieval European perception of Jews and especially of Kabbalists as great sorcerers or magicians. By the late medieval period, one finds not only practices of white magic involving amulets and charms, but also a great many heterodox writings that incorporate Islamic and Germanic or Slavic demonology and witchcraft with Jewish kabbalistic traditions. Scholem lists a great many works that fall under the general rubric of practical Kabbalah, some of which do include "invocations of demons . . . formulas for private gain . . . discovery of hidden treasure . . . and even sexual magic and necromancy."[29] Idel in his book *Messianic Mystics* further makes a convincing case that magic and mysticism cannot be easily separated, particularly when incorporated into messianic traditions, because magical means are often used to help bring about messianic aims.[30]

SCHOLASTIC MAGIC

That there are numerous connections between Jewish and Christian forms of magic is, by now, well known. Of course, it remains an open question whether we are looking at a form of magic or rather, of magico-mysticism both in Jewish and in Christian texts. After all, an important form of Jewish "magic" from late antiquity into the medieval period is detailed in a literature called "Sar-Torah," or "Prince of the Torah," discussed in detail by Michael

Swartz.[31] These texts outline how a practitioner could conjure an angel, who would bestow on him not only exceptional memory and learning, but also esoteric cosmological and metaphysical knowledge. In other words, through recitation of specific divine names and through a particular magico-mystical ritual, the practitioner could reach union with the angel of the Torah and realize knowledge of the divine, or gnosis. A number of quite famous rabbis were held to have gained their wisdom and knowledge in this way.

One finds analogous magico-mystical practices in medieval Christianity as well, as becomes clear when we look at the work of John of Morigny, a Benedictine monk who between 1304 and 1317 wrote a chronicle of his experiences called *Liber visionum*.[32] John practiced a form of proscribed magic called the *Ars notoria*, in which the practitioner undertakes a regimen of ritual prayer and fasting in order that the Virgin Mary might bestow upon him knowledge of the seven liberal arts, as well as divine knowledge. Connected to these practices is also oneiromancy, or the proper interpretation of dreams or visionary experiences. Scholars Claire Fanger and Nicholas Watson have made the text of the *Liber visionum* available, accompanied by a detailed introduction, so for the first time we can see this instance of what is sometimes called "medieval magic" but certainly could also be described as "magico-mystical."

There are clear similarities between Jewish and Christian medieval forms of magic or magico-mysticism, and indeed, there are obvious points of transfer as well. Thus some of the best-known Christian magical works draw on the figure of Solomon, invoking Solomonic wisdom, and many medieval Christian works include Hebrew words and letters, as well as various kinds of "pidgin" Hebrew. One also sees similarities in sociocultural terms, since both Jewish and Christian magicians virtually by definition belonged to the clerisy and had access to texts that were self-restricted through the knowledge of languages these texts inherently required, but that were also often restricted or even banned by some in the respective religious tradition or hierarchy. Of course, it was not always entirely clear whether a work was banned or not— John of Morigny's *Liber visionum*, although it was in fact burned publicly, turned up again in monastic use elsewhere not much later. And we should keep in mind that these and similar works are suffused with a reverential attitude—it is for this reason, among others, that the word *magico-mystical* might be appropriate.

At the same time, as Michael Swartz points out in relation to Jewish Sar-Torah magico-mysticism, the same kinds of rituals and invocations also are found in works that invoke angelic or divine help for financial or other more mundane matters that it is more difficult to describe as having "mystical" aspects. And a similar observation can be made regarding medieval Christian magical works, which is presumably why the Roman Catholic Church decided to err mostly on the side of proscribing magical texts, regarding them as fundamentally attempting to accomplish even respectable ends through what the Church officials regarded as the disreputable or suspect means of magical invocation.[33]

Consider some of the catalogue of "experiments" listed in the fifteenth-century Christian *Munich Handbook of Necromancy* edited and translated by Richard Kieckhefer: "for gaining knowledge of the liberal arts," "for arousing a woman's love," "for arousing hatred between friends," "for obtaining a horse," "for invisibility," "for opening all locks," and so on. The catalogue also includes a "mirror of Lilith" and a discourse on "the name Semiforas," the latter word derived from the Hebrew *Shem ham-M'forasch*. As Kieckhefer notes, "there is some reason to suppose that these divinatory practices show the influence of Jewish divination in particular," and he adds that there is a series of Jewish magical texts closely resembling those in the *Munich Handbook*.[34] One finds similar practices outlined in the thirteenth- or fourteenth-century *Sworn Book of Honorius*, which Gösta Hedegård describes as

> a text concerned with acquiring benefits, material as well as spiritual, through the mediation of the holy Trinity and the Virgin Mary and by means of diverse angels and spirits. This is achieved by the use of certain magic seals and circles, which are described in the book, but first and foremost by reciting a great number of prayers and invocations, both of a general and a more magical/mystical nature.[35]

For the most part, the medieval magi-mystics often, perhaps largely saw themselves as engaging in ritual practices for divine ends. From this other perspective, "magic" might be the means of realizing God's will on earth, or of manifesting angelic powers for redemptive or transformative ends. Not surprisingly, then, the whole area of scholarship on "magic," and in particular on early and medieval forms of "magic," remains as contested today as it has ever been. But the profound links between Jewish and Christian forms of magic are self-evident in a great deal of the literature.

Thus it is not at all surprising that Jewish mysticism and practical Kabbalah also had an extensive influence on the formation of later (nineteenth and early twentieth century) Western magical traditions like that of the Golden Dawn and related groups, as well as a somewhat less visible but also substantial earlier influence on Christian theosophic and Rosicrucian currents. Such influence is visible from the widespread appearance of Hebrew letters and terms throughout the illustrations of the seventeenth and eighteenth centuries. But arguably the most visible influence of Kabbalah is to be found in such pivotal works as Pico della Mirandola's Kabbalistically influenced *Theses* (1487), or Heinrich Cornelius Agrippa's *Three Books of Occult Philosophy* (1533), which represents the juncture of folk, scholarly, and practical Kabbalah magical traditions and was to be a central source work for much that was to follow in the Christian world. But before we turn to the Renaissance, we must consider heresy during the medieval period.

MEDIEVAL HERESIES

If on the one hand, medieval Roman Catholic authorities found it necessary by the fifteenth century to stamp out witches, they had found it necessary much earlier to attack heresies, of which witchcraft might be considered a kind of variant. The term *heresy* derives from the Greek word *hairesis*, meaning "sect," which derives from the Greek word *hairein*, to "take" or to choose, referring to a school of thought. In other words, the word *heresy* has at its heart only the meaning of someone choosing a particular school of thought or perspective; and it is only as Roman Catholicism took on the force of dogma did dissent become not merely an individual's choice but a crime punishable by death. From the period of Constantine onward—after Christianity became more or less the official religion of Europe—the official Church certainly did not endorse heresies, but only from the twelfth and thirteenth centuries did the machinery of the Inquisition emerge and then, as many historians have shown, more out of political-social than doctrinal motivations.

The basic premise of heresy, from the Roman Catholic perspective, was that the heretic was inspired and led by the devil—thus the true heretic had to be proud and obstinate in his error, just like the devil. Of course, such a view of the heretic left relatively little room for tolerance: either one assented in its entirety to Church dogma, or one placed oneself in direct opposition to the Church as a whole. There was no median ground, only the either/or dichotomy, and hence even such a profound, indeed, astonishing figure as Meister Eckhart could be condemned as a heretic; not on "this side," he must be on the "other side," or so the rationale went. One might well argue that this represented the true dualism of the period, not the so-called dualism of the heretics, but that of the Church itself. Yet, how, given that there was little prior tradition of capital punishment for heretics in Europe, did the notorious and extremely dualistic medieval apparatus of the Inquisition and the burning of heretics come about?

Part of the answer to this question might well be found in Orléans, France, in the battle for power of Robert the Pious, King of France in 1022, in a struggle with his rival Eudes II, Count of Blois. This struggle came to involve the bishops and clergy, and the King's men began to root out "heresy" in Orléans with the help of an informer by the name of Aréfast. Aréfast infiltrated a group in Orléans who, he claimed, conducted nocturnal orgies and burned the infants born of the orgies in order to make a kind of Satanic sacrament of their ashes. While these kinds of lurid accusations hark back to similar claims against the Gnostics in antiquity and back to accusations of Romans against Christians in general, they remain as dubiously sensational now as they were then. However, some other elements of Aréfast's account are more interesting, among them the heretics' central insistence on the primacy of gnosis, conferred by the laying on of hands. They held that Christ was not born in a human body but is to be experienced directly for oneself in visionary experience. The Church sacraments meant nothing, they held; what matters is one's own direct spiritual experience. For these views, which are quite gnostic, the King had the group burned to death outside the walls of Orléans, except for two who recanted, thus beginning a practice that the official Church was to sanction throughout Western Europe.

This little saga is particularly interesting because it so closely parallels the conflict in antiquity between the various Gnostic sects and what came to be known as orthodoxy, and because it presages much that was to come. It is unclear where the concept of gnosis in the Orléans group came from; Malcolm Lambert recounts scholarly speculation that it may have come from the Bogomils in the East but concludes that it probably did not. The perspective espoused by Ioan Culianu in his *The Tree of Gnosis* is undoubtedly in any case quite reasonable: that inherent in Christian tradition are certain elements or "building blocks" that periodically recur, and among these may be counted gnosis, visionary experiences, a docetic denial of the incarnation of Christ, and so forth. Certainly these are the elements one finds in Orléans and, for that matter, in a great variety of later medieval "heresies" to come. Thus the heresy of Orléans does not require a direct lineage traceable to antiquity or to the Bogomils; certain patterns are bound to recur in Christianity, and this is but one instance of that fact.

Without question, the various medieval heresies to come—Brethren of the Free Spirit, Catharism, the Albigensians, to name only the most prominent— like that at Orléans, were esoteric in the strict sense of the word. That is, whether they belonged largely to an educated clergy or to the laity, "heretical" groups by their very nature saw themselves as possessing the secret truths not recognized by the exoteric Church with its emphasis on dogma and ritual. And because such stringent penalties for heresy were possible, the groups and individuals had rather good reason to divulge their inclinations not publicly, but only to those who had proven themselves worthy of knowing what they saw as the truths they had come to realize. Central to the various medieval heresies was an emphasis on direct experience and transmutation of the individual, be it through gnosis or through much greater moral austerity than was endorsed by the Church. Heretical groups tended to insist on the primacy of direct individual experience and transmutation as opposed to the Church's insistence on the primacy of the Church and ritual as mediator between humanity and God, and in this sense such groups may even be spoken of as proto-Protestant.

Arguably the most important of the medieval heresies is that of the Cathars, which emerged in Western Europe, chiefly France, Germany, and Italy, from the mid-twelfth into the thirteenth centuries. The Cathars have been claimed by some scholars as a revival of Manichaeism, and there are without doubt many parallels, but so too there are many potential links with the Bogomils as well as with Gnosticism. Critical to understanding the Cathars is their tradition of the *perfecti*, who were admitted to this status by the rite of the *consolamentum*. The *consolamentum* did away with the consequences not only of the individual's sins, but also of the prior fall of the angels and of the reign of Satan over the individual in this world. To be a *perfect* required a strict regimen both to achieve and to maintain this status, which was by no means easy, including as it did total celibacy, periodic fasting, and a stringently restricted diet devoid of all products of coition like dairy products, eggs, or meat. Moreover, for those who "fell" there was only a limited rite of confession and absolution for major transgressions, unlike Catholicism, precisely so that the *perfecti* had the strongest possible incentive to remain perfected and die in an unlapsed condition. The two other classes of Cathars were those who sympathized with Catharism, and those who were believers but had not yet taken the rite of the *consolamentum*.

The Cathars, like the Orléans circle, espoused a Docetist view of Christ as a transcendent spiritual figure but developed also an elaborate metaphysics that saw this world as the domain of Satan. Like the Gnostics of antiquity, they generated a vast number of myths and symbolic or allegorical parables to illustrate their perspectives. Their mythogenic and, one may also say, literary inclinations link them fairly closely with the troubadour movement of the thirteenth century, which celebrated chastity in the service of romantic love; in troubadour poetry, abstention and the absence of one's lover transformed the romantic relationship into something otherworldly and at its height, into a spiritual experience. It is undoubtedly no coincidence that Catharism and the troubadour movement flourished in close proximity in Southern France; in some areas, particularly Languedoc, the Cathars governed with impunity.

By the 1230s, the Church and the Inquisition descended upon the Cathars in southern France, developing an antiheresy police and court system, requiring oaths of fidelity to the Church, and requiring no deviation from Catholic doctrine. By the 1240s, the heresy was being brutally routed, with such tactics as the interrogations of thousands, the burning alive of two hundred

Cathars at Montségur, and the burning of eighty in Agen in a single day in 1249; the last Cathar was burnt in Languedoc in 1330.[37] Various hypotheses have been offered by scholars as to why Catharism did not survive, including observations that the European economies were developing during this period, and that during this time the development of the Franciscan order, as well as of a piety based on the earthly details of Christ's life and death, offered Catharism a competition that it could not, in the end, resist. While these theories undoubtedly bear in them some truth, they also might incline one to overlook the obvious: Catholic persecution via the Inquisition, and the murder of thousands, was successful. To a substantial degree, this persecution came about as Catharism (originally esoteric as a movement) also became exoteric and thus a socioreligious threat to Roman Catholic hegemony in France and Italy.

But if the Cathars were eventually wiped out, other heresies also emerged subsequently that bear examination here. Among them are the "Brethren of the Free Spirit," and the Waldensians. Robert Lerner and Malcolm Lambert each argue flatly that the Brethren of the Free Spirit simply did not exist as an organized group like the Cathars; in their view, as a sect, they were a fiction created by Church authors as a kind of heretical bogeyman.[38] But this is not to say that the Free Spirit adherents did not exist at all; they existed, Lerner holds, as individuals informally in contact with like-minded colleagues. The inquisitors, bound and determined to find heresy, hunted around and took on the most literal-level, paradoxical, or even superficially shocking statements by advanced gnostics in order to condemn them. A very well-known example of this is the *Mirror of Simple Souls*, a very profound work by Marguerite Porete (d. 1310) that made its way into many cloisters throughout the late medieval period, whose author was burnt at the stake as a heretic.[39] Her work in fact is very much a part of the Christian gnostic current that runs from Dionysius in late antiquity to the twentieth-century gnostic Bernadette Roberts, but like Eckhart, Porete was condemned as a heretic. Thus Lerner's argument makes sense: that the prosecution of heretics of the Free Spirit proceeded along similar lines.[40]

In this context one can better understand the emergence of the Neoplatonic Renaissance in Italy and elsewhere in Europe. For if Aristotelianism and a blanket condemnation of all magic and heresy led to the witch persecutions, the counterbalance to this extreme is represented by figures like Marsilio Ficino and Pico della Mirandola, whose Neoplatonism and Christian Kabbalah led in quite a different direction, one of openness to magic and the various Western esoteric traditions. It is not surprising that some of the groups and individuals persecuted as heretical insisted that the devil and demons would eventually be saved in a universal restoration—this is a recurrent theme in

Christian theology, one linked to such figures as Origen and the Neoplatonist Eriugena. Fundamentally, Neoplatonism allowed for a more subtle worldview that did not separate solely into two camps but recognized a spectrum of perspectives, and it is in the Neoplatonic Renaissance that much of later Western esotericism finds its intellectual ancestors.

NOTES

1. See Emma Clarke, John Dillon, et al., trs., Iamblichus, *De Mysteriis* (Atlanta, GA: Society of Biblical Literature, 2003). References are to chapters and sections.

2. See R. W. Dyson, trs., Augustine, *The City of God against the Pagans* (Cambridge: Cambridge University Press, 1998). References are to book and chapter divisions—e.g., Book X, chapter 11.

3. See Bengt Ankarloo and Stuart Clark, *Witchcraft and Magic in Europe: Ancient Greece and Rome* (Philadelphia: University of Pennsylvania Press, 1999), 320 ff.

4. Ankarloo and Clark, *Witchcraft and Magic in Europe,* 323.

5. See Gershom Scholem, *Kabbalah* (Jerusalem: Keter, 1974), 20.

6. See Moshe Idel, *Messianic Mystics* (New Haven, CT: Yale University Press, 1998), 127.

7. Idel, *Messianic Mystics,* 130–31.

8. See Eriugena, *Periphyseon,* I. P. Sheldon-Williams, trs. (Washington, D.C.: Dumbarton Oaks, 1987).

9. Cf. *Periphyseon,* Book V.936A, 613–14.

10. See the "space trilogy" of C. S. Lewis for a modernized version of the Sylvestrian medieval angelic cosmology, in particular *That Hideous Strength,* where the planetary angelic beings are agents in the midst of modern spiritual warfare.

11. See *The Cosmographia of Bernardus Sylvestris,* W. Wetherbee, trs. (New York: Columbia University Press, 1990), 105–8.

12. For more on this ambience, see the introduction to *The Cloud of Unknowing,* J. Walsh, ed. (New York: Paulist Press, 1981), 49.

13. There are a number of translations of Eckhart's sermons and treatises; in English I would suggest M. O'C. Walshe's *Meister Eckhart: Sermons and Treatises,* 3 vols. (Shaftesbury, UK: Element, 1979). See I.121–123. For the original, see Josef Quint, Ernst Benz, et al., *Meister Eckhart: Die deutschen und Lateinischen Werke* (Stuttgart: Kohlhammer, 1936).

14. See O'C. Walshe, I.1–2

15. See Johannes Tauler, *Sermons,* M. Schrady, trs. (New York: Paulist Press, 1985), esp. 39, 80, 89.

16. See *The Cloud of Unknowing,* 104. I am drawing here on the translation by James Walsh (New York: Paulist Press, 1981). There are a number of translations of the *Cloud,* including those of Evelyn Underhill (London: Watkins, 1912), and Phyllis Hodgson (London: Oxford University Press, 1944), as well as more "psychological" versions like that of Ira Progoff (New York: Dell, 1957).

17. See Jeffrey Burton Russell, *Witchcraft in the Middle Ages* (Ithaca, NY: Cornell University Press, 1972), 14–17, 23–25.

18. Russell, *Witchcraft*, 59, 304 n. 24.

19. See *The Book of Secrets of Albertus Magnus*, M. Best and F. Brightman, eds. (New York: Oxford University Press, 1973), 6.

20. *Book of Secrets*, 104.

21. See Russell, *Witchcraft*, 220.

22. Carlo Ginzburg, *I Benandanti: Ricerche sulle stregoneria e sui culti agrari tra Cinquecento e Secento* (Turin: Einaudi, 1966).

23. See Scholem, *Kabbalah*, 12.

24. On such practices, see Moshe Hallamish, *An Introduction to the Kabbalah* (Albany: SUNY Press, 1998), 49 ff., 75 ff. See also Moshe Idel, *Kabbalah: New Perspectives* (New Haven, CT: Yale University Press, 1988), 74 ff., 268 ff.

25. In this description of the Sefirot, I am drawing on, among other works, Hallamish, *Introduction to the Kabbalah*, 128 ff.

26. See *Early Jewish Kabbalah*; see also Scholem, *Kabbalah,* 55–56.

27. See Scholem, *Kabbalah*, 235.

28. Scholem, *Kabbalah*, 182–89.

29. Scholem, *Kabbalah*,184 ff.

30. Moshe Idel, *Messianic Mystics* (New Haven, CT: Yale University Press, 1998), esp. 126–29, on the "magico-Kabbalistic" model of praxis.

31. See Michael Swartz, *Scholastic Magic* (Princeton, NJ: Princeton University Press, 1996), 3–4, 209–11.

32. Part of the *Liber visionum*, translated and introduced by Claire Fanger and Nicholas Watson, is available in pdf form in *Esoterica* at www.esoteric.msu.edu

33. See Valerie Flint, *The Rise of Magic in Early Medieval Europe* (Princeton, NJ: Princeton University Press, 1991).

34. See Richard Kieckhefer, *Forbidden Rites: A Necromancer's Manual of the Fifteenth Century* (Thrupp: Sutton, 1997), 27–28, 115.

35. See Gösta Hedegård, *Liber Iuratus Honorii: A Critical Edition of the Latin Version of the Sworn Book of Honorius* (Stockholm: Almqvist, 2002), 26.

36. See Malcolm Lambert, *Medieval Heresy: Popular Movements from the Gregorian Reform to the Reformation* (London: Blackwell, 1977; New York: Barnes and Noble, 1992), 10–16, 15.

37. See Arno Borst, *Die Katharer* (Stuttgart: Hiersemann, 1953), 136.

38. See Robert Lerner, *The Heresy of the Free Spirit in the Later Middle Ages* (Los Angeles: University of California Press, 1972); see also Lambert, *Medieval Heresy*, 186.

39. See Marguerite Porete, *The Mirror of Simple Souls*, Robert Lerner, trs. (New York: Paulist Press, 1993).

40. Lambert, *Medieval Heresy*, 186.

Chapter Five

The Renaissance

NEOPLATONISM AND SCHOLARLY MAGIC

One cannot write about the history of Renaissance Neoplatonism and scholarly magic without discussing its most influential figures, chief of whom is Marsilio Ficino (1433–1499), but who certainly also include Gemistus Pletho (1360–1452) and Pico della Mirandola (1463–1494) as well as Lodovico Lazzarelli (1450–1500). In many respects, these figures may be seen as the heart of the Renaissance itself, not least because they rediscovered, translated, and interpreted a wide range of ancient traditions, among them Platonism, Neoplatonism, Hermeticism, the Chaldean Oracles and Hymns and, in the case of Pico, Jewish Kabbalism. By rediscovering what they saw as the *prisca theologia*, or ancient theology, they were to have a profound impact on the humanities as a whole, including the fine arts, but also on virtually all who were interested in magic or magico-astrological ways of viewing the world.

One has to begin, however, with Nicholas of Cusa (1401–1464), whose work is exactly in the stream of Dionysius the Areopagite and John Eriugena—that of the *via negativa*. Cusanus, a mathematician and theologian, drew upon the Neoplatonic, hierarchic cosmos as perceived by Eriugena and as it informed medieval theology, but from this point of departure he struck out into the territory of Meister Eckhart. He demonstrated that Aristotelian logic is merely a discursive logic referring to the finite realm and is not applicable to the transcendent. He denied the possibility of logic allowing one to describe or understand the infinite—the "docta ignorantia" of his first and most influential book, *De docta ignorantia* (1440). Cusanus also opposed to Aristotelian-derived medieval logic of the excluded middle his own doctrine of the *coincidentia oppositorum*, or coincidence of opposites, and, in the tradition of Ramon Lull, he endorsed themes of universal concordance and eclecticism that were to be woven into the various strands of esotericism to come.

In his *De visione Dei*, Cusanus gives the example of a portrait he saw in Brussels, Belgium, the eyes of which seemed to follow an onlooker. Such a portrait seems to be looking at everyone in a room individually—very much like the relationship between the infinite and the finite, for each individual bears a unique relationship to the infinite. Thus, Ernst Cassirer points out, for Cusanus

> all [religious] institutions and all customs are merely sensible signs for the truth of faith; and whereas the signs are subject to change and to modification, what they signify is not. There is no form of faith so low, so abominable, that it cannot find its relative justification from this point of view. Even polytheism is not excluded. For wherever *gods* are honored, the thought, the idea of the divine must be presupposed.[1]

The immense acceptance of diversity within unity that Cusanus embraced in turn set the stage for the eclectic esotericism of the late Renaissance and the modern era. But Cusanus was fundamentally a negative theologian in the tradition of Eckhart, brought up in the Brotherhood of Common Life that was founded by a follower of Ruysbroeck, whereas figures like Ficino and Campanella represent very much more the *via positiva* that lends itself to magic or theurgy. And thus although Cusanus's metaphysical gnosis sets the foundations for later forms of esotericism based on what Faivre calls the "praxis of concordance" [between religious traditions], the cosmological gnosis of Ficino, Bruno, and Campanella correspond much more to the major magical, alchemical, and other cosmological currents of esotericism in the modern period.

Ficino's work began in earnest in 1450, when his patron Cosimo de Medici charged him with heading a new Platonic Academy in Florence, and later with the translation of Platonic and Hermetic manuscripts. The first of these translations was in fact the *Corpus Hermeticum*, which Ficino published in 1463 with a dedication to his patron and a portrayal of Hermes as a great sage who belonged to the "golden chain" of sages that included Moses (envisioned as Hermes's contemporary), Orpheus, Pythagoras, and Plato. Thus Ficino endorsed what became a common theme in esoteric works to follow, namely the view of sages in antiquity as originating a Western lineage of initiates in a "golden chain," not a lineage in the Asian sense of master and disciple, but what might better be termed an "ahistorical continuity." Ficino went on to publish Plato's dialogues in 1484, and in 1489, *De Triplici Vita*, a work in three parts of Ficino's own composition, the first on maintaining one's health, the second on extending one's lifespan, and the third on astrological influences. The third of these is *De Vita coelitus comparanda*, and it is from this latter work that we have a window into Ficino's own astrological magic.

Knowledge of Ficino's astrological magic came to general awareness among modern scholars with the publication of D. P. Walker's *Spiritual and Demonic Magic from Ficino to Campanella* (1958), which outlined in detail the magical perspectives that pervaded the major Renaissance figures' thought. Walker, a student of Frances Yates, surveyed not only Ficino's work but also that of Lazzarelli, Pico della Mirandola, and Tommaso Campanella in order to document just how pervasive magical cosmology was during this period. These figures all drew to a greater or lesser extent on the Neoplatonic theurgy of Iamblichus (in particular his *De Mysteriis*), as well as the works of Proclus, Porphyry, Synesius, and Plotinus, among others. Neoplatonism provided a philosophical framework, so to speak, by which astrological magic might be seen as part of Christianity rather than as its demonically inspired nemesis.

Of course, Ficino and his colleagues or successors had to negotiate their language and cosmology carefully so as not to present themselves as sorcerers, and one sees this in Ficino's cautious, even hesitant navigation through loaded terms like *magic*. After outlining Ficino's view of astrological magic—Ficino's belief that through Orphic singing, proper diet and clothing, and astrological awareness, one could effect beneficent magic without the use of demons but only through attracting beneficent "natural" planetary powers— Walker then remarks: "It is clear that Ficino is strongly attracted by this kind of magic or theurgy, that he considers it valuable, and also it is clear that he is aware that it is dangerous. His conclusion seems to be that its dangers might be avoided if it remained within a learnèd, philosophical circle, and were kept secret from the ignorant *vulgus*, who would distort it into idolatry and superstition."[2] Thus in Ficino's perspective we can see both his emphasis on a cosmological gnosis and the need for its restriction to a comparatively elite group—in brief, we can see that he very clearly belongs to the current of esotericism.

But Ficino represents a particular stream, that of spiritual and natural, not demonic magic, a cultured and philosophical stream that inspires and relies upon music and the arts. Walker memorably differentiates this philosophical stream from "demonic magic [which] combined with medieval planetary magic, led to the overtly demonic, recklessly unorthodox magic of Agrippa and Paracelsus."[3] Walker's characterization of Agrippa and Paracelsus is somewhat extreme, for in fact one has to wonder just how great is the difference between Ficino's use of planetary magic and that espoused by Agrippa or Paracelsus, or that of Tommaso Campanella (1568–1639), who in some respects might be seen as Ficino's successor. For all of these figures sought to incorporate into Christianity the practice of planetary magic; all of them saw it as a natural aspect of a religious worldview; in short, all of them espoused a Christian philosophy of magic.

Campanella's magic is noteworthy because he combined it with a millennialist agenda that he presented in his well-known *City of the Sun* (1623), and because he sought to actually implement this agenda by magical work with Pope Urban VIII in order to ward off the negative effects of eclipses and to bring about a Christian millennium. In Pope Urban VIII Campanella had an ally because this particular pope was a strong believer in astrology, and from 1626, astrologers had begun to predict his death. Campanella was a worthy ally because he believed that his magic, which he defended as entirely legitimate Christian practice, was a means to offset the negative influences of malign planetary alignments. According to reports from the period, in 1628 Campanella and the pope sequestered themselves in a sealed room, which they fumigated with incense, decorated with silk, and lit with seven torches and candles to represent the seven planets. They also had Jovial or Venusian music played to disperse the negative planetary influences and used various other means, including gems, plants, and liquors, to create an atmosphere unaffected by an eclipse. All of this Campanella himself described in a chapter of his book *Astrologica* (1629), a chapter he did not intend to be published but that was added to his book without his knowledge so as to discredit him for a public position—as indeed it did.[4]

One should not, from this unusual incident, assume that Campanella's magical efforts or views were generally accepted or even tolerated. For unlike Ficino, Campanella dreamed of a utopian society, a "city of the Sun" that united Europe through beneficent Christian magic, and he long sought to make this dream a reality. Thus in 1599 he had been imprisoned in Naples for conspiring to create a revolution, and in fact he was tortured and remained imprisoned until 1626, not long before his rendezvous with the pope. Campanella was fortunate that he did not meet the fate of another great esoteric figure of the day, Giordano Bruno, who was burned at the stake as a heretic on Ash Wednesday, 1600. Of course, whereas Campanella's magic stayed more or less in the sphere of Christianity, that of Bruno embraced a magical worldview that harked back to ancient Egypt and that thus represented a theological threat to Catholicism that perhaps Campanella's did not—even if Campanella actually went so far as to foster a Calabrian revolt.

One cannot offer a brief survey of the Italian Renaissance without further reference to Pico della Mirandola (1453–1494), who is perhaps best known for his explicit incorporation of Kabbalism into his Christian Neoplatonic and Hermetic writings, chiefly his essay "On the Dignity of Man," a definitive classic of the entire Renaissance period, and his nine hundred theses, in which he drew directly on Jewish Kabbalism in order to create a syncretistic Christian Kabbalism with its roots not only in Judaism and in Neoplatonism but also in Hermeticism—even if as Ernst Cassirer points out, he also rejected many aspects of such a central esoteric tradition as astrology.[5] Pico's nine hundred theses represent an extraordinary concerted effort of universal syncretism, an effort at a union of all the major philosophical-religious traditions in one overarching system. Recent evidence uncovered by Steven A. Farmer suggests that Pico's work was tampered with by pious Christian editors after his premature death, and that as a result, the truly radical nature of Pico's theses has not been recognized.[6] Certainly it becomes clear from reading Farmer's new edition of the nine hundred theses that Pico is far more radically syncretic and indebted to Jewish Kabbalah even than one might have gathered before.

But Pico's work as a whole may best be described as representing for the first time in a concentrated form the universalist outlook that came to characterize modernity as a whole. By this I mean that Pico was able and willing to draw on the panoply of inherited religious traditions from antiquity; he was able to look over them as from above and draw upon each of them to illustrate his larger point. This is a uniquely modern viewpoint, this syncretist universalism, and it is with Pico as much as with any one figure that we see its inception. This tendency of his is visible even in his commentary on the first seven days of creation in the book of Genesis. For there, in his *Heptaplus*, he draws on the *Timaeus* of Plato as well as Pythagorean and other teachings from antiquity. And in his best-known work, *On the Dignity of Man*, he writes that "surely it is the part of a narrow mind to have confined itself to a single Academy," going on to allude to Islamic philosophers like Avicenna and "Alfarabi" (Ibn Arabi), to Platonists like Porphyry, Iamblichus, Proclus, Hermias, and Olympiadorus, to Hermes Trismegistus, to the Chaldeans, to Pythagoras, and to Judaism.[7]

There are several other authors whose work we should not pass over here, not least among them Lodovico Lazzarelli, Giambattista Della Porta (1538–1615), and Johannes Reuchlin (1455–1522), each of whom illustrate in different ways the universalist syncretism that came to characterize the modern era and that has its roots here in the Renaissance. Lazzarelli, about whom Wouter Hanegraaff has written at length, was the student of a messianic figure and drew for his own work on the *Corpus Hermeticum*.[8] Della Porta is best known for his *Magia naturalis*, published in 1568, in which he drew on Greek antiquity to develop an early form of what was to become *naturphilosophie*. Reuchlin, of course, is known for his publication of Kabbalistic teachings that in turn became central for the emergence of Christian Kabbalism.[9] All of these figures represent variants of the Renaissance drive

toward a unified understanding of religions under the sign of an esoteric synthesis, an effort toward a higher spiritual understanding via an esoteric concordance of traditions. This is a tendency that, far from disappearing in the
modern period, in fact was to continue to develop and expand.

AGRIPPA: JOINING OF FOLK MAGIC
AND SCHOLARLY MAGIC

It may well be said that all the various strands of folk, scholarly, and Kabbalistic magical traditions are joined together in the major work of Agrippa
(1486–1535), his *Three Books of Occult Philosophy* [*De occulta
philosophia*]. Agrippa's work was first published in 1531, and its first English
edition was in 1651, but it has remained one of the most important works in
the entire Western magical tradition even while it was long out of print. In it,
Agrippa covers an encyclopedic array of subjects, including not only planetary energies, stones, herbs, and other aspects of natural magic, but also the
nature of spirits, magical squares, and numerology. Agrippa's genius lay in
his ability to conjoin much of the full spectrum of contemporary and prior occult philosophy—in Agrippa's compendium, one finds discussed nearly every
magical topic imaginable, drawing from a plethora of ancient and medieval
authorities. His work remains the single largest and most important compendium of magical thought and knowledge in the West.

Agrippa was, of course, indebted for his knowledge at least in part to another remarkable figure, Abbot Johannes Trithemius (1462–1516), whom he
met in 1509, and to whom he dedicated *De occulta philosophia* (first published when Agrippa was only twenty-four!). Trithemius is an influential and
fascinating figure in his own right, best known for his cryptographic
Steganographia, by various interpretations a book of secret codes or a coded
handbook for magical operations.[10] Trithemius was subsequently attacked as
having hidden in his *Steganographia* and *Polygraphia* demonological conju-
rations, but he himself saw his cryptographic writings as means to overcome
the limitations of terrestrial life, to communicate at long distances, to gain supernatural powers, and to transcend human limitations. Trithemius offered the
young Agrippa much advice after their many hours of conversation, admonishing him among other things to keep that which is arcane from vulgar eyes
and to preserve it for the noble. As Noel Brann articulates in *Trithemius and
Magical Theology*, Trithemius and Agrippa both sought to "effect an accord
between magic and Christian doctrine," to restore magic to its rightful place
in the Christian world, and to develop what amounts to a magical theology.[11]
Together, Trithemius and Agrippa are without doubt among the most influential authors on magical topics in their period.

While we do not have room here for a full analysis of Agrippa's magnum opus, we certainly must offer an overview of the book's most salient characteristics. The book itself is divided into three primary sections, the first being on the natural or elemental realm; the second being on the mathematical and planetary or celestial realm; the third being on spirituality or religion. This threefold division into elemental, celestial, and intellectual, or terrestrial, astrological, and spiritual, corresponds to the tripartite nature of Agrippa's cosmology as reflected in his many illustrations and charts. In fact his book is remarkably well organized, given its encyclopedic scope.

Agrippa begins *De occulta philosophia* by defining magic as "the most profound contemplation of most secret things," the "knowledge of all nature," the "most perfect and chief science," and "the absolute perfection of all most excellent philosophy" (I.ii).[12] He discusses, in a succession of short chapters, each of the elements (earth, air, fire, water) and how various virtues manifest themselves in various plants or other natural phenomena. It is here, in the elemental section, that he discusses folk magic, offering much on the destructive power of menstrual fluid, and such tidbits as how a stone bit by a mad dog has the power to induce discord among men, or how if one spits in the mouth of a little frog climbing a tree and then lets the frog escape, one will cure a cough (I.li). Some of these folk remedies are traceable to the *Book of Secrets* attributed to Albertus Magnus, but others go back to the ancient Greeks and Romans, or to Northern European folk traditions. Included in this first book are divination, fascination, and subjects like the nature of words.

Agrippa's second section begins, appropriately enough, with mathematics, but this is preparatory for the larger subject of the nature of the planets and stars in relation to earthly life via mathematical relationships. Thus it is in this section that we find the well-known planetary or magical squares, for instance that of Jupiter:

4/14/15/1
9/7/6/12
5/11/10/8
16/2/3/13

Associated with this magic square are various magical "seals" or "characters" that sometimes can be illuminated by superimposing them on the magical square so that one can see the mathematical relationships underlying them. One should note that Agrippa includes the Hebrew versions of the magical squares, as well as the Hebrew names of the sundry spirits to be conjured. Hence the "intelligence" of the Sun is Nachiel, with the numerical value of 111; and the "spirit of the Sun," Sorath, bears the numerical value of 666. This second section, fundamentally astrological, is also full to the brim with the celestial images or knowledge necessary for the practice of sidereal magic.

Hence it is perhaps not surprising that the third and final book is about how necessary and powerful is a religious mind. Agrippa discusses here the secret aspects of religion, including the absolute necessity that a magician know the true God and not be deceived, the nature of the Trinity, and the Divine Names of God as found not only in Hebrew tradition but also within Christianity in the works of Dionysius the Areopagite (III.xi).[13] Here too Agrippa discusses intelligences and spirits, divine as well as infernal, and even outlines the nine orders of the fallen angels and spirits (which corresponds inversely to the nine orders of angels found in the Dionysian writings and in Jewish magical traditions) (III.xviii). Agrippa also explicitly refers to the Kabbalistic art of combining the Divine Names and offers a kind of magical or celestial writing of Hebrew letters (III.xxvii). He outlines how one binds spirits, what purportedly happens to an individual after death, the nature of sacrifices and consecration, and much else that corresponds to the overarching religious theme of the third book. One can see by its scope and inclusiveness how this book might well have formed the basis of subsequent Christian magical traditions.

PARACELSUS

If Agrippa's *De occulta philosophia* places him among the most influential of authors on magic in the European tradition, certainly the many works of Paracelsus place him as central to the Western alchemical and medical traditions. Indeed, one can scarcely imagine the many important figures to follow him—especially those in the wake of Böhme, but also the numerous alchemical writers who flourished over the next two centuries—without the prior example and influence of Paracelsus. Paracelsus remains an enigmatic figure, one famous (or infamous) already in his own day, a man full of certainty about what he had discovered or learned, and a man contemptuous of the growing ratiocentrism and materialism of his time. Although he died young, his work continues to fascinate readers and still awaits a modern interpreter capable of fully recognizing and integrating the various threads of Paracelsus's many works.

Given the birth-name Theophrastus von Hohemheim, Paracelsus was born in 1493/4 in Einsiedeln, Switzerland, and died less than fifty years later in 1541. According to Andrew Weeks, relatively little is known for certain about Paracelsus's early life or education. He later wrote that he was much indebted to his father for his education, and it is said that he graduated with a doctorate from the University of Ferrara, but Weeks points out that in fact there remains little if any documentation to support with certainty his claims of either his graduation from Ferrara or his subsequent visiting of various French, Italian, and German universities.[14] On the other hand, there is also no evidence contradicting Paracelsus's recounting of his life experience or training that led up to his extraordinary series of treatises and unpublished manuscripts on medicine and alchemy, and what he himself writes accounts for all this as well as any alternative interpretation.

Paracelsus's writings might be described as bordering on arrogant in the way that he dismisses his colleagues or competitors. Take this passage from quite early in his works, probably dating from the mid-1520s: "If one wants to be a city physician, a lecturer, and professor ordinarius, one should have the appropriate abilities. [But these] people, inasmuch as some are lazy from pedantry and others puffed up with rhetoric, [still] others accustomed to lying in poetry and so forth. . . . [are] fools."[15] His works are full of his attacks upon those he saw as boneheads who do not think and experiment for themselves but only blindly accept medical or religious tradition, and full too of evidence that Paracelsus himself had no lack of detractors. He writes of "daily cavils and incitements against me" of the confusion and ignorance of those who attack him, and it is clear from the tone of his many works that he was not only convinced of the truth of his own medical theories, he was convinced of the errors of others, which he felt obliged to point out.[16]

One can imagine, then, why he was not necessarily very popular, and in fact Paracelsus was driven out of various cities, rendered poor and homeless, and lived much of his adult life as a wanderer. During this time he did attract a number of disciples and admirers, some of whom wrote down as amanuenses his dictated works—some, it is claimed, dictated after a night on the town in a local tavern. His motto, "let none belong to another who can belong to himself" [*alterius no sit qui suus esse potest*] takes on a certain force and poignance when one considers Paracelsus's biography, for he was indeed his own man. But he also, as Weeks points out, existed within a context of Anabaptist opposition to the institutional Catholic Church, and he reflected a similar bent of thought even if he was motivated above all by his alchemical medical theories and practices.

NOTES

1. Ernst Cassirer, *The Individual and the Cosmos in Renaissance Philosophy* (New York: Harper, 1964), 30.

2. D. P. Walker, *Spiritual and Demonic Magic from Ficino to Campanella* (Leiden: Brill, 1958), 51.

3. Walker, *Spiritual and Demonic Magic*, 75.

4. See Walker, *Spiritual and Demonic Magic*, 207–8.

5. See Ernst Cassirer, *The Individual and the Cosmos in Renaissance Philosophy* (New York: Harper, 1963), 114–18, where Cassirer discusses Pico's rejection of astrology.

6. See Steven A. Farmer, *Syncretism in the West: Pico's 900 Theses (1486)* (Tempe: Arizona State University Press, 1998).

7. See Charles Wallis and Paul Miller, trs., *Pico della Mirandola: On the Dignity of Man and Other Writings* (Indianapolis, IN: Bobbs-Merrill, 1965), 3–34.

8. See Wouter Hanegraaff, *Lodovico Lazzarelli (1447–1500): The Hermetic Writings and Related Documents,* with Ruud M. Bouthoorn (Tempe: Arizona Center for Medieval and Renaissance Studies, 2005).

9. On Christian Kabbalism see François Secret, *Les Kabbalistes chrétiens de la Renaissance* (Paris: 1964).

10. See Noel Brann, *Trithemius and Magical Theology* (Albany: SUNY Press, 1999), esp. 33 ff.

11. Brann, *Trithemius*, 155.

12. See Henry Cornelius Agrippa, *Three Books of Occult Philosophy*, James Freake, tr. (London: 1651), a full version of which is available from the digital archive at http://digital.lib.msu.edu. For a recent republication, see Donald Tyson, ed., *Three Books of Occult Philosophy* (St. Paul, MN: Llewellyn, 1998). References in the text are to book and chapter, respectively, so as to be easily found in any edition.

13. See above.

14. See Andrew Weeks, *Paracelsus* (Albany: SUNY Press, 1997), 5–7.

15. Weeks, *Paracelsus,* p. 39, citing Paracelsus, *Opera*, I.1.150.

16. See Paracelsus, *Sämtliche Werke* (Munich: Oldenbourg, 1929–1933), 14 vols. For an easily available translation of some works of Paracelsus, see Arthur Edward Waite, trs., *The Hermetic and Alchemical Writings of Paracelsus* (Berkeley: Shambhala, 1976), 2 vols.

Chapter Six

Early Modern Esoteric Currents

ALCHEMY

Without doubt, among the central concepts of post-Renaissance Western esotericism is that of the creative imagination, and one of the central figures for
the development of that concept is Paracelsus. The concept of creative imagination defines and links magic, alchemy, and medicine, for all are functions
of mind or psyche. In Paracelsus's works, we see a vast and unified cosmology according to which humanity, the earth, minerals, plants, animals, and the
stars and planets are all manifestations of the divine imagination, united in
humanity itself. Nature is not external to man but at once within and without;
and we are joined with nature through the *lumen naturae*, or light of nature
that reveals inwardly the secret meanings and signatures of all things.

Following Paracelsus, and particularly in the seventeenth and eighteenth
centuries, we see what clearly is the flowering of alchemical writing and imagery in Europe. A bewildering variety of alchemical imagery as well as complex analogical writing was published during this period, and alchemists or
would-be alchemists gathered in the vicinity of royal courts or noble houses,
often looking for sponsors, some claiming to have discovered the Stone of
Wisdom, the Elixir of Life, or the means of manufacturing gold. But as Allison Coudert remarks in *The Philosopher's Stone*, alchemists have sought
wealth, health, spiritual perfection, and eternal life for millennia.[1]

Alchemy is classically esoteric, in that it can be understood or interpreted
as belonging variously to cosmology or to metaphysics, to magic or to mysticism, but in fact it has elements of each. Notwithstanding, modern
commentators have tended toward univocal interpretations of alchemy that
emphasize one interpretation to the exclusion of all others. Thus, in the

nineteenth century, Ethan Allen Hitchcock argues, even more strongly than Karen-Claire Voss in the twentieth, that alchemy had little to do with chemistry but was entirely a spiritual science.[2] Carl Jung, in the twentieth century, argues that alchemy primarily revealed psychological insights, whereas a harsh critic of Jung, historian of science Lawrence Principe, argues in favor of alchemy as chiefly protochemistry.[3] Rather than attempting to prove modern interpreters wrong, one might do better to acknowledge that there is some truth in the arguments of all of them, because alchemical writings and images are so complex and variegated that each interpretation could be seen as offering a different window into some aspect of these mysterious works.

Broadly speaking, alchemy is perhaps best described as mystico-magical, in that alchemical texts often refer both to inner or mystical and to outer, chemical or laboratory work. Take, for instance, the twenty-two alchemical treatises published in the well-known and widely available collection *The Hermetic Museum* (1678). Although many of the treatises do include laboratory instructions, such instructions are side-by-side with injunctions that the secrets of alchemy are not to be found in laboratory equipment like alembics, nor in exotic substances.

Rather, the reader is consistently enjoined to be devout, to pray, to ask for divine help, and to gain the spiritual illumination that alone makes possible the alchemical work. "The Golden Age Restored" (1677) ends with the following:

> And thus, in the Name of the Holy Trinity, we will, in these few words, conclude our exposition of the Great Mystery of the Most Precious Philosophical Stone, and of the Arcanum of the Sages. To the most High and Almighty God, the Creator of this Art, Whom it has pleased to reveal to me, wretched, sinful man (in answer to my prayer), this most precious knowledge, be eternal praise, glory, honor, and thanksgiving; and to Him be addressed a most humble and fervent prayer that He may so direct my heart and mind that I may not speak of this Mystery, or make it known to the wicked.[4]

The Philosophical Stone is said to possess properties one might deem magical, for it is (explicitly in the Paracelsian tradition) "the true Healing and Medicine of all things," but it is also a "Great Mystery" revealed in a visionary sequence as a result of prayer and devotion.

What are the secrets of the numerous enigmatic alchemical treatises and illustrations that so flourished during the seventeenth century? There we see invocations of ancient esoteric lineages that hark back to Moses and Hermes; we see visionary encounters and mysterious dream sequences; we see complex and strange laboratory instructions written in allusive symbolism; we see claims of great longevity or of eternal life, of the transmutation of metals, of universal healing; and we see consistent injunctions that prayer and devotion are essential for success, which depends on divine revelation. *Mystico-magical* is the ideal descriptive term for this genre, though one cannot deny that some alchemical works just as well could be termed magico-mystical. Perhaps more than any other esoteric current, alchemy exists right on the boundary between magic and mysticism.

Alchemists tend to divide their work with nature into two broad categories, which are plant or herbal, and mineral or metal. Plant alchemy works with tinctures drawn from herbs and is chiefly concerned (in the Paracelsian tradition) with medicine. Mineral or metal alchemy is traditionally said to be more dangerous, and more mysterious and subtle. Claims for the transmutation of base metals into precious ones like gold belong to the latter realm, but as part of a much larger repertoire of transmutations that are not reducible only to a greedy quest for gold. There are religious dimensions to alchemical instructions, as we have seen, and those suggest that while chemical or laboratory work is a part of alchemy, the rubric extends beyond that into nonphysical domains. Here we see a tradition under the sign of Hermes that exemplifies above all the third in the triad of faith, reason, and gnosis.

While the heyday of alchemy was indisputably in the early modern period, especially in the seventeenth century, alchemy continued to reappear not only in Europe, but also in the wake of English colonization. Thus we find alchemists among the North American colonists, for instance, and indeed, some of the more important alchemical works of the period came from figures whose name we know, like John Winthrop (1606–1676) and Jonathan Brewster (c. 1593–c. 1659), as well as from those who chose to publish anonymously, like Eirenaeus Philalethes, identified by some scholars as George Starkey (1627–1665).[5] Although it is true that alchemy was most prevalent during the early modern era, one must note that it did continue to reappear right through the modern era into the twenty-first century, combining throughout its long history those twin paths of *ora et labora* (prayer and work).[6]

ROSICRUCIANISM

Along with alchemy, among the most important movements in the history of modern Western esotericism is Rosicrucianism. Rosicrucianism is unusual as a movement not only because it emerged from fictional works, but also because it remains to this day somewhat controversial, even a bit mysterious. From its very beginnings, in three peculiar works—the *Fama Fraternitatis* (1614), the *Confessio* (1615), and the *Chemical Wedding* (1616)—the movement was inextricably interwoven with fictional elements. The *Fama* announced the existence of a shadowy brotherhood devoted to the Rosy Cross; the *Confessio* outlined this group's views and goals; and the *Chemical Wedding* is a densely symbolic novel that is easily read as a spiritual adventure and a chronicle of spiritual awakening at once. Taken as a whole, as its origins in a novel would suggest, Rosicrucianism may well have belonged more to the imagination than to historical reality.

Rosicrucianism swiftly captured the European intellectual imagination. Almost immediately, a wide range of responses to Rosicrucianism appeared in print across Europe, some warning of its dangers, others asking to be admitted, still others claiming to be the movement's representatives. By 1620, a scant six years, there were already nearly two hundred written works in various languages addressing the question of Rosicrucianism, showing the kind of fever induced by the concept of a secret brotherhood of the Rosy Cross as depicted in those enigmatic publications.

Since the texts are so pivotal, we begin by looking at them. The *Fama Fraternitatis* reveals the Rosicrucian (and the Freemasonic) universalism, addressing itself to the learned of Europe, lamenting the disarray of European culture and anticipating a renaissance and a harmonious, spiritually illuminated future society. The *Fama*, with its authoritative tone, announced the existence of the Brotherhood of the Rosy Cross and captured the imagination of the age with its tale of Christian Rosencreutz and his mysterious journeys, as well as with its assertion of a secret order as keeper of profound and powerful knowledge.

Frances Yates rightly argued that the word *Rosicrucian* may more wisely be seen historically as a word describing a particular kind of approach to arcane knowledge than as a specific organized order, even if at times such orders did exist. The Rosicrucians' goal, according to the *Fama*, was to follow Christ by renewing all arts to perfection, "so that finally man might thereby understand his own nobility and worth, and why he is called Microcosmos, and how far his knowledge extendeth into Nature."[7]

Such a universal renewal and extension of knowledge is, generally speaking, the gnostic goal of Kabbalism, Hermetism, and later, of Christian theosophy as well. The *Fama* begins by telling the story of C. R., who travels among the Arabians and the Jews on a quest to Jerusalem, and who goes as well to Egypt—precisely where European esotericism has always located its sources of arcane knowledge, in the Orient, and among Sufis and Kabbalists. It tells the story of a visionary trip to the Orient of the spirit, but it also links the Rosicrucian movement from the very beginning with the most gnostic aspects of Islam and Judaism, underscoring immediately the movement's universalism.

When Christian Rosencreutz died, a century old, he was placed in his tomb with a parchment book, called "I." The tomb is described as incorporating much arcane geometry and architecture, as well as a host of mysterious letters and Latin inscriptions. The description is often hard to follow, as when we are told that every "side or wall is parted into ten figures, every one with their several figures and sentences, as they are truly shown and set forth *Concentratum* here in our book."

But the import is clear: the tomb's architecture itself, full of geometric symbolism, forms "sentences" and a kind of book of the hidden principles of nature and of the microcosm. Interestingly, the *Fama* concludes by asserting that "our building (although one hundred thousand people had very near seen and beheld the same) shall for ever remain untouched, undestroyed, and hidden to the wicked world."

The esoteric themes of universalism, of the uniting of all arts and sciences, and of reading the mysterious book of books, also appear in the *Confessio*. Here too, we find references to exotic lands and secret knowledge (gnosis), and we find this definition of the Rosicrucian philosophy: "No other Philosophy have we, than that which is the head and sum, the foundations and contents of all faculties, sciences, and arts, the which (if we well behold our age) containeth much of Theology and medicine . . . whereof all learned who make themselves known to us, and come into our brotherhood, shall find more wonderful secrets by us than heretofore they did attain unto, . . . or are able to believe or utter."[8] Thus the essence of Rosicrucianism is said to be universal knowledge or gnosis.

The Rosicrucian manifestos announce that there is dawning a *miranda sexta aetatis*, or sixth age, an era that recalls the earlier writings of Joachim of Fiore and his complex theory of a coming "age of the Holy Spirit." Hidden in the Rosicrucian mysteries, these treatises imply, is the real essence of Christianity itself, and that one must approach it with humility or find nothing, or worse than nothing. Throughout, they emphasize reading the divine books of humanity and nature, and writing in a "magic language." Such an idea of a magic language has, of course, a very long history in the West, stretching back at least to the Gnostics, and quite probably to Egypt. It certainly emerges in the Middle Ages in the works of Agrippa and Trithemius, who as we have seen drew upon Kabbalistic sources. Now, Agrippa and Trithemius are well known for their primary and influential works on magic, in which we find the sources of many subsequent works illustrated by sigils and magic squares, stellar and numerical patterns connected to specific angels, demons, or intelligences. By using these stellar and numerical patterns in ritual magic, one is calling upon the language of the stars in order to invoke the powers or intelligences with which they are connected. In short, both magic and mysticism appear in Rosicrucianism.

Magical language also is featured in the writings of Dr. John Dee (1527–1604), who in his controversial "conversations with spirits" along with

Edward Kelley, discovered the "Enochian language" that subsequently played an extensive role in the history of magic in the West. Dee's mysterious Enochian language requires tables or "keys" for its deciphering, and it too has been used in magical workings. For these and a variety of other reasons, Frances Yates concluded that the single most important figure in the appearance of early Rosicrucianism is in fact John Dee.[9] Is it only coincidence that the date given as the discovery of C. R.'s tomb, 1604, is the date of Dee's death? And is it only coincidence that the *Fama* and *Confessio* make so much of a "magical language," one of the most famous instances of which Dee is responsible for?

The third of the three works is *The Chemical Wedding*, a work filled to the brim with symbols piled upon symbols. *The Chemical Wedding* is not a manifesto like its companion works, but an incredibly complex novel that tells the dreamlike story (as the title suggests) of an alchemical wedding acted out in a castle through a variety of strange characters and oneiric occurrences. Like *The Golden Ass* by Apuleius, *The Chemical Wedding* can be read as an initiatory journey in which the reader vicariously participates. This work is so rich that it is nearly inexhaustible, and it certainly can be interpreted as a psychological and spiritual allegory; it is a classic of European literature, and one can see why it continues to enthrall readers many centuries later.

As an immediate social phenomenon, the Rosicrucian furor lasted only a few years, disappearing around 1620, as Frances Yates notes, the time of political upheaval in Germany and the advent of the Thirty Years' War. By 1623, there was considerable anti-Rosicrucian sentiment, especially in France. Anti-Rosicrucianism reflected the emerging rationalist and materialist paradigm of the so-called Enlightenment—almost the exact opposite of the Rosicrucian Enlightenment. The Rosicrucian dream was for a nonsectarian, peaceful, universal culture dedicated to the investigation of the language of nature, written in the microcosm and in the macrocosm. A Rosicrucian culture would be one founded on Kabbalah and alchemy, that is, on a mystico-magical pansophy.

PANSOPHY

Rosicrucianism is pansophic rather than theosophic. Pansophy, in contrast to theosophy, is universal, not specifically Christian, in its aims and sources. Pansophy emphasizes magic, alchemy, herbalism, healing, [Christian] cabala, and inquiry into nature more generally, and it incorporates much earlier "pagan" traditions like those attributed to Egypt and Persia. In many respects, pansophy resembles the aims and works of Giordano Bruno, the Nolan genius of the Renaissance who was burned at the stake for his troubles. Pansophy is the emergence of a universalist Western esotericism willing to draw on all previous esoteric movements, Christian or not, magical, alchemical, cabalistic, and gnostic, in order to form the basis for a new, universal culture like that imaged in Bacon's New Atlantis or other utopias of the time. Although the word *pansophy* mostly vanishes from the European vocabulary after the seventeenth century, what the word signifies certainly did not disappear. A pansophic approach to esotericism represents an alternative to the emergent extreme rationalism and materialism that also gave birth to scientism, mechanism, and technologism.

Pansophy incorporates all the primary streams of esotericism, including, of course, various forms of magic—it is magico-mysticism. It centers on natural magic, or *magia naturalis*, but one also finds the emergence of various other shades of magic, often with Kabbalistic influence. We might recall that, although the Kabbalists we discuss above were almost exclusively interested in what we may call high mysticism, there is a long tradition of Kabbalism as the basis for magical practices including sorcery. And in fact most grimoires (magical handbooks) have a Hebrew basis for the angelic and demonic names and characteristics that they list for invocation or evocation. One also can see in such willingness to incorporate any form of knowledge whatever, including sorcery, the pansophic impetus behind the legend of Johannes Faust, who refused to allow any boundaries to his search for knowledge.

Like Faust, Rosicrucianism sought to penetrate the secrets of the cosmos, as evidenced by its intricate tables, diagrams, and illustrations. Among the first of these, predating the Rosicrucian furor but certainly influencing its later productions, was the *Calendarium Naturale Magicum Perpetuum Profundissimam Rerum Secretissimarum Contemplationem* [*Perpetual Natural Magical Calendar*] of Tycho Brahe, printed by Theodore de Bry in 1582. Here we have a massive compendium of magical knowledge, including the names and seals or sigils of angels in Hebrew and Latin, magic squares, planetary correspondences, and much else. This compilation is of special importance for us because it reveals the far-flung syncretic origins of the pansophic impulse, which later emerged in almost endless detail in the *Geheime Figuren* [*Secret Figures*] of the Rosicrucians.

The *Geheime Figuren der Rosenkreuzer*, a series of extraordinarily complex illustrations, was published at Altona in 1785–1788. It was probably preceded by and certainly followed by other versions, including a French edition, and in all cases is replete with examples of the effort to map universal knowledge not only physical, but also metaphysical. There are a number of such manuscripts with various versions of these illustrations, chiefly under the title *Physica, Metaphysica, et Hyperphysica, D.O.M.A.*, almost all, and perhaps all belonging to the late eighteenth century. Characteristic of these esoteric illustrations is one entitled *Figura Divina Theosoph. Cabball. nee non Magia, Philosophia, atque Chymia* [*Divine Figure of Theosoph. Cabbalistica: Not Only Magic and Philosophy, But Chemistry*]. It is an astonishingly complex illustration, with concentric circles marking divinity at the top, and a series of triangles and concentric circles below, marking a host of alchemical stages and enigmatic sayings as well as planetary and zodiacal symbols.

What we see in such works is the effort to map the unseen. While the eighteenth century was an era of physical cartography, it was also a period of hyperphysical cartography—that is, of efforts to survey the ethereal realms. Thus we find so many diagrams and illustrations proliferating—this was the age of the *mappa mundi*. Hence, when we look at an illustration from *D.O.M.A.* entitled "Unendliche Ewigkeit und Unerforschliche Primum Mobile" ["Infinite Eternity and Unknowable Primum Mobile"], we find a more or less typical series of images: above is the *Prima Materia*, marked also Father, Son, and Holy Spirit, as well as Jehovah in Hebrew, surrounded by winged angelic forms. Below that is an intermediate principial realm marked "Water," "Heavenly Seed," "Animal Seed," "Vegetable Seed," "Mineral Seed," and so forth. This middle realm is marked "Figura Cabbalistica" and has on either side gnomic sayings, like "Ein Prophet gilt nichst in seinem Vaterlande" [A prophet is not honored in his native land.] Below is an elemental sphere marked with the zodiacal signs, and with the word "Chaos." Here *chaos* does not mean total confusion so much as "potentiality"; the lower sphere represents the temporal realm, and earth depicted as a ball exists between the elemental and intermediate realms, partaking in both, that is, in time and in eternity.

Hyperphysical mapmaking like this has predecessors in the medieval era, for instance in the *Summa* of Aquinas or in the *Commedia* of Dante, but the early modern interest in "occult sciences" as mapping the invisible also corresponded in some respects to the contemporary mania for physical cartography. It is symbolically appropriate that Dr. John Dee, the greatest occultist of his day, also was relied upon as Queen Elizabeth's cartographer. The fact is, a number of the early major scientific figures, like Isaac Newton (1642–1727), were in fact also alchemists. One could see Western esoteric currents during the early modern period (in particular those associated with Rosicrucianism or pansophy) as being based in verifiable experimentation, in investigation without regard for dogmatic religious barriers, and in the effort to create a comprehensive map of the cosmos.

During the early modern period, pansophic esotericists imagined a unified cosmology that included religion, science, the arts, and literature synthesized under the sign of universalist spirituality. This is the kind of comprehensive worldview visible in such illustrations as the ones we see emerging during the eighteenth century, represented for example in Georg von Welling's *Opus Mago-Cabbalisticum et Theosophicum* (1784), which is just such a compendium of knowledge chock-full of unusual illustrations and tables. Likewise, John Heydon—author of such works as *Theomagia, or the Temple of Wisdom* (1663–1664), and *The Wise-mans Crown, or the Glory of the Rosiecross* (1665)—attempted to create universal compendiums of the occult sciences.

Indeed, we see universalism as a recurrent theme in Europe from the seventeenth century on, certainly not limited only to works labeled Rosicrucian. Consider, for instance, the vast metaphysical cartography of John Pordage (1604–1681), who in his multivolume *Göttliche und Wahre Metaphysica* (1715/1746) chronicles what it is like to visit the supernal realms. Similar journeys are to be found, of course, in the numerous volumes of Emanuel Swedenborg (1688–1772), who was originally a scientist but, after his visionary entry into discarnate realms, was a prolific chronicler of the unseen. For that matter, we also see efforts to bridge the realms in the works of Franz von Baader (1765–1841) who studied mineralogy, invented an industrial process, and became one of the most impressive writers on religious and spiritual themes of the nineteenth century. And we see an even more explicit universalism in the fragmentary but encyclopedic work of Novalis (Friedrich von Hardenberg) during the same period.

Throughout the early modern period and right into the twenty-first century, in other words, Western esotericism often aims at universal knowledge and also often at the transformation and renewal of European culture and politics. Hence it is not surprising that Rosicrucianism did have a political impact with its utopian literature, and we see its traces later in the development of modern Freemasonry. The fact is that all the movements we have mentioned so far (Rosicrucianism, Hermeticism, nostalgia for Egypt, pansophy, and theosophy) fed into Freemasonry, which—unlike these other more individualistic and even, in the case of Rosicrucianism, quasi-fictional movements—developed a very real organizational hierarchy and structure that continues to the present day.

FREEMASONRY

As is well known, Freemasonry has its origins in the medieval period as one of many craft guilds. Each guild had its secrets, and those of Masonry concern the arts of architecture and building associated with the vast cathedrals of medieval Europe. Of course there were other such guilds with their own rites and mysteries, but the Freemasons endured the longest, in part because of Kabbalistic influence and pansophic impulses that meant Freemasonry would be transformed from a society devoted to the arts of building to a parareligious, universalist occult fraternity. While historians have not yet fully discerned exactly how Freemasonry underwent this transformation, it is clear that like Rosicrucianism, Freemasonry inherited and drew from many prior esoteric traditions. Indeed, one can hardly doubt that Rosicrucianism's dreams of an immediate reform of humanity were tributary to the Masonic stream. Rosicrucianism remained a powerful influence in pan-European culture, and its universalist esotericism was particularly important for Masonic circles.

The first grand lodge of Freemasonry was founded in London in 1717, as the union of four earlier lodges. The first grand master of the lodge was Anthony Sayer, and the second was John Theophilus Desaguliers, who was also a fellow of the Royal Society. The Royal Society itself formed a meeting point for people of like mind, drawn to scientific inquiry, and the grand lodge represented an extension of the same impulse into a sphere that more explicitly had spiritual dimensions. This first grand lodge described itself as "speculative" in order to distinguish itself from "operative" Masonry, and it sought to trace its origins back to great antiquity, through ancient Greece and Rome, and through the medieval period. We see this Masonic parahistory first in James Anderson's *Constitutions of the Freemasons* (1723), which also had a considerable influence in promoting Masonry's nonsectarian tolerance. Freemasonry, according to the *Constitutions*, means that "A *Mason* is oblig'd by his Tenure to obey the Moral Law . . . whereby Masonry becomes the *Center of Union* and the Means of conciliating true Friendship among Persons that must have else remain'd at a perpetual Distance." As Edmund Mazet remarks, there is little in such basic principles of Freemasonry to suggest a specific Masonic esotericism.[10]

However, Freemasonry soon was to develop more esoteric dimensions, especially in France. Andrew Michael Ramsay (1686–1743), a Scotsman, was a member of the Philadelphian Society of Jane Leade and Francis Lee, a theosophic circle in London, and subsequently he went to live in France. Ramsay, who had been initiated into Masonry years before, rose in the French Masonic hierarchy, and in 1737 he gave a famous lecture. In this oration, Ramsay called for a massive project of universal illumination, a joining together of the arts and sciences. He echoes earlier Rosicrucian aims, but there is a more rationalist quality to his work, and it is arguably the case that he served as predecessor for the later French *philosophes* and their *Encyclopédie*. But he also linked Freemasonry to the Knights Templar, to aristocracy, and to a kind of mystical chivalry that was very attractive, particularly to the upper class. Many para-Masonic orders thus were generated.

As is already evident, Freemasonry has a complex relationship with the "Enlightenment" and with modernity. Masonic values of rationalism, deism, and nonsectarianism did help shape the modern era, with its general tendency to reject, suppress, or ignore esotericism. Yet Masonry has esoteric dimensions itself, visible most obviously in its complicated visual and ritual symbolism. Thus, there has continuously existed a tension between exoteric and esoteric Freemasonry. On the one hand we see figures like Jean-Baptiste Willermoz (1730–1824), one of the founders of the Rectified Scottish Rite and a powerful proponent of speculative or esoteric Masonry, and on the other hand we have Masons who emphasize a more exoteric, fraternal Freemasonry.

Freemasonry became an important social nexus, particularly for the wealthy and well connected, and not surprisingly, it was exported to the North American colonies in the eighteenth century. Benjamin Franklin (1706–1790), Paul Revere (1735–1818), George Washington (1732–1799), and many others who were central to the emergence of the United States were also Freemasons. Freemasonry was quite widespread in the American colonies by the time of the revolution, and many in the Continental Army were Masons, which helped to build camaraderie among the officers. When the cornerstone for the U.S. Capitol was laid by George Washington in 1793, he was wearing Masonic regalia and was accompanied by numerous fellow Masons.[11]

But events like this represent glimpses of Masonic social influence, whereas we are most interested in its more esoteric dimensions, which remain partially hidden. Freemasonry is an initiatory tradition, and much of its lore is still transmitted orally. Early Scottish Freemasons centered the mysteries of Freemasonry on the symbolism of Solomon's Temple, and this focus was intensified by later, more speculative lodges, some of which built Masonry into a body of universal knowledge that drew on a wide range of esoteric sources, not only Rosicrucianism and mystical chivalry, but also ancient Egypt and Jewish Kabbalah. Without doubt, as the Masonic current continued through the eighteenth century, it became among the more eclectic of esoteric traditions, especially with the founding of the Orden des Guelden-und Rosen-Cruetzes, the Order of the Gold and Rosy-Cross, a Masonic Rosicrucianism begun in 1757 in Germany that incorporated Templar and alchemical symbolism too. Indeed, the Ancient and Accepted Scottish Rite, the most popular form of contemporary Masonry, still preserves its eighteenth grade as that of the Chevalier Rose-Croix.

Like Rosicrucianism, speculative Masonry is a form of universal esotericism that seeks to unite all forms of knowledge, joining the humanities and the sciences under the aegis of a broadly conceived mystico-magical tradition. The universalist esotericist dream belongs primarily to individuals and circles within the larger stream of Masonic tradition, which in turn exists within the still broader current of Western esotericism that includes the pansophic union of magic and mysticism, both based in the pivotal idea that humans are capable of spiritual regeneration and of attaining gnosis, or direct experiential knowledge of the divine.

Central too, in these pansophic traditions, is the theme of mystical language that secretly unites humanity, nature, and the divine. In such a view, language is not just a means for objectification, but also the means for overcoming that objectification.[12] From this perspective, which is certainly central to Jewish Kabbalah, divine language inheres in the whole of creation—each kind of creature bears within it the divine signature, and this the esotericist unveils through visionary perception. In learning the divine language of creation, the esotericist seeks also to restore the cosmos to its transcendent or paradisal origin. Thus the esotericist plays a central role in the drama of cosmic redemption, a role that we also see being assumed in various ways in the esoteric movements that each also drew upon one or both of the twin currents of magic and mysticism, and that continued to develop and transform in the nineteenth and twentieth centuries.

ASTROLOGY

Another very important current in esotericism, astrology, has its roots in Greco-Roman late antiquity, and in writers like the fourth-century author Firmicus Maternus, whose astrological handbook *Matheseos Libri VIII* was written in 334 A.D.[13] Astrology stands midway between magic and mysticism, for it assumes a profound connection between the individual and the cosmos and, in a religious context, assumes behind that a connection to the divine, as does mysticism. That is, from the viewpoint of Christian, Jewish, or Islamic astrology, the cosmos and humanity are both the handiwork of God, and astrological signs and symbols are written by the divine hand upon both of them. From this perspective, astrology is a matter of discerning the hand of God in the cosmos and in human affairs. But this discernment has more than a little of the magical about it—through astrology, the sage might glimpse aspects of the future, might even alter what before looked like destiny.

Hence there remained in Christianity a tendency to distrust astrology, to see it as a manifestation of human pride that seeks to understand destiny and the hand of God in ways that human beings allegedly were not meant to, in part because astrological interpretation might infringe upon freedom of the will. It is interesting to speculate on the long-standing Christian theological suspicion of astrology, which arguably reflects a tendency within exoteric Christianity to see God as fundamentally separated from humanity and from the cosmos. Astrology, by way of contrast, sees the planets and stars as representing divine principles linking humanity, the cosmos, and the divine; astrologers see the cosmos and human life as pervaded by archetypal principles of consciousness. But such a perspective was resisted by a dominant rationalistic and dualistic strain in Christianity that can be traced back to Augustine, and before him to some of the ante-Nicene Fathers of the Church.

For all that, partly as an inheritance from the deep Platonic current in the West, astrological ways of thinking remained embedded in medieval Christian thought and tradition and emerged again explicitly during the Italian Renaissance. During the Renaissance, astrology was rediscovered and played an important role, especially in the Platonic works of Marsilio Ficino, like his *Three Books on Life* (1489). Here we see a complex union of Platonic philosophy with Christian herbal and astrological medicine, bound up together in what we may call an astrological mystico-magic. Like alchemy, astrology can include both mystical and magical dimensions, as Ficino's foundational work makes clear.

It was in the early modern period, however, that astrology really emerged again into its heyday. During the seventeenth and eighteenth centuries, astrological works were widely available, and astrological almanacs became quite popular in Europe, in England, and in North America. This was the era in which knowledge could be seen as unified by astrology, and so one sees the extraordinary herbals, notably of Nicholas Culpeper (1616–1654), *The English Physitian, or an Astrologo-Physical Discussion of the Vulgar Herbs of this Nation* (1652), organized along Paracelsian astrologico-medical lines. During the same time, we see Christopher Heydon's *An Astrological Discourse* (1650), and William Lilly's important book *Christian Astrology* (1647), as well as a translation of Valentin Weigel's *Astrologie Theologized* (1649).[14] Patrick Curry observes that William Lilly's astrological almanac sold at least thirty thousand copies a year during this period, and that almanac sales were four hundred thousand a year, with total sales in England topping four million almanacs![15]

Astrology was traditionally divided into two categories of natural and judicial. Natural astrology is represented in, for example, Culpeper's herbal—it works as a system of classification via principles like Martial (fiery, warlike), Lunar (watery, feminine), Jupiterian (generous, wealthy), and so forth. Judicial astrology like that practiced by William Lilly draws on the same principles but includes complex calculations regarding horoscopes, the signs of the Zodiac, the twelve houses, planetary conjunctions, trines, sextiles, oppositions, and so forth. A judicial astrologer might predict social upheaval, catastrophes, positive times for holding events, synastry (whether a couple fits harmoniously together), financial trends, career, and likely political outcomes. As might be imagined, such predictions would be of particular use to a king, queen, or other ruling figure. Judicial astrology tended to be frowned upon by the Church, but for all that, it remained in use.

Traditional astrology became less popular as the eighteenth century turned into the nineteenth. In part, this may have been because of the advent of science and scientific rationalism, but it also reflects the emergence of industrialism and the increasing commodification of the world. Astrology by contrast, tends to see the world as informed by hidden principles; one can see why astrology might lose popularity as the commodification and exploitation of the world developed. Of course there were still astrologers and authors writing on astrology, but it was not until the twentieth century, and in particular until the advent of computers, that Western forms of astrology came into their own again.

The twentieth century, broadly speaking, was an era of astrological rediscovery and recovery, arguably the liveliest period of astrological activity ever. During the twentieth century, we also see the Western discovery of Asian forms of astrology, notably Indian astrology *(jyotish),* which emphasized predictive astrology through complex calculations like that of *dashas*, or periods ruled by major and minor planetary influences. In turn, Western astrologers rediscovered more ancient methods of calculation, like traditional planetary periods called *firdaria*, which could be reincorporated into Western astrology. Twentieth- and twenty-first-century astrologers, aided by incredibly fast and powerful computer programs, arguably had access to more astrological databases and calculations than the greatest king's astrologers of the past. In keeping with what we see in the New Age and in new religious movements, one finds astrological syntheses in which an astrologer might well become familiar with and use two or even three traditions, including Indian, Tibetan, and Western, each system contributing a different kind of chart and interpretation.

By the early twenty-first century, one finds astrological associations, scholars, and even college curricula appearing in institutions like Kepler College. Scholarship made available a whole array of Greco-Roman and other ancient methods of calculation, and scholars continued to investigate. Here, as in so many other areas, it was as though the whole of the human past was becoming available to those who wished to delve into it. In the twentieth and twenty-first centuries, the esoteric was increasingly only self-restricted to those with an interest in it.

WEIGEL AND PIETISM

While the Protestant movement from the late sixteenth through the eighteenth century often known as Pietism was not, strictly speaking, a manifestation of the esoteric traditions that we have been tracing, it is nonetheless both instrumental in the formation of later modern forms of esotericism and indicative of the most marked characteristic of the shift from medieval to modern: an emphasis on the individual rather than the collective or communal. This shift is most visible, of course, in the emergence of Protestantism from Catholicism, which represented above all an emphasis on the individual's direct relationship to God without the (or with a severely limited) intercession of the Church as a body.

There are, of course, precedents for such an individual emphasis within Roman Catholicism itself—particularly in the very esoteric figures we have discussed, notably gnostics like Meister Eckhart, Tauler, and the author of the *Cloud of Unknowing*. And in fact, I will go so far as to suggest that Protestantism itself arguably is based on a fundamentally esoteric impulse—that of individual illumination—which might well explain why the seventeenth and eighteenth centuries in Europe witnessed such an explosion of explicitly or implicitly esoterically inspired movements and individuals. Some of the more scholarly of those individuals looked back in Catholic history for predecessors and found them precisely in the traditions of Taulerian gnosis, or, if bolder yet, among figures deemed outright heretical.[16]

Valentin Weigel (1533–1588), a pastor from Chemnitz, represents exactly such an individualizing spiritual impulse in his writings, where he manifests at once a Pietist emphasis on individual faith and spiritual illumination combined to some degree with Paracelsian alchemical thought as well. Other major proto-Pietist or Pietist figures include Kaspar Schwenckfeld (1489–1561), Johann Arndt (1555–1621), Philipp Jakob Spener (1635–1705), and Gerhard Tersteegen (1697–1769), author of various hymns, some of which are still widely sung today. Spener exemplifies as well as any our thesis here: his 1675 sermon is entitled "Pia desideria," which he explicitly acknowledges is inspired by the sermons of Tauler, and by the *Theologia Germanica* (translated by none other than Martin Luther), as well as by the *Wahres Christentum* [*True Christianity*] of Johann Arndt.[17] In this sermon, Spener emphasizes how essential is the *Innerlichkeit* [inwardliness] and the *göttliche Einwohnung* [divine indwelling] that occurs as a result of rebirth in the Spirit.[18]

As the name would suggest, Pietism is not itself an explicitly esoteric movement but rather a movement appealing to the individual's inner faith and spiritual experience and thus attractive to a broad range of society. At the same time, it is a mistake to ignore the esoteric side of Pietism as a whole, an esotericism that is obvious in the theosophic tradition of Jacob Böhme (whose works and some of whose followers are often classed as Pietists) but is also implicitly present in the works of Weigel, Spener, and many others in the movement. One should keep in mind that the esoteric efflorescences beginning around 1600 in Europe and manifesting later in a whole host of esoteric movements from Rosicrucianism to theosophy to various kinds of quasi-Masonic Christian orders virtually all had their origins in a general ambience of Pietist individualism and emphasis upon direct spiritual experience. But a recipient of and a contributor to all these other esoteric currents arose out of Pietism and took on a life of its own: Christian theosophy.

CHRISTIAN THEOSOPHY

When one mentions the term *theosophy,* many people still think solely of the late nineteenth-century organization of Helena Petrovna Blavatsky, which called itself the Theosophical Society. But Blavatsky did not invent the word *theosophy,* she simply appropriated it from a preexisting theosophic tradition that stretches from Christianity's beginning to the present day.[19] This appropriation has created a great deal of confusion over terms. To clear up this confusion, we need not only to define the differences, but also to trace the full extent of the theosophic tradition from antiquity to the present. As we see, the Christian theosophic tradition represents an important, continuous, and integral current that only recently has begun to be uncovered and that is in many respects a synthesis of many earlier esoteric traditions both magical (like alchemy) and mystical.

But let us begin with definitions. In keeping with scholarly conventions concerning Jewish and Islamic theosophy, the term *Christian theosophy* broadly speaking refers to the Christian experiential gnostic traditions that stretch from antiquity to the present.[20] Practitioners and representatives of the Christian theosophic tradition are called "theosophers." More strictly speaking, one can refer to the theosophic tradition of Jacob Böhme (1575–1624) and those who came after him, including such figures as John Pordage, Jane Leade, Johann Gichtel, and the others, known collectively as representatives of Böhmean theosophy. Here, *Blavatskyan Theosophy* refers to the cosmological schemata of the Theosophical Society; *Blavatskyan Theosophist* refers to representatives of the Theosophical Society; and *Theosophical* capitalized refers to the cosmological doctrines of that society. One should clearly maintain such distinctions.

To make these distinctions concrete, we should begin with an example—that of the great twentieth century Russian theosopher Nicolai Berdyaev (1874–1948). Berdyaev wrote that he arrived at his Christianity not through habit or tradition, less yet from any compulsion, but through "an intimate experience of the paths of freedom." His faith, he tells us, "was won through an experience of the inner life of a most painful character."[21] "I regard myself," he continued, "as being a Christian theosopher, in the sense in which Clement of

Alexandria, Origen, St. Gregory of Nyssa, Cardinal Nicholas of Cusa, Jacob Böhme, Saint-Martin, Franz von Baader, and Vladimir Solovyov were Christian theosophers."[22] Berdyaev here, as elsewhere, incontrovertibly reveals himself as part of the Christian theosophic tradition to which we are devoting our attention.

What does Berdyaev think about the Theosophical Society? In the same work in which he identified himself as a theosopher, Berdyaev devotes an entire chapter to the doctrines of the Theosophical Society. He writes quite unequivocally:

> Words often provoke a false association of ideas that do not conform to their ontological meaning. "Theosophy" is a word of this kind, for it may mean many different things. Contemporary theosophical movements have given it a debased significance and have made us forget the existence of an authentic Christian theosophy and a genuine knowledge of the divine. The theosophical tradition runs right through Christian history. . . . Mystical theology . . . has always been theosophical. . . .
>
> But it is clear that contemporary theosophy is different from that of other ages. The spirit of Mme. Blavatsky or Mrs. Besant differs considerably from that of Heraclitus, Plotinus, Origen, Dionysius the Areopagite, Meister Eckhart, Jacob Böhme, Baader, or Solovyov. Its form is quite different; they belong to another type altogether. . . . "Cosmosophy" would be a much better name for it than "theosophy," for it deals with nothing but the composition and development of the cosmos.[23]

Whatever one thinks of Berdyaev's assessment, it is self-evident that in regarding himself as a theosopher, he seeks to completely separate Christian theosophy from the Blavatskyan Theosophical Society. And in his brief listing of Christian theosophers, Berdyaev is right in tracing the lineage that runs from Dionysius the Areopagite through Eckhart and Böhme and Saint-Martin. It is precisely this lineage with which we are now concerned.

As I elsewhere remark, theosophy represents a paradigm with certain common elements that reappear even if various groups are wholly unaware of one another, including (1) the focus upon Wisdom or Sophia, (2) an insistence upon direct spiritual experience, (3) reading nature as a spiritual book, (4) a spiritual leader who guides his or her spiritual circle through letters and oral advice. These elements refer chiefly to the modern theosophic tradition that emerged with Jacob Böhme in the beginning of the seventeenth century. Antoine Faivre has pointed out the primary characteristics of Western esotericism more generally, which naturally hold for theosophy, a major current within the even larger stream of Western esotericism.[24] In fact, modern Christian theosophy represents a synthesis of many other currents, including alchemy, Jewish Kabbalah, chivalry, and the gnostic tradition represented by Eckhart and Tauler.

Often one finds theosophers listing the names of those whom they regard as previous theosophers, just as Berdyaev does in our quotations. In so doing, they situate themselves within a historical tradition, by implication placing themselves in the lineage of theosophers. Indeed, self-identification is one primary way of identifying theosophers. For theosophy—and on this one must be very clear—is not an organized sect but an experiential gnostic path within Christianity. As such, it is open to gnosis where it is found and is indifferent to artificial divisions between Protestant, Catholic, and Orthodox.

Theosophers belong to the gnostic current that stretches from some of the ante-Nicene Fathers onward, beginning with Clement of Alexandria. Clement of Alexandria is important to the theosophic tradition because unlike many of the Church Fathers, he insists on the importance of an authentic (not heretical) gnosis within the Christian tradition. In the *Stromata*, or *Miscellanies*, Clement writes that "gnosis, to speak generally, a perfecting of man as man, is consummated by acquaintance with divine things, in character, life, and word, accordant and conformable to itself and to the Divine Logos. For by it faith is perfected, inasmuch as it is solely by it [gnosis] that the believer becomes perfect."[25]

Clement divides authentic from false gnosis, the latter being characterized by immoral behavior, the former by the highest morality. Clement of Alexandria, like Origen, represents a reference point for later theosophers because like them, the theosophers insisted that there is an orthodox gnosis within Christianity, that historical faith is not the only characteristic of that tradition.

Another early reference point and key for understanding the theosophers is Dionysius the Areopagite who, we will recall, differentiates between the *via positiva* and the *via negativa*, the way of transcendence through affirmation of images and the way of transcendence through negation of images. In "The Celestial Hierarchy," Dionysius writes that one may begin with the affirmation of images—but one proceeds soon enough to dissimilar images, because otherwise one runs the risk of vulgarization. Out of such affirmations of dissimilar images emerges the *via negativa*, the transcendence of all images whatever and entry into the "divine darkness." Thus "everything can be a help to contemplation," Dionysius writes.[26] In other words, the way of negation is not a rejection of nature and the world, but an affirmation of it; all that we see is an aid to realization of divine truth, which is nonetheless beyond all images and forms. We find a similar union of the *via positiva* and the *via negativa* in the tradition that begins with Jacob Böhme.

There is a third predecessor in the Christian tradition who figures strongly in the emergence of the theosophic current, and that is Johannes Tauler (ca. 1300–1361). Tauler was in fact cited by some of the more modern theosophers, and a manuscript attributed to him circulated among the late seventeenth century theosophers in England. Tauler was attractive to the later theosophers because, like Dionysius the Areopagite and Clement of Alexandria, he insisted on direct experiential knowledge of divine things. Tauler insisted on true prayer, which is "a direct raising of the mind and heart to God, without intermediary." According to Tauler, true prayer is "a lifting of the spirit upward, so that God may in reality enter the purest, most inward, noblest part of the soul—its deepest ground—where alone there is undifferentiated unity."[27]

It is not uncommon to separate figures like Tauler and Eckhart from subsequent gnostics like Jacob Böhme or John Pordage, but let us look closely at this passage from Tauler. Alluding to Augustine, Tauler tells us that

> the soul has a hidden abyss, untouched by time and space, which is far superior to anything that gives life and movement to the body. Into this noble and wondrous ground, this secret realm, there descends that bliss of which we have spoken. Here the soul has its hidden abode. Here a man becomes so still and essential, so single-minded and withdrawn, so raised up in purity and more and more removed from all things, for God himself is present in this noble realm, and works and reigns and dwells therein.[28]

Now we should keep the specifics of this passage in mind when we turn to modern Christian theosophy, tracing the course of its various currents, for Tauler's emphasis here on a "hidden abyss, untouched by time and space," his reference to a "secret," "noble," and "wondrous" realm in which God himself lives and works, have their direct correspondences in the subsequent German, French, English, and American theosophic currents.

NOTES

1. See Allison Coudert, *Alchemy: The Philosopher's Stone* (London: Wildwood, 1980), 11 ff. For a commentary coupled with many illustrations, see Stanislas Klossowski de Rola, *The Golden Game: Alchemical Engravings of the Seventeenth Century* (New York: Braziller, 1988).

2. See Ethan Allen Hitchcock, *Remarks on Alchemy and the Alchemists* (Boston: Crosby, Nichols, 1857). For a discussion of Hitchcock, see Arthur Versluis, *The Esoteric Origins of the American Renaissance* (New York: Oxford University Press, 2001), 64–71. See also Karen-Claire Voss, "Spiritual Alchemy," in Roelof van den Broek and W. Hanegraaff, eds., *Gnosis and Hermeticism from Antiquity to Modern Times* (Albany: SUNY Press, 1998), 147–82.

3. Lawrence M. Principe and William R. Newman, "Some Problems with the Historiography of Alchemy," in *Secrets of Nature: Astrology and Alchemy in Early Modern Europe*, eds. Newman and Anthony Grafton (Cambridge: MIT Press, 2001),

385–434; George Starkey, *Alchemical Laboratory Notebooks and Correspondence*, ed. William R. Newman and Lawrence M. Principe (Chicago: University of Chicago Press, 2004); and William R. Newman and Lawrence Principe, *Alchemy Tried in the Fire: Starkey, Boyle, and the Fate of Helmontian Chymistry* (Chicago: University of Chicago Press, 2002).

4. See A. E. Waite, ed., *The Hermetic Museum* (London: Watkins, 1893/York Beach, ME: Weiser, 1990), I.67.

5. For a discussion of these and other figures of the period, see Versluis, *The Esoteric Origins of the American Renaissance* (New York: Oxford University Press, 2001).

6. Many alchemical works were made available at the end of the twentieth century by indefatigable researchers, most notably Adam McLean. Groups like the Philosophers of Nature also sought to draw upon and experiment along the lines of traditional Western alchemy of the seventeenth and eighteenth centuries. Readers might also be interested in the work of practical plant alchemists like Manfred Junius.

7. See Frances Yates, *The Rosicrucian Enlightenment* (London: Routledge, 1972), 238–60, which includes in its appendices versions of the *Fama* and the *Confessio*. For an excellent version of the *Chemical Wedding*, see Joscelyn Godwin, trs., *The Chemical Wedding* (Grand Rapids, MI: Phanes, 1994). Versions of all three Rosicrucian works can be found online at www.levity.com/alchemy

8. See *Fama Fraternitatis*, in Yates, 238–60, or see *Allgemeine und General Reformation, der gantzen weiten Welt. Beneben der Fama Fraternitatis . . .* (Cassel Germany: Wilhelm Wessell, 1614). For the *Confessio*, see *Secretioris Philosophiae Consideratio brevis a Philipp a Gabella, Philosophiae St. conscripta, et nunc primum una cum Confessione Fraternitatis R.C. . . .* (Cassel: Wilhelm Wessell, 1615).

9. See Yates, *The Rosicrucian Enlightenment*, 30–69. Yates's work has been critiqued by subsequent scholars, but remains an engaging introduction to the Rosicrucian phenomenon. See also Christopher McIntosh, *The Rose Cross and the Age of Reason* (Leiden: Brill, 1992).

10. See Edmund Mazet, "Freemasonry and Esotericism," in Antoine Faivre and Jacob Needleman, eds., *Modern Esoteric Spirituality* (New York: Crossroad, 1992), 248–76.

11. See Mark Tabbert, *American Freemasons: Three Centuries of Building Communities* (New York: New York University Press, 2005), 44.

12. On this point, see Arthur Versluis, *Restoring Paradise: Western Esotericism, Literature, Art, and Consciousness* (Albany: SUNY Press, 2004).

13. See Jean Rhys Bram, trs., *Ancient Astrology: Theory and Practice, Matheseos Libri VIII by Firmicus Maternus* (Park Ridge, NJ: Noyes Press, 1975).

14. See Ann Geneva, *Astrology and the Seventeenth Century Mind: William Lilly and the Language of the Stars* (Manchester, UK: Manchester University Press, 1995).

15. See Patrick Curry, *Prophecy and Power: Astrology in Early Modern England* (Princeton, NJ: Princeton University Press, 1989), 21.

16. See Versluis, *Wisdom's Children: A Christian Esoteric Tradition* (Albany: SUNY Press, 1999), 178–80, for a discussion of how late seventeenth and eighteenth century English theosophers explicitly drew upon apocryphal works attributed to

Tauler or others. For more heretical influences or connections, see for instance Gottfried Arnold, *Unpartheiische Kirchen und Ketzer Historien* (Frankfurt: 1699–1700).

17. See *The Theologia Germanica of Martin Luther*, Bengt Hoffmann, ed. (New York: Paulist Press, 1980).

18. For a few brief excerpts from Spener in German, see Gerhard Wehr, *Mystik im Protestantismus* (München: Claudius Verlag, 2000), 75–78. For more on Spener and the Pietists in general as well as copious examples of their work in English see Peter Erb, *Pietists: Selected Writings* (New York: Paulist Press, 1983). Erb includes almost all of this sermon in his anthology; see 31–49.

19. See on this point James Santucci, "On Theosophia and Related Terms," *Theosophical History* II.3 (1987): 107–10; see also Santucci, "Theosophy and the Theosophical Society" (London: Theosophical History Center, 1985); among Antoine Faivre's numerous publications on theosophy and related topics, see especially "Le courant théosophique (fin XV–XX siécle): Essai de périodisation," in *Politica Hermetica* 7 (1993): 6–41; and for an overview of the Western esoteric traditions, see Faivre's *Access to Western Esotericism* (Albany: SUNY Press, 1994).

20. The word *gnostic* here refers not to Gnosticism, but to Christian gnosis, representative of which is Meister Eckhart, for instance. I prefer this word to *mysticism,* in that *gnostic* refers to direct experiential knowledge of divinity and is perhaps less freighted than *mystic*. There are parallels between modern Christian theosophy and ancient Gnosticism; on this see my "Christian Theosophy and Ancient Gnosticism," *Studies in Spirituality*, 7 (1997): 228–41.

21. Nicolai Berdyaev, *Freedom and the Spirit* (London: Bles, 1935), x.

22. Berdyaev, *Freedom and the Spirit,* xix.

23. Berdyaev, *Freedom and the Spirit,* 270–71.

24. See Antoine Faivre, *Access to Western Esotericism*; see also Faivre, *Esotericisme: Qui sai'je?* (Paris: Presses Universitaires de France, 1992), and in particular, Faivre, *Theosophy, Imagination, Tradition* (Albany: SUNY, 2000).

25. *Ante-Nicene Fathers* (Grand Rapids, MI: Eerdmans, 1990 ed.), II.538; Strom. VII.x.

26. Dionysius the Areopagite, *The Complete Works* (New York: Paulist Press, 1987), "Celestial Hierarchies," 140c, 151.

27. Tauler, *Sermons* (New York: Paulist Press, 1985), Sermon 24, 89.

28. Tauler, *Sermons,* 89–90.

Chapter Seven

Modern Christian Theosophy

GERMAN THEOSOPHY

The modern theosophic movement begins at the turn of the seventeenth century, chiefly in Germany, where one finds the most influential or seminal of the theosophic writers, Jacob Böhme (1575–1624). Böhme, the "illuminated cobbler," came from Görlitz, a town near the border between Eastern and Western Europe. Böhme's spiritual illumination came after a bout of depression, and it resulted in his first book, *Morgenröte im Aufgang, oder Aurora*, written in 1612. Böhme's remarkable work provoked great wrath in a sour local Lutheran minister named Gregor Richter, and in fact Böhme was forbidden to write more. But he eventually developed quite a circle of followers, who asked him for advice, and so he came to write many more treatises.[1]

As Andrew Weeks points out in his intellectual biography of Böhme, Görlitz had become a kind of center for those with mystical leanings, and Böhme's own circle eventually included some remarkable people, among whom we should note Balthasar Walter, who had traveled to the Near East (Arabia, Syria, and Egypt) in search of "Kabbalah, magic, and alchemy" during the late sixteenth century. Walter came to know Böhme after 1612, and stayed in Böhme's house for several months during 1619 or 1620. Other important members of Böhme's circle include Johann Huser, editor of an edition of Paracelsus's works, Carl von Ender, a nobleman, and Dr. Tobias Kober.

Eventually, Böhme produced a body of work that was to inspire the whole of subsequent theosophy. It is revealing that many later theosophers claimed their spiritual lives really began only with their discovery of Böhme's vast body of writings.[2] In 1618 Böhme began *The Three Principles of the Divine Being*, and between 1619 and his death in 1624, he completed numerous treatises and assorted other manuscripts and letters, including *Forty Questions on the Soul*, *The Signature of All Things*, and *Mysterium Magnum*, a commentary on Genesis, as well as various other works.[3]

We cannot here survey Böhme's writings, which require each reader to work with them individually over an extended period in order to reveal themselves. Böhme's corpus is richly complex and has a specialized Latin-based vocabulary rich in neologisms, so each reader will see different aspects of Böhme's insights.[4] But Böhme's works fuse alchemical, Paracelsian, and Hermetic terms with what we may call high German mysticism, so that his writing possesses extraordinary depth and range. Böhme insists throughout his writings that his readers directly experience for themselves the truth of which he writes. And indeed at the center of his works is spiritual rebirth.

Böhme, in his *Aurora*, elaborates on the process of spiritual rebirth. We are, he tells us, born into the darkness of physicality, "wherein Lucifer and his angels, as also all fleshly or carnal wicked men lie captive."[5] But we are also born into the astral realm, which is of a mixed nature, including both love and wrath contending with one another. This realm is characterized by the seven spirits, outwardly symbolized by the planets, which color or condition the nature of existence. The devil, via wrath, can only reach halfway into this realm; the other half lies hidden from him and from us; and accordingly as we live our lives in love or in wrath will we live in this primordial element after death. But both love and wrath have their origin and transcendence in the third realm, the "holy heart of God," which is beyond all that could be said about it.[6]

Böhme sees the entire cosmos tinctured by love and by wrath, with humanity participating in both. The key to this participation is imagination, symbolized by Mercury. Mercury, representing the principle of consciousness, is in its proper or true nature the "Word" or "Logos"—that is, if Mercury is permeated with love, then it is the means of communication with, indeed, identity with the divine. But when Mercury through imagination allows the wrath to manifest in it, then it becomes poisoned and poisonous; and this is the ordinary, or fallen human condition, our starting point.

Now Böhme discusses in many different ways the process of regeneration and spiritual illumination, one of these being in his *Signatura Rerum*, when he writes of the "philosophic work." Böhme here tells us that although "I in the outward man do yet live in my selfhood, therefore I must also die with the outward man in Christ's death, and arise and live with him."[7] The philosophic work is the process of dying to selfhood and awakening the "inward man." This process, he tells us, is not one he will divulge in detail, but it consists in the "heavenly essentiality" in its virginity permeating the soul's inward nature, transmuting one's wrathful and dead fallenness or disharmony into love's unity. He further remarks that "the poisonous mercurial, martial, and saturnine will and desire die in the blood of Venus in the philosophic work, and both enter together into death, and arise both together in one love, in one will."[8] The seven forms (marked by the planetary energies) must be transformed into one by love, even while remaining distinct; and in this way one's whole being is restored to paradisal wholeness, harmony, and unity.

I am emphasizing Böhme's insistence on spiritual regeneration and on the specific process through which one accomplishes this because this process is the heart of his work and, in turn, reappears as the center of subsequent theosophy. Indeed, the specific process Böhme mentions here as the "philosophic work" recurs again and again in later illustrations and treatises, including those of Johann Gichtel in the Netherlands, and John Pordage in England, as we see below. This process, which is explained using alchemical terms and images, is in fact the work of spiritual awakening through contemplation akin to what we see earlier in the writings of Eckhart and Tauler. Modern Christian theosophy, from Böhme onward, maintains a balance between imagery and the transcendence of imagery, the *via positiva* and *via negativa*.

Another important theosopher was Johann Georg Gichtel (1638–1710), the often volatile "hermit of Amsterdam" whose collected letters of spiritual advice under the title *Theosophia Practica* (1722) comprise seven volumes and several thousand pages. Although there is some repetition in his letters, even a cursory study will reveal Gichtel's authority on a wide range of subjects including spiritual alchemy, which draws explicitly upon Böhme's work. Gichtel and his friend Ueberfeldt edited the first major edition of Böhme's complete writings, published as *Theosophia Revelata* (1682/1730).

A more concise book, often also published under the title *Theosophia Practica*, but actually entitled *Eine kurze Eröffnung und Anweisung der dryen Principien und Welten in Menschen [A Brief Opening and Demonstration of the Three Principles and Worlds in Man]* (1696/1779), is an important guide to Gichtel's spiritual understanding and includes several illustrations that have been linked to Asian traditions of the chakras in the human body. Even though Gichtel's harsh rhetoric might well dissuade the casual reader, a closer examination of this treatise reveals that Gichtel simply is guiding the reader along the spiritual path that he has himself followed.[9] He seeks to show us how to go from the dark or wrathful world of fallen man to divinely regenerated man.

Gichtel's *A Brief Opening . . . of the Three Principles* is a very detailed work on theosophic praxis. Gichtel writes, in the preface to the first chapter, that he wants to show "the first-created image of God before the Fall, which stands hidden in the spirit, which the author knows by praxis and [also will show] in the figures of the completed man, out of the new birth in Christ, which is to be developed in you."[10]

Gichtel's own struggle was difficult from early on, for in youth his uncon-ventional spirituality brought him to the attention of church and city authori-ties, who

> mocked, insulted, and humiliated me, led me over the streets and wanted to force my head down, but because they could not ultimately agree, they finally took everything away from me and banned me eternally from the city. . . .
>
> So now I lay in a stinking hole, locked up, tempted by the devil and tested by gruesome doubts, so much so that I grasped a knife and would have, in order to save my anxious life from suffering, brought my life with a stab to a quick end.[11]

But instead of committing suicide, Gichtel experienced a vision that inspired him to follow a long and difficult path of poverty and spiritual struggle to-ward Sophianic illumination.

Gichtel's outward life began in Ratisbon, Germany, in March 1638, and had three stages: from 1638 to 1664, when he began to encounter difficulties with the clerical authorities in Ratisbon; from 1665 through 1667, when he moved about, staying for a while with the Protestant author Friedrich Breck-ling (1629–1711); and from 1668 to his death in 1710, the time during which he lived, wrote, and taught in Amsterdam. Most of our information about Gichtel comes from this last period, during which he established his commu-nity of the "Brethren of the Angelic Life," the Engelsbrüder, and became more generally known as a theosopher.

Gichtel's biography is entitled *The Wonderful and Holy Life of the Chosen Champion and Blessèd Man of God Johann Georg Gichtel* and includes nu-merous miraculous or paranormal events. Gichtel said that both he and his Angelic Brethren were supported by prayer and divine mercy—money or food or clothing simply appeared when they were necessary, generally do-nated by benefactors (there were rumors that Gichtel was a practicing al-chemist). A querulous man, Gichtel had argued vociferously with nearly everyone he knew by the time he died, and it is at times difficult to reconcile this with his spirituality.

If Gichtel is certainly among the most important practical theosophers, Gottfried Arnold (1666–1714) is arguably the most important scholar among the theosophers. Arnold, an acquaintance of Gichtel, fell in Gichtel's eyes when he married. Arnold's most important books were published in 1699/1700 and include his *Unparteiische Kirchen- und Ketzer-historie* (4 vols.) and *Das Geheimniss der Göttliche Sophia*. Arnold's *Impartial Church and Heretic History* is striking for its affirmations of authors traditionally deemed heretical, and thus it raised some controversy after publication. His *Mystery of the Holy Sophia* is significant for its extensive scholarly treatment of this most central theosophic theme and closely follows traditional Patristic and other sources on the topic of Wisdom.

Arnold was a scholar who sought to place theosophy within the larger context of the entire Christian tradition, and when one considers that Böhme and many of the other theosophers were dismissed by conventional Christians as heretical, one can see how Arnold's assessment of ancient and more recent heresies was a reaction against this contemporary dismissal. Arnold was also known for his spiritual songs or hymns, some of which were published conjointly with his book on Sophia, and one can find his songs in an 1856 edition.[12] His last important theosophic work was *Theologia Experimentalis* (1714). Certainly it is fair to say that Arnold, in his historical method, was influential not only for pietist writers but also for his aim of creating an impartial assessment of Christian mysticism, anticipating much more recent efforts in this direction.

Jewish Kabbalah, itself theosophic, was undoubtedly formative for Christian theosophy from Böhme on. Its most important eighteenth century syncretic exponent within theosophy was Friedrich Christoph Œtinger (1702–1782), whose works represent an attempt to synthesize Kabbalah—especially that of Isaac Luria—with the theosophical tradition of Böhme. Œtinger's works range from his *Aufmunternde Gründe zur Lesung der Schriften Jacob Böhmens* (1731) to his *Theologia ex idea vitae deducta* (1765) and *Biblisches und Emblematisches Wörterbuch* (1765). Perhaps most well known is his *Die Lehrtafel der Prinzessin Antonia* (1763) in which he explains "the most important truths of the holy scriptures according to the knowledge of the Kabbala."[13] Œtinger also wrote about the visionary Emmanuel Swedenborg's (1668–1772) writings in *Swedenborgs und andere irdische und himmlische Philosophie* (1765). We should remark here that Swedenborg was looked down upon by Böhmean theosophers like Louis-Claude de Saint-Martin, who saw Swedenborg's visions as belonging mainly to the astral realm. At any rate, it is fair to say that Swedenborg himself stands outside the main current of theosophy, whereas Œtinger stands within it while drawing upon Swedenborg.

Antoine Faivre has pointed out that Christian theosophy is divisible into main currents. The Kabbalistic line of theosophy represented by Œtinger was carried on in the nineteenth century by Franz Josef Molitor (1779–1860), author of *Philosophie der Geschichte, oder über die Tradition* (1854). What we may call magical theosophy is represented in, for instance, Georg von Welling's (1655–1727) *Opus Mago-Cabbalisticum et theosophicum* (1784) as well as by Karl von Eckhartshausen (1752–1803), whose writings range from *Ausschlüße zur Magie* (1788/90) and *Zahlenlehre der Natur* (1794) to the well known little work *Die Wolke über dem Heiligthum* (1802), in English

The Clouds over the Sanctuary, a work closer to theosophy than to the magical-occult tradition of his early works.

But undoubtedly theosophy's greatest recent German exponent is Franz von Baader (1765–1841).[14] Baader is a grand unifying figure, joining science, religion, and literature, as well as all three traditions of Christianity (Protestantism [particularly theosophy], Roman Catholicism, and Eastern Orthodoxy). A peerless aphorist, Baader is intellectually among the most stimulating and profound of the theosophers. The sixteen volumes of his collected works often are difficult and abstruse but repay closer reading, not least because he joins scientific, religious, and literary concerns. In many respects, Baader was truly a Renaissance man.

Born in 1765 in Munich, the son of a physician, Baader studied mineralogy under such luminaries as Alexander von Humboldt and spent four years in England beginning in 1792, where he witnessed the social effects of the industrial revolution, especially the appearance of a proletariat class. In 1796, he returned to Germany, where he was able through various chemical experiments to develop a patented formula for glass fabrication that brought him a substantial income. Obviously Baader came to theosophy from an unusually scientific viewpoint.

Termed by August Wilhelm Schlegel "Boehmius redivivus," or "Böhme reborn," a complimentary designation still indissolubly linked to Baader's name, Baader was a great reader of Böhme, Saint-Martin, and Meister Eckhart. Most famous as a theosopher, Baader's theosophic writings encompass an unusual range of subjects, from eros to politics to the meeting of Catholicism, Protestantism, and Eastern Orthodoxy.[15] His emphasis on erotic philosophy, and on furthering a religious rather than merely materialist science, is worthy of much further inquiry than it has yet received, although Antoine Faivre has made much headway in this sphere.[16]

But German theosophy does not end with Baader, however monumental his work was in joining countless fields. Baader remains the most towering figure on the German scene in the nineteenth and twentieth centuries, but there are some noteworthy others, including Johann Jakob Wirz (1778–1858), one of the most accessible and charming authors in the whole of theosophic literature. Wirz almost never cites or even alludes to other theosophers; Sophia herself has been his guide and companion, and he writes directly of her, in stories or parabolic teachings that are perhaps most paralleled in world literature by Sufi works, what Henry Corbin called "visionary recitals." His divine inspiration began around the end of 1823, and he soon gathered a small group, called the Nazarene community, which emphasized a simple, humble, and pure way of life. Wirz believed his group incarnated an almost Joachimite "age of the Spirit," inspired and guided by divine Wisdom. To him, God is Father and Mother both, and he held that this mystery was the secret of "urrre-ligion" from time immemorial. A firm believer in the feminine aspect of divinity, Wirz held that the Virgin Mary was the "spiritual-corporeal daughter of divine Wisdom." Wirz's major writings were published as *Testimonies and Revelations of the Spirit through Johann Jakob Wirz [Zeugnisse und Eröffnungen des Geistes durch Johann Jakob Wirz]* (1863–1864).

After Wirz, we could also mention Jakob Lorber (1800–1864), a musician and conductor who, on the fifteenth of March 1840, heard a voice that instructed him as follows: "Pick up your pen and write!" Write he did. His *Johannes, das große Evangelium* (1851–1864) comprises eleven volumes and some five thousand pages, a vast work that derived from his acting as a medium. In keeping with the spirit of theosophy, Lorber's circle founded no church nor sect, although there still exists a group in Germany that maintains his books in print. Occasionally, extravagant claims have been made regarding Lorber's works; he is in my estimation on the periphery of the theosophic current.

We must also take note of Rudolf Steiner (1861–1925), who although he was undoubtedly the inheritor of the theosophic current we are here tracing, did not present himself as part of it. Indeed, one finds in his many books comparatively few references to Jacob Böhme or the other theosophers, even, for instance, in a work entitled *Theosophie: Einführung in übersinnlich Welterkenntnis und Meschenbestimmung [Theosophy: Guide to Supersensible Worlds]* (1922), one finds little to remind one of the theosophic tradition we are here discussing. Instead, Steiner (a member of the Theosophical Society before his founding of the Anthroposophical Society) seems much more interested in astral cartography. Perhaps most revealing of Steiner's approach to theosophy is his work *Die Mystik im Aufgange des neuzeitlichen Geisteslebens [Mystics of the Renaissance and their Religion to Modern Thought]* (1912 trans.), which is devoted to Eckhart, Tauler, Böhme, and others, but is often dismissive and downplays Steiner's indebtedness to them.

Another figure, somewhat enigmatic, is Karel Weinfurter (dates unknown), a Czechoslovakian author of the early twentieth century whose work *Der Brennende Busch [The Burning Bush*, 1930, 1949, 1957], went through numerous editions in German, and who also wrote *Mystische Fibel [A Handbook for Students of Practical Mysticism*, 1954, 1959]. Weinfurter's work was translated into English and published as *Man's Highest Purpose: The Lost Word Regained,* n.d. Weinfurter, unlike our other theosophers either before or after, alluded occasionally to Blavatsky's works, and to those of Annie Besant, but his primary source is a group of practical mystics that met in Prague earlier in the twentieth century.[17]

Weinfurter explicitly drew on the work of J. B. Kerning (1774–1851), originally named Johann Baptist Krebs, an ardent Freemason strongly influenced by the theosophic current, whose books include such titles as *The Way to Immortality and Key to the Spiritual World*. Kerning also wrote *Historical Overview of Freemasonry*, so one can see how he represented a confluence of currents. Much on and by Kerning was brought to light and published or republished in 1902, at the behest of the Theosophic Lodge of the Blue Star, Weinfurter's group in Prague founded in 1891.[18] Weinfurter's group sought throughout Europe for spiritual guidance, and he claims to have ultimately found it, after having practiced numerous ascetic exercises and practices.

In his books, Weinfurter—whose group often originally met in the flat of Gustav Meyrink, the well-known fiction writer—offers an unusual form of theosophy. He elaborates a tradition regarding a mystical alphabet and the use of Western "mantras," as well as offering a discussion of what we may call metaphysiology. According to Weinfurter, who drew extensively on what was available from newly translated yogic works like that of Patanjali, there is an orally transmitted Christian tradition of bodily concentration and awareness that corresponds rather closely to some forms of Indian yoga, as well as in other respects to ancient Gnosticism for that matter. Although Weinfurter is somewhat outside the primary current of theosophy, his work is certainly still worthy of further examination.

While Christian theosophy in general has remained a current separate from movements like the Theosophical Society, during the early twentieth century there were several exceptions, among which were Weinfurter and the founder in 1886 of the German branch of the Theosophical Society, Franz Hartmann (1838–1912). Hartmann's group, the ITV (Internationale Theosophische Verbrüderung), was more rooted in the European esoteric traditions than, for instance, Annie Besant's Adyar group, as we can see from the kinds of books Hartmann published.[19] Hartmann published several books drawing extensively on the works of Jacob Böhme, with copious excerpts, and he also published a book on Paracelsus, this too with many direct quotations. In the latter work, Hartmann defines *theosophia* as

> Divine self-knowledge. The true understanding. Supreme wisdom, acquired by practical experience by which it is eminently distinguished from merely speculative philosophy. Theosophy is not any new creed nor any system of philosophy; neither can it be taught by one person to another. It is not any knowledge relating to any external thing, but the self-knowledge of the awakened spirit in man.[20]

Hartmann's theosophy was very much rooted in the Christian theosophic tradition. In his book on Böhme, Hartmann concludes his introduction by affirming the books of Böhme as "the most valuable and useful treasure in spiritual literature."[21]

Among twentieth-century theosophers, Leopold Ziegler (1881–1958) was arguably the most important, similar in scope to Graf Hermann Keyserling, but much more well read in and influenced by Christian theosophy, and instrumental in what has come to be called "East-West dialogue." Born in Karlsruhe, Germany, and a student at the University of Heidelberg, Ziegler first published *Die Metaphysik des Tragischen [The Metaphysics of the Tragic]* (1902), in which he discussed the significance of suffering in human life, but more characteristic of his work is *Gestaltwandel der Götter [Transformation of the Gods]* (1920), *Überlieferung [Tradition]* (1936), and *Menschwerdung [Becoming Human]* (1948), the latter two his main works, illustrating his focus on Buddhism and Christian theosophy, and on finding a course out of existentialism and nihilism into a spiritual understanding that affirms the whole of life. In *Spätlese eigener Hand [Late Harvest From My Own Hand]* (1953), Ziegler discusses the spectrum of Sophianic spirituality.[22] Too little known today, Ziegler remains an important figure in twentieth-century thought.

There are some important German scholarly studies including discussions of theosophy that we cannot overlook. All of these have in common an inclusion of and even an emphasis on the magical elements of this tradition or current. One major such study is Will-Erich Peuckert's *Pansophie: Ein Versuch zur Geschichte der Weissen und Schwarzen Magie* (1956). Another is Karl Frick's vast multivolume surveys entitled *Licht und Finsternis* and *Die Erleuchteten* (1975). Frick's work in particular includes reference to numerous figures not mentioned elsewhere, and what his study necessarily lacks in depth, it certainly makes up for in breadth.

Finally, we may note three primary German figures of the twentieth-century's second half: Ernst Benz (1908–1978), Gerhard Wehr, and Peter Koslowski. Ernst Benz is author of a vast number of articles and books, many of which focus on specifically theosophic subjects or authors. Gerhard Wehr has edited and republished popular editions of Böhme's works and has also written books on Christian mysticism, including *Esoterisches Christentum* (1975/1995). But Peter Koslowski, in books like *Die Prüfungen der Neuzeit* (1989), has incorporated the theosophic current—particularly the works of Molitor and Baader—into a contemporary philosophical synthesis of great significance for us because it reveals how theosophy speaks to philosophical and spiritual issues of the present day and is not simply a subject for retrospective perusal. Koslowski speculates that Christian gnosis can point the way for a true postmodern cultural renaissance. Thus, although somewhat muted in Germany in the aftermath of the Second World War, theosophy continues nonetheless and will undoubtedly emerge again in new forms when the time is ripe.

ENGLISH THEOSOPHY

Although Böhme marks the beginning of modern theosophy, he was not the only theosopher at the beginning of the seventeenth century. Böhme was part of a larger circle of theosophers in the vicinity of Görlitz, but there was a broader movement of which his work is a striking instance. Exemplary of this is a manuscript entitled *Aurora Sapientia,* or *The Daiebreak of Wisdome,* dated 1629, that is by one hand attributed to Dr. John Dee, and by another to one Robert Ayshford, but is signed "P knowen in the Grace of God." This manuscript includes a number of letters revealing a theosophic circle existing in England much earlier than previously thought, one without direct allusions to Böhme, but nonetheless showing very similar references to the "three principles" and to "theosophie" "to the service of the sixt Church att Philadelphia."[23]

As its title suggests, *Aurora Sapientiae* is concerned with the revelation of Wisdom, and its author exhorts us to read the cosmos, or physisophia, Scripture, and Man, in whom is hidden theosophia. He writes that through the "third Book," Man, "wee maie learne to understand the theosophia, the secret and hidden wisdome of the Mysterie of God the Father, and of Christ, and of his Church . . . withall the onlie whole and great Librarie of us all wherewith wee who are the Scholars of the true Wisdome ought to be contented."[24] There is here no direct reference to Böhme, but its "three principles," its preoccupation with wisdom, and its emphasis upon reading the book of nature, certainly place it as a predecessor to the Böhmean theosophic tradition.

The work's reference to the "sixt church att Philadelphia" is especially striking because less than half a century later there was another group of English theosophers that had gathered around Dr. John Pordage (1608–1681), later to be led by Jane Leade (1623–1704) under the name "the Philadelphians." Whether there is any historical continuity between these groups remains unclear, but certainly there is a parallelism in language and ways of thinking, similar to what Ioan Coulianu wrote about more broadly in *The Tree of Gnosis* (1990).[25] Bluntly put, theosophic groups tend to think along similar lines, often quite independently of one another. *Aurora Sapientiae* represents a hitherto unremarked early instance of English theosophy.

Böhme became reasonably well known in England by the middle of the seventeenth century primarily through the efforts of men like John Sparrow, Humphrey Blunden, John Ellistone, and Charles and Durant Hotham. But it was in John Pordage, a minister until he was forcibly removed from his post due to charges of heresy, that Böhme found his greatest English expositor and fellow visionary. Written in English, the manuscripts lost, Pordage's vast works like *Göttliche und Wahre Metaphysica* (3 vols., 1715), are now found only in German translation. They detail his visionary experiences, his cosmology, and his process of spiritual alchemy.

In his work entitled *Sophia* (ca. 1675) (in a passage later excerpted by the great French theosopher Saint-Martin), Pordage explains how it is that one breaks through into spiritual illumination. The soul continually seeks to rise upward and break through the wall separating it from the heavenly principle, he asserts. But eventually it realizes that it cannot so ascend, and

> because it thereupon finds that through ascending out it had been constantly misled and had missed its goal, that it is not on the right path ([even] if it were privy to revelations and glimpses of the heavenly countenance). It realizes that the Wisdom of God . . . can be attained [only] through descending and sinking into one's own inward ground, and no longer seeking to rise out of oneself.
>
> Whereupon it now thus sinks into itself and before it the gate of Wisdom's depths is opened directly and in the blink of an eye, and it is led into the holy eternal principium of the lightworld in the wine-cellar of the New Lebanon, in the new magical Earth wherein the Virgin Sophia or the Virgin of God's Wisdom appears and announces her message.[26]

This "new magical earth" bears a striking resemblance to what Henry Corbin wrote of Islamic visionary Sufism in his book *Spiritual Body and Celestial Earth*. Indeed Corbin was himself influenced in his interpretations of Islamic theosophy by his familiarity with Christian theosophy.[27]

Surrounding Pordage were a number of significant figures, including Thomas Bromley (1629–1691), whose *The Way to the Sabbath of Rest* (1650/1692/1710) represents an enduring classic elaboration of the stages in the spiritual transmutation of an individual in a theosophic community.[28] Much of this work is published in an appendix to my book *Theosophia: Hidden Dimensions of Christianity* (1994), as in an anthology of theosophic writings entitled *Wisdom's Book*. Bromley wrote about the process of spiritual transmutation that he himself, and the little circle around him and Pordage, had experienced:

> And they that are in this near Union, feel a mutual Indwelling in the pure Tincture and Life of each other: And so, the further we come out of the animal Nature, the more universal we are, and nearer both to Heaven, and to one another in the Internal; and the further instrumentally to convey the pure Streams of the heavenly Life to each other, which no external Distance can hinder: For the Divine Tincture (being such a spiritual Virtue, as Christ imprinted into the Heart of the Disciples with whom he talked after his Resurrection, making their Hearts to burn within them) is able to pierce through all Distance, and reach those that are far absent; because it is not corporeal, nor subject to the Laws of Place or Time.[29]

Bromley here discusses a kind of spiritual communion characteristic of theosophic communities, focused as they are on contemplative practice.

The theosophers, unusual for their time, were as willing to be led by a woman as by a man, and so Pordage was succeeded as leader by Jane Leade, whose visions were recorded in numerous books published around the turn of the eighteenth century, with titles including *The Revelation of Revelations* (1683), *The Laws of Paradise* (1695), and *A Fountain of Gardens* (3 vols.) (1696–1700). Leade's visionary revelations and her insistence on the doctrine of universal restoration (apocatastasis) were opposed by some other theosophers, including her contemporary Johann Georg Gichtel. Also in Leade's circle were Anne Bathurst; the brilliant scholar of Hebrew, Francis Lee (1660/1–1719); Richard Roach (1662–1730), active in establishing the Philadelphians; and Dionysius Andreas Freher (1649–1728), known for his commissioning of various esoteric theosophic illustrations and for his commentaries on Böhmean doctrines, nearly all of which remain unpublished.[30]

Initially, under Pordage, this English theosophic circle was quite reclusive and intent on contemplation, but Jane Leade and her companions established a slightly more formal association under the name "The Philadelphian Society," including a loose charter and organizational structure. The Philadelphians published a journal called *Theosophic Transactions* and even attempted a kind of evangelism, including an unsuccessful attempt to establish their association on the continent in Germany.[31] Often seen as associated with French millennialism, then current in England, the Philadelphians were poorly received in England, at some points even being physically and verbally attacked by small mobs. Of course, many continental theosophers saw such efforts at theosophic evangelism as less than wise; Gichtel, for example, vociferously opposed establishing what would amount to just another sect.

No discussion of English theosophy is complete without mention of William Law (1686–1761), the well-known Anglican author whose deep indebtedness to Freher and Böhme is not always mentioned, not least because Law himself rarely called attention to their influence on his writing. His most well-known work is *A Serious Call* (1729); and his *The Spirit of Love* (1752/4) is certainly influenced by theosophy.[32] Law was born in King's Cliffe, Northamptonshire, and was educated at Emmanuel College, Cambridge, of which he became a fellow in 1711. Law's life is in some respects interestingly parallel to that of Dr. John Pordage. Like Pordage in the previous century, Law refused to swear allegiance to King George I in 1714. A Nonjuror, Law was forced to resign his college position and kept from other public positions as well. Law then lived in Putney, near London, at the home of Edward Gibbon from 1727 to 1737, where he tutored the historian Gibbon's father. In about 1740, Law moved back to King's Cliffe, where he lived a celibate and quiet life shared with Hester Gibbon, the historian's aunt, and Mrs. Hutcheson, a rich, pious widow. Law's later years were spent studying Böhme and writing in relative seclusion until his death in 1761.

In the latter years of his life, Law attracted a sort of Protestant monastic community of lay people that, situated at King's Cliffe, was renowned for its generous charity. Law and an anonymous patron established a poorhouse for young girls, teaching them to read, knit, sew, study the Bible, and attend church. He was also responsible for establishing an almshouse that fed and clothed the poor. Indeed, Law and Mrs. Hutcheson gave away to the poor all but a tenth of their income. Law awoke every day at 5 A.M., and spending much of his day reading in his large library of mystical authors, writing, and praying.

Law was succeeded, in some respects, by James Pierrepont Greaves (1777–1842), who had been a London merchant but accepted bankruptcy before he was thirty and lived thereafter on a small stipend. He traveled to visit the renowned educational pioneer J. H. Pestalozzi in Switzerland, where he lived for eight years, after which he returned to England and became active in educational reform there, as well as in large-scale charity efforts, and in theosophic practice. His posthumously published books, taken from his voluminous diaries and papers, include *Letters and Extracts from the Manuscript Writings of James Pierrepont Greaves* (1845) and *The New Nature in the Soul* (1847). Greaves, as I point out in *The Hermetic Book of Nature*, was especially influential for the American Transcendentalists Ralph Waldo Emerson and Bronson Alcott, particularly the latter. It is no coincidence that one of Greaves's English educational experiments was called the "Alcott House."

After Law and Greaves, English theosophy in the nineteenth century owes something to the person of Christopher Walton (1809–1877), who came from a Methodist family background, and who, having happened across John Wesley's anthology from William Law's writings, came eventually to the works of Böhme, and then Freher and all the other theosophers. By trade a goldsmith and jeweler, Walton devoted his money and efforts to the furtherance of theosophy, bringing out a book entitled *Notes and Materials for an Adequate Biography of the Celebrated Divine and Theosopher William Law* (1854/1856). A strange, voluminous work composed in tiny type and highly disorganized, *Notes and Materials* is nonetheless chock-full of source materials from Freher and elsewhere and includes some original contributions to theosophy by Walton himself, tinged to some degree by his interest in "animal magnetism" and similar phenomena.[33]

Mid-nineteenth century England also was home to a group of loosely connected theosophers that included Thomas South (ca. 1785–ca. 1855), his

daughter Mary Ann South (later Mary Ann Atwood, 1817–1910), Isabel de
Steiger (1836–1927), and Edward Burton Penny (1804–1872) and his wife
Anne Judith Penny (1825–1893). In some respects, one could refer to this
time as a kind of English Renaissance in theosophy, for all of these people
knew or had corresponded with one another; some had met at Greaves's theosophic group in Kent, others through corresponding via letters; and all of
them published books. Important among these are Mary Ann South's *A Sug-
gestive Inquiry into the Hermetic Mystery* (1850/1918); Ann Judith Penny's
Studies in Jacob Boehme (London: Watkins, 1912); and Edward Burton
Penny's translations of Saint-Martin's *Theosophic Correspondence* (1863)
and *The Spiritual Ministry of Man* (1864). Although some members of this
circle, notably Mary Ann South and her friend Isabel de Steiger, lived into the
twentieth century and during the founding of Blavatsky's Theosophical Society, like Charles Massey (1838–1905; author of *Thoughts of a Modern Mystic* [1904]) their primary interest remained Christian theosophy in the tradition of Böhme. Another figure who represented a fin-de-siècle Christian
esotericism was Anna Kingsford (1846–1888), founder of the Hermetic Society and author of *The Perfect Way* (1881).

   The twentieth century also saw some representatives of theosophy in England, as well as some Böhmenist influence in widely known figures like Evelyn Underhill (1875–1941), whose classic works include the massive study
Mysticism (1911) and the aptly named *Practical Mysticism* (1915). Underhill
was not a theosopher in the strict sense (that is, in the tradition of Böhme,
Saint-Martin, Baader, and the others) but she drew extensively on the works
of Böhme and cited Jane Leade, William Law, and other theosophers at some
length as well. Lesser known but also significant was G. W. Allen, vicar of
Bretby near Burton on Trent and editor of a theosophic journal entitled *The
Seeker*. Another figure who brought Böhme into the public eye in England
during the twentieth century is Robin Waterfield, whose selections from
Böhme's works are prefaced by his own sketch of theosophical history and
significance.[34] Finally, one must mention the remarkable Scottish independent researcher Adam McLean, who republished some important theosophic
works, including Jane Leade's *Revelation of Revelations*, and although without formal academic training or position is himself a repository of biblio-
graphic knowledge.

FRENCH THEOSOPHY

Theosophy is a movement whose main stream unquestionably flows through
the German tradition, but its literature has been written in numerous lan-

guages, including French—and any account of primary literature must consider the remarkable French author Louis-Claude de Saint-Martin (1743–1803) whose spiritual life was early on influenced by the occult school of Martinez de Pasqually (1710–1774) but who attributed his spiritual rebirth and his profound later writings to his contact with the works of Jacob Böhme. Late in life, he learned German and translated Böhme into French. Saint-Martin, who wrote as "le philosoph inconnu," sought to combat modern rationalist and materialist reductionism with his many books, including *Des Erreurs et de la Verité* (1775), *Tableau Naturel* (1782), *De l'esprit des Choses* (1800), and *Le Ministère de l'Homme-Esprit* (1802), the last two of which translated theosophic thought into terms accessible to his contemporaries. Among the most delightful of Saint-Martin's works is his correspondence with the Swiss Baron Kirchberger during the French Revolution, testimony to the spiritual balance theosophy provided them during the most turbulent of eras. Saint-Martin did not come to the works of Böhme until relatively late in life; his early works were written from the perspective of his theurgic school, founded by Martinez-Pasquales, a sect that employed theurgic rituals and "operations." This school, called Martinists, or later, Elects Cohens, fought vigorously the growing atheism of contemporary France, and in this battle Saint-Martin played a major role.

Saint-Martin's public role began with his books *Des Erreurs et de la Vérité, ou les Hommes rappelés au Principe universel de la Science* (1775), and *Tableau Naturel des Rapports entre Dieu, l'Homme, et l'Univers* (1782). In these works Saint-Martin explained the traditional doctrine of correspondences between man and nature, and the idea of man as a microcosm. He sought to oppose the reductionist atheist assertion—which incidentally has by no means disappeared since—that religion originated in mere delusion inspired by a fear of nature's powers. His works alluded to the scriptures but were couched in a parabolic Hermetic language that, because it referred to God, for instance, as the active intelligent cause, was designed to lead a materialistic, atheistic, or scientistic readership back toward authentic religion.

It was not until the mid-1780s that Saint-Martin was introduced to Böhme's works, but he immediately recognized in the theosopher "the greatest human light that had ever appeared," and the revelation in toto of what he had glimpsed in his earlier theurgic school. From this time on, St. Martin's works and life were increasingly informed by Böhmean theosophy, seen especially in such books as *De l'Esprit des Choses, ou Coup-d'œil philosophique sur la Nature des tres, et sur l'Objet de leur Existence* (1800), and *Le Ministère de l'Homme-esprit* (1802). In the latter book especially, one sees Saint-Martin emphasizing the necessity for human regeneration in the Logos, which is the Gospel way and the simple key to wisdom—something not seen in the spiritism of the day nor in authors like Swedenborg. In his later years, Saint-Martin learned German and translated several works of Böhme into French, and there is in this a special symbolism.

For Saint-Martin's later works are also, in a different way, an effort to translate Böhme into modern terms. Here is a characteristic passage from *Le Ministère de l'Homme-esprit [The Ministry of Spiritual Man]* (1802):

> The original generation or formation of the planets and all stars was, according to our author [Böhme], in accord with the way that the wondrous harmonic proportions of Divine Wisdom have been engendered from all eternity.
>
> For when the great change took place in one of the regions of primitive nature, the light went out in that region, which embraced the space of the present nature, and this region, which is the present nature, became as a dead body, unmoving.
>
> Then Eternal Wisdom, which the author sometimes calls SOPHIA, Light, Meekness, Joy, and Delight, caused a new order to be born in the center, in the heart of this universe or world, to prevent and arrest its entire destruction.
>
> This place, or center, according to our author [Böhme], is the place where the sun is kindled. Out of this place or center all kinds of qualities, forms, or powers, which fill and constitute the universe, are engendered and produced, all in conformity with the laws of divine generation; for he admits in all beings and eternally in the Supreme Wisdom, a center in which a sevenfold production or subdivision takes place. He calls this center the Separator.[35]

If we were to characterize the overarching significance of Saint-Martin's work, beyond what we have here suggested, it would be to say that in him one sees how an extraordinarily chaotic social milieu like the French Revolution need not be a barrier to the theosophic path. For instance, Saint-Martin writes to his friend Baron Kirchberger that "I am freezing here for want of firewood," warns his friend that he must be careful what he puts into letters, and still finds room to discuss his own translation of Böhme's *Drei Principien* as well as his own marriage to Sophia.[36] When one recalls that Saint-Martin's father died during this time, and he himself was in some danger during the political upheavals of the time, the serenity of his correspondence on such matters as the works of Böhme, Gichtel, Pordage, Leade, and the other theosophers becomes all the more striking.

After Saint-Martin, there are some other French authors influenced by theosophy during the nineteenth and twentieth centuries, including Madame de Staël, who discusses theosophy in a chapter of *De l'Allemagne* (1820) entitled "Des Philosophes religieux appelés Théosophes," as well as Joseph de Maistre, who alludes to theosophy in his famous *Les Soirées de Saint-Pétersbourg*.[37] But none of these have the breadth or depth of influence that Saint-Martin had, nor his originality and genius for clear expression. Indeed, many represented more the influence of Emanuel Swedenborg (1688–1772), the Swedish scientist turned visionary, than the current of theosophy. This is the case with such authors as J. F. E. Le Boys des Guays (1794–1864). Saint-Martin did have an arithmosophic mysticism that is also represented in figures like Höné Wronski in his *La Clef de l'infini* (1814). But Saint-Martin's work included and transcended the themes of these more cosmologically inclined authors.

If the central current of theosophy unmistakably runs through Germany from Böhme through Baader and right into the twentieth century with a figure like Ziegler, twentieth-century scholarship on esotericism generally, and theosophy in particular, belonged very much to France. In scholarship on Jacob Böhme, there are two major French figures: Alexander Koyré, *La philosophie de Jacob Boehme* (1929/1971) and Pierre Deghaye, *La Naissance de Dieu ou La doctrine de Jacob Boehme* (1985). Koyré's study is widely regarded as one of the best twentieth-century works on this seminal figure; in the latter half of the twentieth century, Deghaye, whose style of writing is strikingly direct, is undoubtedly among the most important interpreters of Böhme's works. There have also been some important shorter studies, notably Antoine Faivre's "Boehme en Allemagne" and other articles in two collections.[38]

There are a number of books in French on later theosophers than Böhme, including in particular Bernard Gorceix's *Johann Georg Gichtel: Théosophe d'Amsterdam* (1975), an extensive study of this important theosophic figure. Another important book, this one chiefly on the English theosophers Pordage, Leade, and the others, is Serge Hutin's *Les Disciples anglais de Jacob Boehme* (1960). It is indicative of the state of scholarship on theosophy in the English-speaking world that until recently, the only available discussion of the English theosophers was in French!

Without doubt the most important scholar of esotericism, who held the first chair at the Sorbonne dedicated to this transdisciplinary field, is Antoine Faivre. Faivre's books and articles are far too numerous to list here, but those searching for works in English ought to look first to two primary studies, one, *Access to Western Esotericism* (1994), a masterly encyclopedic survey of esotericism that includes a very important introduction to and study of Franz von Baader. Also important is the edited volume *Modern Esoteric Spirituality* (1992), which includes articles by Deghaye, Edighoffer, and others that cover theosophic topics.

We should also mention here the work of the specialist in Islamic esotericism, Henry Corbin. Corbin's focus, as is well known, was Sufism and Ismaili gnosis, but he interpreted these with an eye to the European theosophic tradition, specifically referring to such figures as Œtinger and Baader. Indeed, Corbin was not only a scholar of Islamic esotericism but also a creative thinker in his own right, giving to us such concepts as the "imaginal," a realm intermediate between the material and the spiritual and to be distinguished from the imagination as fantasy. In creating such concepts, Corbin drew tacitly, and sometimes explicitly, on the Böhmean theosophic tradition.

RUSSIAN THEOSOPHY

Naturally, it is not possible here to discuss every Russian theosopher, but certainly we cannot consider the history of Christian theosophy without at least sketching the primary Russian figures, not least because they are so influential outside Russia. Chief among the Russian theosophers are four major ones, upon whom we focus: Vladimir Soloviev, Sergei Bulgakov, Pavel Florensky, and Nicolai Berdyaev. These four figures, almost contemporaneous, are united by their emphasis on and development of what is called "Sophiology," that is, by the centrality of Sophia or Wisdom to their thought.

The first of these, Vladimir Soloviev (1853–1900), whom J. D. Kornblatt terms "certainly one of the greatest Russian thinkers of all time," is at least partly within the theosophic tradition.[39] Soloviev was born into a large and prominent Moscow family; his father was a well-known scholar, and his family had strong ties to Orthodoxy. At the age of nine, during a liturgy, Soloviev had the first of three visions of Sophia that were to define the rest of his life. After graduating from Moscow University in 1873, Soloviev attended seminary for a year, after which he went to England to study theosophy. There, he became familiar with the works of such figures as Pordage, Leade, and Law, whose influence on his work is as yet not at all thoroughly explored. In the British Library, he had a second vision of Sophia, who instructed him to go to Egypt, where he had in the desert his third vision.

After his visionary quest, Soloviev returned to Moscow, where he delivered from 1877 to 1880 his *Lectures on Godmanhood*, and in 1880 he defended his doctoral dissertation. For a time, it appeared that Soloviev had a promising academic career, but eventually he was to be forced out of academe because of political indiscretions like urging clemency for the killers of Czar Alexander II. Thereafter, he spent his time writing, publishing, and lecturing, producing such books as *The Meaning of Love*, *Russia and the Universal Church*, and *The Justification of the Good*.[40] Much of Soloviev's writing has a somewhat abstract quality; the following is characteristic both of style and of ideas: "It is this abnormal attitude towards all around us, this exclusive self-assertion or egoism, all-powerful in practical life even if it is rejected in theory—this contra-position of self to all others and the practical negation of these others—it is this which constitutes the fundamental evil of our nature."[41]

Soloviev clearly drew on Böhmean theosophy—as when he wrote of the "three modes of existence," his abstract version of Böhme's "three principles"—but he also was an original thinker, as here, when he insists on the transcendence of selfhood as the definition of deification.[42]

After Soloviev, the leading Russian Sophiologist was Sergei Bulgakov (1871–1944), whose masterwork was *Unfading Light* (1917). Bulgakov's father, grandfather, great-grandfather, and so on for six generations, had been priests, but Bulgakov himself studied economy and law. In 1900, he published his first major book on capitalism and agriculture; shortly thereafter he and Nicolai Berdyaev, to whom we will turn momentarily, published together the journal *The New Way*, and then another, *Questions of Life*. This was a heady time in Russia, full of religious ferment and innovative thought, in which Bulgakov himself played a key role.

But in 1922 he was banished from the Soviet Union, and in 1925 he helped found the Paris Orthodox Theological Institute, where he served as chair of dogmatic theology. He died in 1944, a controversial figure in Orthodoxy even though he insisted that his Sophiology, influenced by Böhme and Baader, was certainly not heretical. And Bulgakov's work does demonstrate that a synthesis of Orthodoxy and theosophy is entirely possible through Wisdom. In his book *The Wisdom of God* (1937) Bulgakov held that "the future of living Christianity rests with the sophianic interpretation of the world and of its destiny. All the dogmatic and practical problems of modern Christian dogmatics and ascetics seem to form a kind of knot, the unraveling of which inevitably leads to sophiology."[43]

Another figure we can't ignore is Pavel Florensky (1882–1937), although the degree to which he was influenced by theosophy is by no means as clear as in the case of Soloviev or Bulgakov. Florensky was an enigmatic man, trained in the hard sciences and mathematics, inventor of a noncoagulating machine oil that he called Dekanite, yet also a man trained in the Moscow seminary, an art historian and a poet. It is as a theologian that Florensky became famous, chiefly for his masterwork, published in 1914 and entitled *The Pillar and Foundation of Truth*. Central to Florensky's thought are the concepts of antinomy and synthesis—that is, of duality resolved in a third. One may say that there is in Florensky's theology something mathematical, as in his technique there is something artistic and theological. It is a great pity, and yet another indictment of the totalitarian Soviet Union, that in 1937 he was murdered by the KGB after having been sent to a Gulag.

The most original and important of the Russian theosophers—also the one most explicitly a theosopher—was Nicolai Berdyaev (1874–1948). Berdyaev was born to a well-to-do Russian family, his mother a princess of French origin, his father an officer in the Russian army. Never at home in school, Berdyaev nonetheless was a precocious reader and lived an aristocratic life until he became something of a Marxist while living as a student in Kiev. In 1904, he moved to St. Petersburg, where he and Bulgakov published a journal entitled *The New Way*. During this time Berdyaev formed his thought and became involved in the lively religious ferment of the time, meeting all of the major Russian members of the "New Religious Consciousness" that had emerged in people like Dmitri Merezhkovsky and his wife, as well as many others. But in 1922, he and his wife, Lydia, moved to Berlin, and in 1924 they moved to Paris, where they were to remain thereafter in exile, and where Berdyaev was eventually to die.

As discussed in chapter 6, Berdyaev called himself a theosopher in the sense of Böhme and Baader and explicitly separated himself from the Theosophical Society, from Anthroposophy, and from similar movements. In his monumental dissertation entitled *Nicolas Berdyaev: Theologian of Prophetic Gnosticism* (1948), Charles Knapp defends Berdyaev against the "serious prejudice" aroused by the use of the term *theosophy,* pointing out that Berdyaev meant not the "modern eclectic system of thought . . . quite devoid of historic sense or real philosophic, theological, or scientific rigor," but "a mystical theology that has had its orthodox representatives in all ages of the church."[44]

But Berdyaev was not entirely Orthodox, as his friend Bulgakov was. Influenced by Orthodoxy, Berdyaev was more a theosopher who, like his fellow Russian theosophers, sought in theosophy a Christianity that speaks clearly to the modern world. The range of Berdyaev's work is remarkable, as can be seen in the collection *Christian Existentialism*, a pastiche of his writings on numerous subjects. His primary thesis, to which he returned time and again in his writings, is that the modern world (communist and capitalist alike) objectifies everything, quantifying and therefore separating us from all objects. The path of gnosis is the path of overcoming this disastrous and destructive dualism between subject and object that is at the root of evil.

Berdyaev's first book, written in a kind of visionary ecstasy, was *The Meaning of Creativity* (1914), in which he outlined most of his major themes, including the nature of human freedom, the power of creativity, and the significance of mysticism. A much more mature work is his *Freedom and the Spirit* (1935), in which he explicitly identifies himself as a theosopher, and in which the influence of Böhmean theosophy is quite evident. Berdyaev's life is recounted, along with many fascinating glimpses of well-known Russian and European figures, in his book *Dream and Reality* (1950), and perhaps the most mature statement of his philosophy is to be found in his very profound book *The Beginning and the End* (1941/1952).

Berdyaev's writings were unjustly ignored during the last half of the twentieth century, even though nearly all of his works had been translated into

English and published before 1960, and even though he is the most lucid, penetrating, indeed brilliant of all the Russian theosophers. Whereas Soloviev's work is often opaque and verbose, Berdyaev is a model of clarity, and although he is indebted to theosophy, he applies theosophy to the modern situation with great insight. It is typical, and outrageous, that a book entitled *Russian Religious Thought* could be published in 1996 and allude to Berdyaev with but a single sentence.[45] More just is the assessment of Knapp, who devotes more than five hundred pages to Berdyaev's work: "With a tremendous catholicity of mind, Berdyaev draws intellectual and spiritual power from a score of sources."[46]

Among those sources is certainly Jacob Böhme, from whom Berdyaev took his central concept of Ungrund.[47] It may well be that Berdyaev was the first to recognize how critically important Ungrund is to understanding not only Böhme, but the radical and long-standing errors of Western philosophy and cosmology from antiquity onward. Ungrund, for Berdyaev, means the divine centrum that precedes being, that indeed precedes even God, and is prior to all division or differentiation. Ungrund is the source of all existence, and the source also of our primordial human freedom, the essence of humanity and the means for our potential deification. Both ancient and modern philosophies committed the fundamental error of descending into objectification, for only Ungrund allows for a transcendence of this subject-object dualism.

In short, with Berdyaev we see a brilliant synthesis of theosophy with contemporary philosophy, combined by a penetrating mind. It may well be that Berdyaev's time is yet to come, for of all the theosophers we have discussed in this survey, Berdyaev is the one whose work is most applicable to the present era. And as theosophy is rediscovered by scholarship, and perhaps even renewed in yet another synthesis (as it takes on new forms to suit new conditions), one can have little doubt that this new synthesis will draw heavily on Berdyaev and his insistence on the primacy of freedom, creativity, and gnosis in human life. For we have not seen the last of Russian theosophy.

AMERICAN THEOSOPHY

The history of American theosophy begins, of course, with emigration from Europe to North America during the seventeenth century. The influence of Jacob Böhme has yet to be thoroughly charted, but his works, as well as those of some other theosophers, were carried over to the colonies very early on, chiefly by German Pietist settlers. The leader of the first Pennsylvanian group of theosophers was Johannes Kelpius, a remarkable, learned young man who led a group of German theosophers to England and then to Pennsylvania, where he headed the first theosophical community in the New World for four-teen years until his death in 1706. Often romanticized, and held by some to be a Rosicrucian, Kelpius was in fact a theosopher in the classical Böhmean tradition, whose life and primary works are well worth documenting here.

Kelpius was born in Denndorf, Germany, in 1670, and after studying at the Gymnasium, in 1687 went to the University at Tübingen, then to Leipzig, and finally to Altdorf, now the University at Helmstadt, studying theology. Since his father died when he was young, Kelpius was sent to the university by family friends. Important among others in his life were the renowned Professor Fabricius, Philipp Jakob Spener, and the Christian Kabbalist scholar Knorr von Rosenroth. Kelpius set sail for America with a group led by Johann Zimmermann (1634–1694), and when the latter died, Kelpius became head of the group, which then settled in Pennsylvania along the Wissahickon River.

The Kelpius settlement took no name, and its members said that they belonged to no denomination. But because their sermons or exhortations often referred to Revelation 12:1–6, they became known by other settlers, German or otherwise, as "the woman in the wilderness" community on the Wissahickon. A later manuscript of the Ephrata colony (which succeeded the Kelpius group) explained their unnamed way of life as follows:

> While giving up their souls to their Creator, and devoting their whole lives to a preparation of their hearts for the glorious inheritance prepared for the faithful, they mutually instructed each other, and cemented a bond of brotherly love and holy affection. They professed love and charity toward all denominations, but desired to live without name or sect. "The Contented of the God-loving Soul" was the only name they acknowledged.[48]

This account suggests not only how they lived but underscores their refusal to participate in sectarianism, a refusal characteristic of all theosophers.

Kelpius, who died young, did not publish a great deal, but his treatise on prayer is a model of economy and demonstrates quite clearly the profound parallels between his Protestant mysticism, the German Catholic mysticism that preceded the theosophers, and the Greek Orthodox mysticism that influenced them. For Kelpius affirms the different forms of prayer, and holds—like the mystics of other faiths—that

> Forasmuch as internal prayer is so weighty a point that one may call it the only means to attain perfection in this life and to kindle the pure and disinterested love in our hearts, and as all Christians . . . are called to this state of pure love and perfection, and will, by the power of this call, have the necessary grace offered to them to attain such a state: so this inward prayer suits all persons, even the most simple and ignorant, who are also capable of performing this order or manner of prayer.[49]

According to Kelpius, all Christians are called to the same inward form of prayer, the unceasing prayer of the heart.

The Wissahickon group was succeeded by another, this one at Ephrata, Pennsylvania, which was to have a long history. Central to the history of Ephrata was another German immigrant, Johann Conrad Beissel (1690–1768), who set sail for America in 1720 and was baptized in the Wissahickon River in 1724. Beissel gathered a small group around him and organized it into a semimonastic community on the Cocalico River. It was to become the most important of the American theosophic communities, famous for its music, reputed to be angelic-sounding, and for its ascetic ways of life and emphasis on prayer. Ephrata grew to be a very prosperous enclave and eventually came to have (despite Beissel's disapproval) quite a number of businesses, including a printing press and a lumber mill. The printing press, run by Christopher Sauer (sometimes spelled Sower) brought out works by Gottfried Arnold and Thomas Bromley, among other theosophers, and was one of the more important presses in early America.

We possess much more documentation of Beissel's thought and writing than we do of Kelpius's, which perhaps explains something of Kelpius's mystique. In 1743, the press of Christopher Sauer brought into print one of the first Bibles published in America. 1745 saw the publication of several books by Conrad Beissel, including *Mystische Abhandlung über die Schopfung und von des Menschen Fall und Wiederbringungen durch des Weibes Samen . . . [Mystical Treatise on the Creation, Fall, and Restoration of Man through the Woman's Seed]*, and *Die Hohe Zeugnüsse [The High Testimonies]*, and *Die Weiderstellung Der Reinen Paradisischen Menschheit, oder des Jungfräulichen Ebenbildes Gottes . . . in einer Sammlung geistliche und Theosophischer Episteln [The Restoration of the Pure Paradisical Humanity, or the Virginal Image of God . . . in a Collection of Spiritual and Theosophic Letters]*, which includes thirty-seven meditations and sixty-seven letters on theosophic topics.[50]

Ephrata was important in theosophic history because it represented a documented, long-lived theosophic community, and its significance has not yet been fully assessed.[51] But much of theosophic history in America remains underground and indeed may never be known more widely. Certainly it is the case that theosophy's influence among German Pietist immigrants to America was substantial and passed on from generation to generation. It is unclear to what degree this influence corresponds to the transmission of esoteric traditions more generally, but it is undoubtedly true that theosophy continued to be found on the periphery of American Anabaptist communities like the Amish right into the twentieth century.

Theosophy was also influential in American Transcendentalism, although this fact is rarely recognized. Indeed, one nearly could term Bronson Alcott

(1799–1888), author of *Tablets* (1868), *Concord Days* (1872), and *Table-talk* (1877), a theosopher. In *Concord Days*, Alcott includes a letter from the British theosopher Christopher Walton praising Böhme to the skies, and Alcott himself writes that

> Mysticism is the sacred spark that has lighted the piety and illuminated the philosophy of all places and times. It has kindled especially and kept alive the profoundest thinking of Germany and of the continent since Boehme's first work, "The Aurora," appeared. Some of the deepest thinkers since then have openly acknowledged their debt to Boehme, or secretly borrowed without acknowledging their best illustrations from his writings . . . he has exercised a deeper influence on the progress of thought than anyone since Plotinus.[52]

Alcott in turn influenced Ralph Waldo Emerson, whose essays—particularly the 1836 "Nature"—include some indebtedness to Böhme. All of these connections I detail elsewhere; suffice it here to say that theosophy certainly was one of the currents that fed into American Transcendentalism.[53]

Indeed, theosophy always has sprung up unexpectedly and almost irrespective of circumstance, in Europe, England, America, Eastern Europe, and elsewhere. One can distinguish, however, between more popular forms of theosophy and more speculative forms. Exemplary of popular theosophy is a Southern American evangelist of the late twentieth century named Larry Hodges, a former welder who felt called to distribute (and preach based on) the writings of English theosopher Jane Leade. Hodges, who republished some of Leade's treatises, holds that her theosophic visions and prophecies refer not to Leade's own time, but to the late twentieth century. And Hodges is not alone; Böhme's influence in American Christianity continues, among others through the works of Norman Grubb.

There are a number of twentieth-century American contributions to speculative theosophy or theosophic studies, beginning in the 1950s, when an American at Columbia University named Charles A. Muses published a perceptive book on Jane Leade's contemporary and spiritual son, Dionysius Andreas Freher, entitled *Illumination on Jacob Boehme* (1951), as well as a journal devoted to the works of Böhme. And in 1999, Arthur Versluis published *Wisdom's Children: A Christian Esoteric Tradition*, a general introduction to the theosophic tradition. In fact, late twentieth-century America saw something of a renaissance in Sophianic studies, not only with the advent of feminist interest in Sophia, but also in books by Barbara Newman and Robert Sardello, in lectures and publications by Christopher Bamford, founder of Lindisfarne Press, and in an anthology compiled and introduced by Robert Faas, a clinical psychologist, as well as in the publication of numerous important source materials in this theosophic current.[54]

Given the burgeoning interest in Sophianic spirituality and in theosophy particularly, not only in scholarly but also in popular circles, we can well expect that the Christian theosophic current will continue to emerge, oftentimes in the most surprising places. To return to the remarks of Nicolai Berdyaev with which we began—those remarks so sternly separating the Christian theosophic current from that of the Theosophical Society—we can see that indeed there is at least some truth in his assessment. Although there were some occasional links between the Theosophical Society and writers like Hartmann, such connections are circumstantial and, one may even say, accidental. For the Christian theosophic current clearly is visible as a particular lineage and, having traced its emergences thus far, we can be certain that we have not seen the last of it.

NOTES

1. See Böhme, *Sämtliche Schriften*, 8 vols., Will-Erich Peuckert, August Faust, eds. (Stuttgart: Fromann, 1955–1961); see also in English, for example, Jacob Böhme, *Aurora* (London: John M. Watkins, 1910), *Dialogues on the Supersensual Life*, W. Law, ed. (New York: Ungar, 1957), *Six Theosophic Points* (Ann Arbor: University of Michigan Press, 1958), and *The Way to Christ*, P. Erb, trans. (New York: Paulist Press, 1978).

2. See, for instance, Basarab Nicolescu, *Science, Meaning, and Evolution, the Cosmology of Jacob Böhme* (New York: Parabola, 1992); and Peter Koslowski, *Die Prüfungen der Neuzeit: Über Postmodernität, Philosophie der Geschichte, Metaphysik, Gnosis* (Wien: Passagen, 1989); see also Versluis, *The Hermetic Book of Nature*, in which I discuss in detail Böhme's influence on Emerson, Alcott, and American Transcendentalism in general. See also Versluis, "Bronson Alcott and Jacob Böhme," *Studies in the American Renaissance* 16 (1993), Joel Myerson, ed., 153–59.

3. See Werner Buddecke, ed., Jakob Böhme: *Die Ur-Schriften* (Stuttgart: Frommann, 1963).

4. On Böhme see Pierre Deghaye, *La Naissance de Dieu* (Paris: Albin Michel, 1985); Alexander Koyré, *La Philosophie de Jacob Boehme* (Paris: Vrin, 1979); Andrew Weeks, *Boehme: An Intellectual Biography of the Seventeenth-Century Philosopher and Mystic* (Albany: SUNY Press, 1991); on Böhme's predecessors see Alexandre Koyré, *Mystiques, spirituels, alchimistes du xvi siècle allemand* (Paris: Gallimard, 1971).

5. Böhme, *Aurora*, xx.57; see also xx.50, and for the subsequent discussion of the three realms, xx.57–72.

6. Böhme, *Aurora*, xx.72.

7. Böhme, *Signatura Rerum*, xii.10.

8. Böhme, *Signatura Rerum*, xii.25.

9. See Johann Georg Gichtel, *Eine kurze Eröffnung und Anweisung der dryen Principien und Welten in Menschen [A Brief Opening and Demonstration of the Three Principles and Worlds in Man]* (Berlin/Leipzig: Christian Ulrich Ringmacher, 1779).

10. Gichtel, *Eine kurze Eröffnung*, preface, I.3, 4.

11. Gichtel, *Eine kurze Eröffnung*, III. 47, 48.

12. See Arnold, *Sämmtliche geistliche Lieder*, C. Ehmann, ed. (1856).

13. See Œtinger, *Die Lehrtafel der Prinzessin Antonia, Sämmtliche theosophische Schriften* (Stuttgart: Steinkopf, 1858), 2nd ed., I.86.

14. See *Die Philosophie, Theologie und Gnosis Franz von Baaders: Spekulatives Denken zwischen Aufklärung, Restauration und Romantik*, Peter Koslowski, ed. (Wien: Passagen, 1993), esp. Antoine Faivre, "Franz von Baader und die okzidentale Esoterik," 221–42.

15. See Franz von Baader, *Sätze aus der erotischen Philosophie* (Frankfurt: Insel, 1966), introduction.

16. See Antoine Faivre, *Access to Western Esotericism*, part of which is devoted exclusively to an examination of Baader's extraordinary writings. See also Faivre, *Theosophy, Imagination, Tradition* (Albany: SUNY Press, 2000), 99–161.

17. For Weinfurter's references to the Theosophical Society or its members, *see Man's Highest Purpose: The Lost Word Regained* (London: Rider, n.d.), 34, 43, 48.

18. Weinfurter quotes liberally from Kerning's books in his *Man's Highest Purpose*. Franz Hartmann also presented Kerning's works in *his Lichtstrahlen vom Orient* (Leipzig: n.d., reprint; Stuttgart: Manes, 1984); see Gottfried Buchner, *J. B. Kerning: Leben und Schriften* (Württemburg: Renatus, 1927). A variety of Kerning's works were republished in the 1990s, including *Das Buchstabenbuch: die Wiedergeburt* (Bad Münstereifel: Edition Magnus, 1994).

19. See Karl Frick, *Licht und Finsternis* (Graz: Akademische, 1978), II.305 ff.

20. Franz Hartmann, *The Life and Doctrine of Paracelsus* (New York: U.S. Book, 1891), 54.

21. Franz Hartmann, *Personal Christianity: The Doctrines of Jacob Boehme* (New York: Unger, 1957), 44.

22. A sample of Ziegler's writing from this volume can be found in Arthur Versluis, ed., *Wisdom's Book: The Sophia Anthology* (St. Paul, MN: Paragon House, 2000).

23. Robert Ayshford, *Aurora Sapientia, that is to saie, The Daiebreak of Wisdome of the three Principles and beginning of all in the mysterie of wisdome in which the ground and key of all wisdome is laid open, directing to the true understanding of God, of Man, and of the whole world, in a new and true triune wisdome Physisophie, Theologie, and Theosophie. tending to the Honour of God, Revelation of the true wisdome and to the service of the Sixt Church att Philadelphia By Her Minister called by the Grace of God to beare witness of God and of Jesus Christ*, 1629.

24. Ayshford, *Aurora Sapientia*, chap. 1, "Of the threefold Book of Wisdome."

25. See Ioan P. Coulianu, *The Tree of Gnosis: Gnostic Mythology from Early Christianity to Modern Nihilism* (San Francisco: Harper, 1992), originally *Les Gnoses dualistes d'Occident* (Paris: Plon, 1990).

26. See John Pordage, *Sophia: The Graceful Eternal Virgin of Holy Wisdom, or Wonderful Spiritual Discoveries and Revelations That the Precious Wisdom Has Given to a Holy Soul* (London: n.p., ca. 1675), in Versluis, *Wisdom's Book*, chap. 5.

These paragraphs by Pordage also appear in the *Theosophic Correspondence of Louis Claude de Saint-Martin* (Exeter, UK: William Roberts, 1863), 92–93.

27. See Henry Corbin, *Spiritual Body and Celestial Earth, From Mazdaean Iran to Shi'ite Islam* (Princeton, NJ: Princeton University Press, 1977).

28. See also *A catalogue of Mr. T. Bromley's Library* (London: n.p., 1691). *Bromley's The Way to the Sabbath of Rest* was a popular work in England and in America and was even translated into Swedish and smuggled into Sweden during the eighteenth century. It is worth noting that there was a close connection between theosophy and alchemy, as evidenced for instance in Edmund Brice's translation of Ali Puli, *Centrum Naturae Concentratum* (London: J. Harris, 1696).

29. See Versluis, *Theosophia: Hidden Dimensions of Christianity* (Hudson, UK: Lindisfarne, 1994), 199.

30. See C. A. Muses, *Illumination on Jacob Böhme: The Work of Dionysius Andreas Freher* (New York: King's Crown, 1951).

31. For an account of the Philadelphians' abortive missionary effort in Germany, see Nils Thune, *The Behmenists and the Philadelphians: A Contribution to the Study of English Mysticism in the 17th and 18th Centuries* (Uppsala: Almquist and Wiksells, 1948), 114–35.

32. Much of the Rosicrucian movement also found inspiration in theosophy, and the deep affinities between Rosicrucian works—particularly the tables of correspondences and illustrations—and theosophic works remains an area ripe for further exploration. See Christopher McIntosh, *The Rose Cross and the Age of Reason* (Leiden: Brill, 1992).

33. See, on Walton, Joscelyn Godwin, *The Theosophical Enlightenment* (Albany: SUNY Press, 1995), 235–41.

34. See Robin Waterfield, *Jacob Boehme: Essential Readings* (Wellingborough: Aquarian, 1989).

35. From Versluis, *Wisdom's Book.*

36. Letter dated 4 Jan. 1795, in *Theosophic Correspondence* (Exeter, UK: William Roberts, 1863), 153.

37. See Antoine Faivre, "Le Courant Théosophique (Fin XVI–XX Siècles): Essai de Périodisation" in *Politica Hermetica* 7 (1993): 6–41, esp. 38–39.

38. See *Jacob Boehme ou l'obscure lumière de la connaissance mystique* (Paris: Vrin, 1979), esp. 135–54. See also Gerhard Wehr and Pierre Deghaye, *Jacob Böhme* (Paris: Albin Michel, 1977).

39. See J. D. Kornblatt and R. Gustafson, eds., *Russian Religious Thought* (Madison: University of Wisconsin Press, 1996), 27.

40. Nearly all of Soloviev's works have been translated into English: see *The Antichrist*, W. Barnes and H. Hayes, trans. (Edinburgh: Floris, 1982), *The Crisis of Western Philosophy*, B. Jakim, trans. (Hudson: Lindisfarne, 1996), *The Meaning of Love*, J. Marshall, trans. (Stockbridge: Lindisfarne, 1985), *Russia and the Universal Church*, H. Rees., trans. (London: Bles, 1948), *The Justification of the Good*, N. Duddington, trans. (London: Constable, 1918), *War, Progress, and the End of History*, A. Bakshy, trans. (Hudson: Lindisfarne, 1990).

41. V. Soloviev and P. Zouboff, trs., *Lectures on Godmanhood* (London: Dobson, 1948), 166.

42. V. Soloviev and P. Zouboff, trs., *Lectures on Godmanhood,* Lecture Six. "Deification" is an Orthodox concept succinctly expressed in the saying that God became man so that man could become God.

43. Sergei Bulgakov, *Sophia: The Wisdom of God* (Hudson: Lindisfarne, 1993), 21.

44. Charles C. Knapp, "Nicolas Berdyaev: Theologian of Prophetic Gnosticism" (Ph.D. diss., Toronto, 1948), 40.

45. Knapp, "Nicolas Berdyaev," 40.

46. Knapp, "Nicholas Berdyaev," 7.

47. On this topic, see Knapp, "Nicolas Berdyaev," 275 ff. See Berdyaev's introduction to Jacob Boehme's *Six Theosophic Points* (Ann Arbor: University of Michigan Press, 1958). See also Nicholas Berdyaev, *The Destiny of Man* (New York: Scribners, 1935), 25 ff.; *Freedom and the Spirit* (New York: Scribners, 1935), 194 ff.

48. Julius Sachse, *The German Pietists of Provincial Pennsylvania* (Philadelphia: Sachse, 1895, I. 80–81.

49. See Johannes Kelpius, *A Short, Easy, and Comprehensive Method of Prayer*, Christopher Witt, trs. (Philadelphia: Christopher Sower, 1761), 1.

50. Sachse, III.176 ff., 238 ff.

51. See Peter Erb, *The Pietists* (New York: Paulist Press, 1983); see also Peter Erb, *Johann Conrad Beissel and the Ephrata Community* (Lewiston, NY: Edwin Mellen, 1985).

52. Alcott, *Table-talk* (Philadelphia: Saifer, 1971, rpt. of 1877 edition), 132.

53. See Versluis, *The Esoteric Origins of the American Renaissance*, see also Kirby Don Richards, *A Method of Prayer: A Mystical Pamphlet from Colonial America* (Philadelphia: Wordsmiths, 2006).

54. See Robert Sardello, *Love and the Soul* (San Francisco: Harper, 1995), in which Sardello writes at length on Sophia; Robert Faas, *The Divine Couple: Writings on the Christian Mysteries of Eros* (St. Paul, MN: Grailstone, 2001), a collection of works from the Sophianic tradition. This and other books in the theosophic tradition can be found at www.grailbooks.org. Robert Powell, an anthroposophist in the line of Steiner, is author of the pamphlet "The Most Holy Trinosophia" (Great Barrington: Goldenstone, 1990), and apparently is bent on generating a "new cult of the virgin" (48). A collection of theosophic writings on Sophia is to be found in Versluis, *Wisdom's Book*. See also Pavel Florensky, *The Pillar and Foundation of Truth* (Princeton, NJ: Princeton University Press, 1997); Sergei Bulgakov, *Sophia: The Wisdom of God* (Hudson: Lindisfarne, 1993). For a history of the topic that excludes the theosophic current, see Caitlín Matthews, *Sophia: Goddess of Wisdom* (London: Aquarian, 1992). And finally, see Versluis, *Theosophia* and *Wisdom's Children*.

Chapter Eight

Western Esotericism Today

MAJOR WESTERN MAGICAL FIGURES AND CURRENTS

Through the late medieval and renaissance periods into early modernity, Western magical traditions were for the most part closely aligned with and perhaps even inseparable from the monotheistic religious traditions of Judaism and Christianity. We have already seen how practical Kabbalah played an important role in Jewish communities—even in some Christian circles— and when we turn to a close inspection of the kinds of Christian magic that emerged in the late medieval period, we can see that for the most part these are deeply indebted to their Jewish origins. Works like the *Spiritus Familiarus* of Daniel Caesaris (1730), *Der goldene Habermann* (Kapuzinerkloster Füßen, 1505/Sachsen-Weimar, 1601), the *Trinum Perfectum Magiae Albae et Nigrae* (1534), and *Das Geheimniss der heiligen Gertrudis* (1809) all are works said to be preserved by and in some cases attributed to Capuchin, Jesuit, and Carthusian monastics—the dates associated with such works are often dubious, but the implication is clear: ceremonial magic remained closely associated with Christianity and Christian monasticism. The history of magical currents in modernity is largely the history of how ceremonial magic became secularized.

Such late medieval/early modern magical handbooks or grimoires often evidence a deep indebtedness to Hebrew and to Kabbalistic sigils and also often reproduce the kinds of planetary sigils we saw in Agrippa's *Occulta philosophia*. In fact, one could reasonably argue that the history of Western ceremonial magic since the sixteenth century is one of variations on themes and, to put it even more precisely, of books that derive from and even plagiarize their predecessors. Writing on late nineteenth and early twentieth century ceremonial magicians, Brad Verter argues that the history of magic in the

West is fundamentally one of books—far more even than scriptural religious traditions, what came to be known as modern occultism begins and is continued by means of books.[1] Certainly exemplary of this tendency is Francis Barrett's *The Magus, or, Celestial Intelligencer* (1801), which was closely indebted to (read: plagiarized) Agrippa's earlier compendium on magic.

If Barrett's book was of value for its baroque illustrations and its collection of information, of much greater influence was Alphonse-Louis Constant (1810–1875), known as Eliphas Lévi. Lévi was known in his youth as a utopian revolutionary, for which he was at one point jailed. But later in life, Lévi became a major figure of European magical circles, his popular books including *Dogme et rituel de Haute magie* (1854–1856), *Histoire de la magie* (1860), and *La Clef des Grands Mystères* (1861). Particularly in the first of these, Lévi offered not only a compendium of information, but a systematized approach to magic that was to figure in virtually every subsequent major Western magical figure, even if they did not acknowledge this. Lévi was also one of the first to draw explicitly and extensively on the images of the Tarot as a key to esoteric knowledge, a theme that was to be continued by numerous other authors throughout the nineteenth and twentieth centuries.

While one must mention such figures as Gérard Encausse (1865–1915), an occultist known as Papus and author of *Traité de science occulte* (1888), in Prague one finds also various esoteric or initiatory circles, including those inspired by the work of Johann Baptist Krebs (1774–1851), mentioned earlier. In fin-de-siècle Prague, one also found a number of other significant figures whose work crosses over between magic and theosophy, among them Karel Weinfurter and the novelist Gustav Meyrink, both of whom were much influenced by Kerning's works and who founded an initiatory order called the lodge of the Blue Star. During this period, magical currents are often not easily separable from a whole complex of esoteric forms of knowledge; the practice of magic is often bound up with various esoteric lodges or groups that nonetheless might not best be described as only magical, but as mystico-magical.

Representative of a mystico-magical current is the work of Rudolph Steiner (1861–1925), who was at one time a member of the Ordo Templi Orientis, the magical lodge associated with Aleister Crowley (1875–1947) as well as with Carl Kellner (1850–1905) and Theodore Reuss (1855–1923). Although it is relatively little known or remarked upon in circles devoted to the work of Steiner, who in 1914 founded his own Anthroposophical Society, Steiner in fact led the German wing of the OTO prior to this time. While Steiner's voluminous work includes much that can be classified as "occult" knowledge—clairvoyance, and so forth—he cannot be classified as a magus in the strict way that Crowley certainly can be.

Indeed, the end of the nineteenth century represents a burgeoning of various Western magical groups as well as of syncretic movements like the Theosophical Society of Helena Blavatsky (1831–1891) or the Anthroposophical Society of Steiner, both of which themselves included magical elements and even, in the case of the Theosophical Society, a special magical wing called the "Esoteric Section" and headed by William Q. Judge. This semisecret magical group within the Theosophical Society undoubtedly arose as a reaction to the growing recruitment power of the Order of the Golden Dawn, which was founded in 1888 by William Wynn Westcott (1848–1925) and Samuel Liddle MacGregor Mathers (1854–1918), both already members of the Societas Rosicruciana in Anglia. The Order of the Golden Dawn has a somewhat legendary beginning in the finding of a hidden and encoded manuscript bearing the keys to the work of the Abbott Trithemius; but the Golden Dawn itself as a group practiced ceremonial magic with a pronounced Masonic ritual flavor, drawing also upon Christian Kabbalah and a number of preexisting magical or "occultist" traditions.[2] Arguably the most important contribution of the Golden Dawn was its systematization of magic in a series of Masonic grades.

But the Golden Dawn's systematization of ritual magic owed at least something to its predecessors, among these the African American magician Paschal Beverly Randolph (1825–1875) and the Hermetic Brotherhood of Luxor.[3] Randolph certainly deserves discussion here, as out of his work emerged the sexual emphases of many subsequent twentieth-century magical groups and individuals. Randolph was born in New York and learned various occupations before, in the early 1850s, taking up a spiritualist vocation, eventually serving as an onstage trance medium and then as a psychic and healer. Randolph's various books and treatises—in which he also claimed himself as heir to the secrets of Rosicrucianism while later acknowledging that his Rosicrucianism came out of his own head—were chiefly about sexuality. In such works as *The Ansairetic Mystery*, *Eulis*, and *The Golden Secret*, Randolph outlined his perspective on the mysteries of sexuality, which included sexual magic. Randolph insisted on the importance of women's sexual satisfaction and included in some of his works directions for sexual magical practices that ran him afoul of local New England legal authorities at least once. After the Civil War, Randolph was for a short time the principal of Lloyd Garrison Grammar School in New Orleans, but for our purposes he is perhaps most important not for his various achievements nor for his "Rosicrucianism," but for his establishing the general outlines of sexual magical practices to be followed and developed by subsequent groups both European and American.

One of the most complicated avenues of Randolph's influences has been to a considerable degree unraveled by Joscelyn Godwin, Christian Chanel, and John Deveney in their collection of documents entitled *The Hermetic*

Brotherhood of Luxor (1995). In this work, the authors trace how Randolph's cosmological and sexual teachings made their way to England, to a small group of occultists who drew upon them and even plagiarized them in creating an esoteric order and their own system of magical practice. It is by no means clear whence Randolph himself drew his own cosmology of how the individual "monad" evolves toward immortality—he himself claimed that he learned it during his travels in the Near East during 1861, and it is true that his post-travel teachings entailed something of a rejection of his previous spiritualism and the embrace of what he called "blending" or "atrilism," meaning the union of the earthly personality with a transcendent entity, as well as a far more complex cosmology of uncertain origin. Randolph's writings were directly taken over by those who established the first mail order school of practical magic: Peter Davidson (1837–1915) and Thomas Henry Dalton [alias Burgoyne] (1855?–1895?), in connection with the somewhat mysterious French figure Max Theon (1847/8?–1927), very likely of Polish Jewish origin.

Many teachings of the Hermetic Brotherhood of Luxor (HBL) were taken wholesale from Randolph's works without attribution and sent back to America from Britain as HBL inner teachings. Arguably one of the most influential ideas expressed by this group, common to the HBL as well as to the Theosophical Society, was the notion that esoteric orders could have discarnate or invisible "masters" existing elsewhere and directing the activities of the order. Thus the HBL had an interior and an exterior circle, the latter by and large the business of Davidson and Burgoyne, the former that of Max Theon and the invisible masters themselves. This concept of hidden masters, popularized by Blavatsky with her "Koot Humi," almost certainly owes much to the earlier precedence of spiritualism in Europe and North America, as well as to Randolph's concept of "blending" with higher spiritual entities, a variant form of spiritualism. The second primary contribution of the HBL in its various documents was its emphasis on sexual magic and on the primacy of sexuality in the nature of the cosmos itself.[4] This emphasis of the HBL, derived directly from Randolph, disseminated Randolph's ideas much more widely in Europe and North America.[5]

Aleister Crowley joined the Order of the Golden Dawn in 1898, with which he had a very turbulent relationship, after which he went on to found his own order, the Astrum Argentinum (incorporated into the Ordo Templi Orientis [OTO], founded by Carl Kellner [1850–1905] and Theodor Reuss [1855–1923]). Crowley continued the emphasis on sexuality in magical ritual. Crowley's OTO developed a luciferian tendency that manifested not only in his writings, but also in the incorporation of rituals like the Gnostic Mass, the ritual consumption of wafers reportedly consisting in part of semen and menstrual fluid. Hardly averse to bad publicity, he styled himself "the Great Beast," becoming a favorite subject for tabloid journalism. But his voluminous writings remain an important part of the history of twentieth-century magical esotericism, and the OTO continues to the present day, if occasionally rent asunder by schism.

An allied order in many respects, founded somewhat later than Crowley's group (in 1926) is the Fraternitas Saturni (FS), started and led by Gregor Gregorius (Eugen Grosche) until his death in 1964. The FS is a relatively little-known and rather sinister group, arguably among the most influential of contemporary magical orders, along with the OTO. Yet it was only at the end of the twentieth century that information about the teachings of the FS became more widely known, not only through the publication of documents and teachings in book form, but also via the Internet.[6] Whereas many occult groups, like the Society of the Inner Light, focus exclusively on the light, the FS includes also use of what has been called the "dark side," and their sexual rites are said to reflect this. It is clear, in any case, that the FS has a luciferian as well as a cold, austere, Saturnian quality, and that sexual rites play at least some role in the order's structure.[7]

The late twentieth century saw the emergence of various other neo-Gnostic groups like that of Latin American author Samael Aun Weor (1917–1977), not to mention Satanism, or the development in the late twentieth century of Wicca or witchcraft as a movement, all of which drew or draw upon sexuality as a primary basis for mystico-magical power. We do not have room here to outline all of the various groups and individuals who represent the continuation and development of magical orders or movements in the late twentieth century, as this is a task best accomplished individually by recourse to the internet and other sources, or by a book devoted exclusively to the subject. Here, it is enough to note the primary tendencies of many of these groups, which are (1) to assert a Nietzschean superiority over conventional forms of morality; (2) to hold sexual rites of one sort or another for purposes of magical power; and (3) to explicitly react against conventional forms of organized Christianity, even if insisting upon the necessity of attaining gnosis of one kind or another. One also can discern an increasing tendency away from the eighteenth-century Masonically inspired hierarchic orders that persisted throughout the twentieth century, and toward an eclectic or syncrasic individualism. Perhaps nowhere is that individualism more apparent than in chaos magic, but it is also visible in the long-standing American folk magic traditions.

AMERICAN FOLK MAGIC

American folk magic traditions, notably those in the Eastern and Southeastern United States—including various permutations of Powwow, Pennsylvania German traditions, and Appalachian folk magic—are well known for their syncretic and synthetic qualities. As we saw above, the American colonies and the subsequent United States were long a home for religious refugees, and for esoteric practitioners of alchemy, astrology, mysticism, and magic. When such traditions waned in mainstream America under the waxing influence of rationalist philosophy, science, and industrialism, they were continued nonetheless in certain areas that were conducive to them, among those regions being backwoods Pennsylvania, Appalachia, the Southeast, and the Deep South.

Much work yet remains to be done on the intersection of African American, Native American, Muslim, and European magical traditions that variously mingled in North America during the eighteenth, nineteenth, and twentieth centuries. Recent authors who have worked on North American folk magic include David Kriebel and John Richards, who have each uncovered aspects of different folk magical traditions.[8] Important to many American folk magical traditions is individualized synthetic praxis that incorporates elements of astrology, herbalism, magic, and religion as transmitted through family or other intergenerational lineages. Although these folk magical traditions often draw on elements that were once transmitted in a European and Roman Catholic ambience, in the United States they often were conveyed in a Protestant ambience that encouraged individual praxis and experience. As John Richards has shown, Appalachian folk magic in particular exists within a Protestant religious context, and for that matter, so too do the Pennsylvania and Southern folk magical traditions. Behind practical folk magic traditions like "burn doctoring" is a mystico-magical current that, akin to and perhaps even indebted directly to Böhmean Christian theosophy, joins together practical cosmology such as the astrological "signatures" of herbs and illnesses with mystical invocations of Biblical verses and names, and with transmuted states of consciousness. Traditions like these, some centuries old and continued in the remote backwoods or mountain country, would seem to be worlds removed from a more jaded late twentieth-century phenomenon like chaos magic.

CHAOS MAGIC

Just as the turn of the nineteenth century saw an efflorescence of various magical orders that represented in part innovation and in part a synthesis of earlier traditions—most notable of which was the Golden Dawn—the turn of the twentieth century once again saw the emergence of a bewildering variety of new groups and orders. Among the most prominent of these is certainly chaos magic, which generated a number of magical orders, among them the order of the Illuminates of Thanateros. In the introduction to his book *Liber Null and Psychonaut* (1987), one of the defining works of this movement, Peter Carroll writes that "The Illuminates of Thanateros are the magical heirs to the Zos Kia Cultus [of Austin Osman Spare] and the A.'. A.'."[9] But whereas the Golden Dawn drew upon Renaissance white magic and Jewish Kabbalism, the Chaos magic movement reflects a distinctly darker nature, sometimes referring to itself as "grey magic."

Chaos magic is more or less free-form in nature and might perhaps be best described as a kind of neoshamanism. According to Phil Hine in his book *Condensed Chaos,*

> The simple message of Chaos Magic is that, what is fundamental to magic is the actual *doing* of it. . . . Carroll's *Liber Null*, therefore, presented the bare bones of the magical techniques which can be employed to bring about change in one's circumstances. *Liber Null* concentrated on techniques, saying that the actual methods of magic are basically shared by the different systems, despite the differing symbols, beliefs, and dogmas. What symbol systems you wish to employ is a matter of choice, and . . . the webs of belief that surround them are means to an end.[10]

Chaos magic draws freely from whatever traditions or ideas seem useful to it, from science fiction and quantum physics to Crowley's writings or Tibetan Buddhism, but characteristic of the movement is its moral relativism or, as others may describe it, nihilism. Whereas the Golden Dawn was closely allied to, perhaps even inseparable from a Judeo-Christian context, chaos magic is definitely not connected to any particular religious tradition.

One of the more innovative elements of chaos magic is its use of quantum or particle physics in the elaboration of magical theory. A developed instance of this is to be found in the second half of Peter J. Carroll's *PsyberMagick*, where he even offers equations derived from particle physics, astronomy, and chaos mathematics, but applied to what he calls "off-white magick." There is a tongue-in-cheek quality to such expositions, but there is also a serious element, to be found also in Phil Hine's writings. Hine, who works with computers, developed the term *servitor* as a descriptor for a nonphysical agent or force controlled through sorcery, a rather more technological term than, say, *demon*. There is a technological and semiscientific aspect to the writings of these and other chaos magician authors that cannot be ignored; indeed, William S. Burroughs wrote in response to Hine's book *Condensed Chaos* that it corresponded to his own hope that "science will become more magical and magic more scientific."[11]

Perhaps the most significant aspect of chaos magic is its resistance to organizational hierarchies and its emphasis on individualism. In this it is a modern departure from earlier magical or esoteric orders that emphasized initiatory lines of transmission from the past. One thinks of the hierarchic initiatory grades of the Golden Dawn, or those of the orders of Martinism, as well as those of the various orders that call themselves Rosicrucian, all of whom claim an initiatory chain going back to hoary antiquity. One joins as a neophyte and rises through the initiatory grades; this is the structure, too, of such early twentieth century magical groups as Dion Fortune's Society of the Inner Light. Chaos magic is different.

There is precedent for chaos magic's individualist ethos, of course. When one reads a nineteenth century figure like Eliphas Levi closely on the subject of initiation one finds him appearing as self-initiated, as a figure like Agrippa, emerging into the world not as a scion of this or that order, but as a kind of "self-made man." He insists on the importance of "hierarchy and initiation," yet one cannot but leave his works, particularly *Dogme et Rituel de la Haute Magie* (1861), except with a sense that this is a modern who is fashioning a new synthesis of magic based on his own direct experiences and experimentation.

Chaos magic draws upon and develops this kind of synthesis to an anarchic degree. If Lévi, like so many before him, later in life sought to integrate or reintegrate his magical practices with the spiritual practices of the Church, the chaos magicians of the early twenty-first century eschewed, even scorned taking refuge in traditional religions. Carroll, for instance, is openly derisive of Christianity and fundamentalism in particular.[12] One is struck by the individualism that resonates throughout the chaos magical movement to such a degree that one can hardly speak of a chaos magical *tradition* even if there is an order of "Magical Pact of the Illuminates of Thanateros." In this movement, the term *initiation* takes on the neoshamanic meaning of a period of trial and growth rather than an institutionalized series of hierarchic degrees; chaos magic is, as much as anything, based on what one could call social deprogramming. Chaos magic represents an anarchic and radical individualist mystico-magical movement that is by self-definition antitraditional, but that nonetheless draws from religious traditions and emphasizes transformations of consciousness. Thus it is especially interesting to find during the same time an almost exactly antithetical movement, that of "Traditionalism."

SYNCRETISM AND UNIVERSALISM

Traditionalism

Without doubt, one of the most significant intellectual movements of the twentieth century was that form of perennialism generally known as Traditionalism. Traditionalism as a movement appeared with the singular voice of the French author René Guénon (1886–1951), whose books and articles all reflect the certainty of a man utterly convinced of the truth of what he had to say. In his youth, Guénon became familiar with the phenomena associated with spiritualism as well as with magical, Masonic, and Gnostic orders. Having been trained in mathematics, Guénon left behind the possibility of teaching or a university post and investigated the various esoteric groups available to him; he studied at the Ecole Hermétique of Papus (Gérard Encausse) and became a member of the Martinist Order, later became the leader of the Ordre du Temple Renové; he became a bishop in the Eglise Gnostique (which claimed to be a restitution of Catharism); he joined the Grand Lodge of France as a Mason; and he began a journal entitled *La Gnose*. During his formative period, he also became familiar with Hinduism as well as with Taoism and then Islam both through books and through, for instance, Albert de Pouvourville (1862–1939), who had studied Taoism in China, and through Shaikh Elish Abder-Rahman el-Kebir, an Egyptian Sufi, by way of Ivan Aguéli, a Swedish painter.[13]

In terms of overall intellectual influence within Traditionalism and outside it, Guénon is the most important figure, not least because he in many respects is responsible for the movement's inception. Guénon's many works include his overview of Vedanta, *Introduction générale à l'étude des doctrines hindoues [Man and His Becoming According to Vedanta]* (1921), his attack on the Theosophical Society entitled *Le Théosophisme, histoire d'une pseudo-religion [Theosophy]* (1921), his criticisms of modern society, *La Crise du monde modern [Crisis of the Modern World]* (1927) and the apocalyptic *Le règne de la quantité et les signes des temps [Reign of Quantity and the Signs of the Times]* (1945), as well as his studies of traditional symbolism, *Le Symbolisme de la Croix [Symbolism of the Cross]* (1931) and *La Grande Triade [The Great Triade]* (1946). His most abstract metaphysical treatise was *Les états multiples de l'étre [Multiple States of the Being]* published in 1932, but all of Guénon's works have an abstract and cold quality that paid little attention to art or the forms of Western esotericism we have discussed to this point.[14]

Indeed, one could well argue that Guénon's works, like Traditionalism as a whole, represent to a large degree a rejection of prior Western esoteric traditions in favor of an intellectual universalism not much interested in cosmological gnosis. Whereas earlier figures like Papus or Eliphas Lévi—not to mention much earlier figures like John Dee or Agrippa—existed in an almost exclusively Western European context, Guénon and the Traditionalist school exist in a global context. It is significant, for instance, that Guénon, a Freemason from a Catholic background, first published a work devoted to Vedanta, and that he himself left Europe entirely to live the last part of his life in Cairo, Egypt, as a traditional Muslim. Guénon was certainly aware of the various esoteric orders and traditions of Europe, but he placed himself as much as possible outside and beyond them. In his works one has the sometimes uncanny sense of a dispassionate intelligence surveying the entire human religio-cultural landscape, and his writing is alluring by virtue of its clarity, certainty, and simplicity, even if, as Antoine Faivre has aptly remarked, Guénon's thought "encourages too readily the abandoning of complex realities, cultural richness, esoteric or otherwise, for the benefit of metaphysical certitudes having the value of dogma."[15] From Guénon onward, Traditionalism has been characterized by antimodernism, a sense that modernity represents not progress, but rather a profound decline corresponding to the Iron Age or the *Kali Yuga*.

If Guénon represents a largely apolitical perspective, the same cannot be said in quite the same way of Julius Evola (1898–1974), roughly Guénon's contemporary and certainly a correspondent with him. Evola ultimately did insist on a more or less apolitical viewpoint, but he is associated with the extreme political right in ways that other Traditionalists are not. As H. T. Hansen has documented, Evola was in fact distrusted by Himmler and the German Nazis, and he wrote against fascism, but for all that he did espouse views that place him on the far right of the political spectrum.[16] Evola, sometimes titled Baron because of his Italian family line, was author of a series of works bearing considerable resemblance to Guénon's even if he paid a great deal more attention to the Hermetic, alchemical, magical, and warrior traditions of Europe. Like Guénon, Evola wrote an overview of a major Asian religious tradition, in Evola's case, Buddhism in his *The Doctrine of Awakening* (1943). However, Evola's rendition of Buddhism is far from accurate, being more a vehicle for his own theory of personal immortality—and much the same can be said of his work on Hermeticism. Probably Evola's most interesting books are his *The Metaphysics of Sex* (a work one can hardly imagine the intellectual ascetic Guénon having written) and *Revolt Against the Modern World* (1969), a work whose title is self-explanatory, and which owes a considerable debt to Guénon's *Crisis of the Modern World* and *Reign of Quantity*. Evola also wrote *Cavalcare la Tigre* (1961) [*Ride the Tiger*], a book that insists not on abandoning the degenerate modern world to its own imminent destruction, but on harnessing it, drawing on the Tantric expression that one must ride the tiger of passions rather than run away from it.

Evola, like Guénon, has remained fascinating to a significant if not large audience. Many of Evola's books were translated into English and published in the United States in the last quarter of the twentieth century, and like Guénon, he retains a devoted following in Europe. The attraction of Traditionalists in general, and of Evola and Guénon in particular, is their sense of self-assuredness or certainty as writers. In his foreword to *Revolt Against the Modern World*, for example, Evola dismisses what he calls modern "knowledge" in toto, asserting that "I do not want to have anything to do with this order of things, as well as with any other that originates from [the] modern mentality."[17] He insists instead on "nonmodern forms, institutions, and knowledge" because these exemplify "what is superior to time and to history"; these alone can produce a "real renewal . . . in those who are still capable of receiving it. Only those capable of this reception may be totally fearless and able to see in the fate of the modern world nothing different or more tragic than the vain arising and consequential dissolution of a thick fog, which cannot alter or affect in any way the free heaven." "So much," Evola writes, "for the fundamental thesis [of this book]."[18]

By asserting the fundamental superiority of the traditional over the modern, Evola has a means of attacking the totality of modern existence, and he does not hesitate to do so. The resulting sense of superiority in the author translates to the reader, who becomes an intellectual initiate by virtue of reading these kinds of books or articles. As reader, if one enters into Evola's perspective, one enters into a new if reactionary way of seeing the world, for the sense of absolute certainty and superiority of Evola (or Guénon) as author places one inevitably in opposition to the entirety of the modern world—one becomes a member of the intellectual elite who can see beyond the fog of the immediate. It is true that Evola's kind of globalist comparativist writing is itself a function of the modern world that offers knowledge of so many different religious traditions, but this internal contradiction is superceded by the sense of universal knowledge that Evola and Traditionalism more generally offer; one rarely notices that Evola himself is a particular manifestation of the modern world—a reaction against it that could not exist without it—because of the giddy sense that here is universal knowledge, here is the key to understanding our era. It is easy to be seduced by this sense of intellectual superiority, a kind of esotericism unique to the modern period.

This intellectual esotericism has its avatar, if one may so put it, in Frithjof Schuon (1907–1998), whose severe and abstract works are seen by some Traditionalists as the culmination of the movement. Schuon was born in Basle, Switzerland, and was trained as a textile designer; he worked in Paris, where he corresponded with Guénon, later meeting Guénon in Egypt. He evidently had some contact with Sufis in Islam, and his many books are infused with an abstractness that owes a great deal to the aniconic Islamic tradition. Among his books are *Understanding Islam* (1963), *Islam and the Perennial Philosophy* (1976), *Christianity/Islam: Essays on Esoteric Ecumenicism* (1985), as well as *In the Tracks of Buddhism* (1969), *The Feathered Sun: Plains Indians in Art and Philosophy (1990)*, and *Light on the Ancient Worlds* (1966). His abstractly esoterist works include such books as *Esoterism as Principle and as Way* (1981) and *Survey of Metaphysics and Esoterism* (1986), as well as *To Have a Center* (1990) and *The Play of Masks* (1992).

Only in the early 1990s, late in his life, did it become publicly known that Schuon was the center of a *tariqah*, or esoteric group based in Bloomington, Indiana. Schuon's books give the sense, as one can see from the titles listed above, that he wrote from a universalist or transcendent position, as more or less pure intellect removed from the modern world. What one does not see from the books is what emerged publicly in the 1990s with the release by an erstwhile disciple of Schuon's in Bloomington of a more or less scandalous dossier of photos and texts circulated to document Schuon's visions, as of a nude Virgin Mary, his "spiritual wives," and a Sufi or para-Sufi universalist initiatic group with an elderly Schuon at its center as spiritual shaikh. As a result of these revelations, assessments of Schuon have tended to be bifurcated into either deifying or demonizing, and so one awaits a balanced account and analysis of Schuon's life and work that takes into account and perhaps even reconciles what seem to be its disparate and almost irreconcilable elements.

If Schuon, Evola, and Guénon represent the most flamboyant of the Traditionalists, each of them generating a devoted and even cultish following, one cannot help but mention other figures who, if sometimes less well-known, are also perhaps a bit more modest in their approach. Among these are Titus Burckhardt (1908–1984), who published on art, alchemy, and the architecture of sacred cities or cathedrals; Marco Pallis (1895–1990), who recounted his experiences in Tibet and his Buddhist perspective in his books *Peaks and Lamas* (1939), *The Way and the Mountain* (1960), and *A Buddhist Spectrum* (1980); and Seyyed Hossein Nasr (b. 1933), a noted Islamic scholar living in the United States, who has published a large number of academic books on Islamic philosophy, spirituality, and related themes. And there are quite a few other authors who belong, more or less, to the Traditionalist camp, among them Martin Lings, William Stoddart, Gai Eaton, Lord Northbourne, and Leo Schaya.

When one looks at the Traditionalist school as a whole, one is struck by its apparent relative unanimity, an impression that is fostered by adherents and by the school's universalist attitude, as well as by the sense of intellectual initiation that it encourages and, indeed, is based upon. By reading these works, one becomes a kind of "insider." But as a series of contentious articles in a late-twentieth/early twenty-first century Traditionalist journal, *Sacred Web*, shows, one does not have to poke around too much in the movement to find some dissent; if there are "insiders," there also are factions and dissenting voices among them. Nonetheless, Traditionalism does represent a uniquely modern phenomenon, an antimodern, explicitly esoteric intellectual approach that presents a coherent and powerful critique of much that usually remains unexamined in the modern world. As a result, regardless of one's personal reaction to Traditionalism, it remains an important development in the history of esotericism, one whose significances are only now beginning to be explored. A pioneering academic work in this regard is Mark Sedgwick's *Against the Modern World* (2004).[19]

NEW AGE UNIVERSALISM

If Traditionalism tends toward the arguably pessimistic view that the modern world represents the latter stages of a descent into the Kali Yuga, or degenerate time cycle—the view expressed in Guénon's *The Reign of Quantity and the Signs of the Times* or in Evola's *Revolt Against the Modern World*—the congeries of very different figures and groups under the rubric of "New Age" represent in general the opposite, optimistic view that modern society is on the brink or cusp of a new era in human "evolution" or progress, that just around the corner is a literal New Age sometimes associated with the Zodiacal precession from Pisces to Aquarius (the so-called Age of Aquarius). But while Traditionalists in general tend to be harshly critical of New Age figures and movements, seeing them as more or less demonically inspired, the fact is that however opposed in many respects they might be, these two movements do share tendencies toward syncretism and universalism. Like Traditionalism, the New Age movement is peculiarly modern and to some extent reactionary in its origin and nature.

In his monumental book *New Age Religion and Western Thought* (1996/1998), Wouter Hanegraaff surveys the entire New Age movement in detail and comes to the general conclusion that

> All New Age religion is characterized by the fact that it expresses its criticism of modern western culture by presenting alternatives derived from a secularized esotericism. It adopts from traditional esotericism an emphasis on the primacy of personal religious experience and on this-worldly types of holism . . . but generally reinterprets esoteric tenets from secularized perspectives. Since the new elements of "causality," the study of religions, evolutionism, and psychology are fundamental components, New Age religion cannot be characterized as a return

to pre-Enlightenment worldviews, but is to be seen as a qualitatively new syncretism of esoteric and secular elements. Paradoxically, New Age criticism of modern western culture is expressed to a considerable extent on the premises of that same culture.[20]

Put even more succinctly, his primary conclusion is this: "The New Age movement is characterized by a popular western culture criticism expressed in terms of a secularized esotericism." If Hanegraaff is right, then the New Age movement is at bottom a secularizing current of thought that nonetheless shares common origins with Traditionalism itself.

For both Traditionalism and the New Age movement have common antecedents in the nineteenth century, antecedents so extensive that we can here only allude to a few. Probably the most important antecedents for both are to be found in German *Naturphilosophie* and European Romanticism, in the late nineteenth century New Thought movement, in the various syncretizing "occult" or esoteric figures and lodges of the late nineteenth and early twentieth centuries, as well as in pivotal figures like Emanuel Swedenborg, William Blake, and above all, Ralph Waldo Emerson. All of these various currents of thought have in common tendencies toward individual syncretism and synthesis, toward joining together apparently disparate perspectives in a more general overview that takes on a universalist flavor. One sees the emergence of syncretic universalism throughout the nineteenth and twentieth centuries in figures as diverse as Rudolph Steiner, Frithjof Schuon, and Ken Wilber, each of whom presented himself as a surveyor of the entire human religiocultural inheritance, figures differing not least in their degree of incorporation or rejection of scientific-evolutionist premises.

The pivotal figure in the nineteenth century, however, is Ralph Waldo Emerson (1803–1882), in whose work one can clearly see the origins of virtually all the major subsequent New Age trends, even if Emerson's own work transcends them. It is clear from Emerson's essays that there is a millennialist tinge to them; a perennial optimist, Emerson expects, from his first book, *Nature* (1836), onward that we shall "come to look at the world with new eyes," that we shall soon enter "a dominion such as now beyond [our] dream of God," that there are "auspicious signs of the coming days, as they glimmer already through poetry and art, through philosophy and science, through church and state."[21] It should, then, come as no surprise that the mid- to late nineteenth century New Thought movement—as manifested variously in (or derived from) the mesmeric healing of Phineas Quimby (1802–1866), the "harmonial religion" of Andrew Jackson Davis (1826–1910), the rather cult-like esoteric communities of Thomas Lake Harris (1823–1906), and the Christian Science of Mary Baker Eddy (1821–1910), as well as the evolutionist fantasies of John Fiske (1842–1902)—had its origins to a significant degree in Emerson's writings.[22]

The New Thought movement, with its pastiche of influences from spiritualism, mesmeric healing, various Western esoteric traditions, Asian religious traditions, and evolutionist science, represents the nineteenth century fin-de-siècle predecessor and counterpart to the twentieth century fin-de-siècle "New Age" movement. But one can trace many of the themes of both movements directly back to Emerson. What themes? (1) That direct spiritual experience of the individual is more important than adherence to organized religious traditions. (2) That behind or within all traditions is a "perennial philosophy" or esoteric center, which the individual can come to realize. (3) That we are moving toward a new era in human understanding, an era that unites science and spirituality. (4) That suffering does not have any ultimate reality and that we can choose to overcome or transcend difficulties or suffering. (5) That we can draw from Asian religious traditions such concepts as *karma* or enlightenment and place them in an individualistic modern context. These are only a handful of such themes, but this list does at least outline the filial strands of thought here that could be seen, in the way Harold Bloom has argued in a book of that title, as something like *The American Religion*.

There are, of course, numerous such strands linking earlier esoteric traditions, the nineteenth century American New Thought movement, and the late twentieth century American New Age movement. One can, for instance, as Hanegraaff has suggested, trace the filiation between such figures as Friederike Hauffe (1801–1829)—known as the "Seeress of Prevorst," who had become a medium and a kind of "channel" for "higher beings" after having been magnetized by the German doctor and poet Justinius Kerner—and much later figures like Jane Roberts (1929–1984), who became well-known as the "channel" for the "spiritual teachings" of a discarnate spirit named "Seth."[23] Between these two figures stands the nineteenth-century work and life of Andrew Jackson Davis, also a medium or channel who became a widely known author and public figure of his time, and who claimed to have spoken with none other than Emanuel Swedenborg in the afterlife. One can see, here, in other words, a series of linked figures who represent common tendencies, not just the fact that they were famous "spirit mediums" or "channels," but also that their works emerged from and reflected the fundamental premise that the individual, without the intermediary of the church, contact higher beings and reveal spiritual truths.

Given that Emerson himself disliked spiritualism, which he derisively termed the "rat hole of revelation," certainly I am not willing to lay the spiritualist movements (including "channeling"), let alone the entire New Age movement at his feet. But one can nonetheless trace what we might call a legacy of radical spiritual individualism to which Emerson belongs and to which he contributed—and to which all of these "channelers" also belong. One of Emerson's premises, expressed in his "Divinity School Address," was that we should not consider revelation as being only frozen in the past, for in fact it is present to us now as well. Emerson, of course, is thinking of direct divine inspiration of the individual, whereas these various spiritualist movements or figures are concerned more with intermediary revelation from discarnate beings, but in both cases the individual has access to some form of direct revelation, even if it is from the rathole rather than from on high.

Emerson thus, for many reasons, may be seen as an ancestor of the New Age as a whole, particularly in its strands of syncretism, perennialism, radical spiritual individualism, and above all, its cosmic optimism. What is more, Emerson inaugurated what became more or less a staple of the New Age movement—its grafting of various elements of Asian religious traditions (concepts like karma or reincarnation, for instance) into what remains a fundamentally Western millennialist current of thought. One sees such millennialism in authors like David Spangler, who wrote that "The New Age is a concept that proclaims a new opportunity, a new level of growth attained, a new power released and at work in human affairs, a new manifestation of that evolutionary tide of events which, taken at the flood, does indeed lead on to greater things, in this case to a new heaven, a new earth and a new humanity."[24] And one sees a similar if perhaps less extreme millennialism in such various late-twentieth-century New Age authors as Shakti Gawain, Shirley MacLaine, and George Trevelyan.

But the term *New Age* is actually at least as much a marketing category as it is a school of thought.[25] While one might not wish to go so far as some scholars in this argument, it is certainly true that the term *New Age* did become a category for a whole potpourri of merchandising possibilities, and that while the river of this merchandise might look fairly wide—carrying along in its current everything from crystals and scented candles to quasi-scientific tomes by figures like Fritjof Capra to various forms of Chinese herbalism or acupuncture, from "channeled" books dictated by various discarnate entities claiming great antiquity and wisdom to cultish Western figures claiming themselves to be representatives of Hindu or Native American or other traditions—the river is also fairly shallow. While one cannot be sure where this broad and shallow river is heading, one can see that it has been harnessed more than once as a means of making money, and sometimes one wonders if that is not, in the end, its primary function.

It is for this reason that it is ultimately unjust to place too much emphasis on the origins of the New Age movement in the thought of Emerson or, for that matter, in Western esotericism as a whole. There is naïveté, crassness, and superficiality in the New Age movement that one simply does not find in the same proportions in earlier Western esoteric traditions or in the works of Emerson. Hanegraaff is convincing in his magnum opus showing the filiations between earlier Western esoteric currents and the bewildering gamut of New Age figures, groups, and tendencies in the late twentieth century. But he is also convincing in arguing that the New Age movement is fundamentally a secularization of preexisting Western esoteric currents.

I would go further and suggest that the New Age movement also represents a manifestation of what the influential Tibetan Buddhist teacher Chögyam Trungpa, Rinpoche, called "spiritual materialism." By this I mean that whereas traditional Western esoteric traditions like Christian theosophy in the tradition of Böhme or Pordage, for example, entail the individual's effort toward and process of self-transcendence in a community with shared symbols and means of transcendence, the New Age movement largely represents the accumulation of objects or experiences that tend to bolster the self. The entire New Age industry itself bespeaks this: people who accumulate crystals, books, workshops, tourist experiences, new clothes, and so forth may be somewhat transformed in the process, but they may also be engaging in a kind of spiritual materialism that in the end is far indeed from the kind of quiet work of self-transcendence that one finds delineated in works like the *Cloud of Unknowing* on the one hand or alchemical treatises on the other.[26] If the various currents of esotericism we have seen throughout Western history have tended to encourage the transcendence of self, the New Age movement tends to encourage adorning, massaging, acupuncturing, flattering, and extending the life of the self indefinitely. This is, it would seem, a significant difference between the two.

LITERARY ESOTERICISM

Clearly esotericism is present in the works of most of the major American authors of the mid-nineteenth century American Renaissance, from Edgar Allan Poe, Nathaniel Hawthorne, and Herman Melville to Emerson, Emily Dickinson, Alcott, and Margaret Fuller. By drawing upon alchemy, astrology, theosophy, Swedenborgianism, Mesmerism, Rosicrucianism, Freemasonry, and many other esoteric movements and ideas, these authors expressed in their published work basic themes that had enormous resonance in the popular mind and remained as living forces in the American imagination.

Many important nineteenth-century American authors clearly inscribed esoteric themes in their works. There are certainly esoteric dimensions to the works of Herman Melville (1819–1891), notably in *Moby Dick*, but also in his

poetry. We see this in poems like his "Fragments of a Lost Gnostic Poem,"
"The New Rosicrucians," or "Clarel." Melville had many voices in his fiction
and poetry, so perhaps we should not be surprised that some drew on esoteric
traditions, even if his own views were probably most clearly set forth in that
sardonic, almost nihilistic book, *The Confidence Man.* Margaret Fuller
(1810–1850) also wrote poems that are indisputably esoteric, perhaps most
notably "Winged Sphynx," "My Seal Ring," "Sub Rosa-Crux," and above all
"Double Triangle," probably the best of her poems, meant to explain the esoteric illustration that originally appeared at the beginning of *Woman in the
Nineteenth Century.* Part of the poem reads:

> When the perfect two embrace,
> Male and Female, black & white,
> Soul is justified in space,
> Dark made fruitful by the light;
> And, centred in the diamond Sun,
> Time & Eternity are one.[27]

Fuller was quite interested in magic and in astrology. Emily Dickinson
(1830–1886) was also a poet with esoteric themes who, like Melville, was
very much influenced by the delightful essayist and collector of esoteric lore,
Sir Thomas Browne (1605–1682). Dickinson did not pursue scholarly investigation into esotericism, but she was interested in such topics as witchcraft
and posthumous existence, and her poetry reveals much evidence of spiritual
trauma and spiritual awakening.[28]

   In twentieth century American literature, there are three representative figures I would emphasize: modernist poet H. D. (1886–1961), the Beat novelist William S. Burroughs (1914–1997), and the science fiction writer Philip
K. Dick (1928–1982). H. D.'s work contains many traditional Western esoteric currents, including alchemy, astrology, and sexual mysticism, while Burroughs's later work contains more contemporary magical currents, and Dick's
work has modernized projected Gnosticism. Arguably, the most deeply aware
of Western esoteric currents was H. D. That H. D.—born Hilda Doolittle—
was fascinated with esoterica is well known. Susan Friedman outlines the in-
tertwining of H. D.'s biography and her fascination with mysticism, the Tarot,
numerology, astrology, magic, psychic insights or visions, various heresies of
antiquity including the Ophites and other Gnostic groups, Rosicrucianism,
and the Christian theosophy of Count Nikolaus von Zinzendorf (1700–1760)
and the Moravians.[29] H. D., like Margaret Fuller before her, was fascinated
with numerology, astrology, and what we might term esoteric correspondences or patterns in life. She created a hermetic emblem for herself and was
very interested in doctrines of occult or hidden sympathies between human-

ity and nature. We see H. D.'s esoteric interests in her poems *Trilogy* and *Vale Ave* as well as her novel *The Gift*, but the much earlier work *Notes on Thought and Vision* help to make clear H. D.'s gnostic perspective in relation to literature. *Notes* is a very unusual work; written in July 1919 in the Scilly Islands, it argues for the characteristically Emersonian idea of an "overmind" as a model of higher consciousness, and it includes sexual mysticism as well.

During the London blitz in the Second World War, H. D. wrote the collection of three long poems later published as *Trilogy*. These three poems were "The Walls Do Not Fall," "Tribute to the Angels," and "The Flowering of the Rod." In "The Walls Do Not Fall," H. D. develops many of the themes that were initially sketched in *Notes on Thought and Vision*. These themes are clearly esoteric: she writes of her experience of "nameless initiates" as her "companions," of the "alchemist's secret," and of "the most profound philosophy," of the stars as beings who can be invoked by spells, and much else.

H. D.'s most important work was the esoteric novel *The Gift*, which was not published until the late twentieth century in a full version that included H. D.'s complex mysticism drawn from her family's Moravian tradition. H. D. was herself a baptized Moravian, but the Moravian Church of the twentieth century was vastly different from the Herrnhuters of Count von Zinzendorf (1700–1760), who settled in Bethlehem, Pennsylvania, in the middle of the eighteenth century. Zinzendorf and his group were far more esoteric in their interests than those who followed them. H. D. avidly read a great deal about eighteenth-century esotericism and much else in order to fashion an extraordinary novel that embodies many currents of Western esotericism, most notably those of Christian theosophic mysticism. In H. D.'s work, we see a fusion of some magical and many mystical themes.

By contrast, the later works of William S. Burroughs incorporate magical and alchemical elements, as well as some aspects of Egyptian religious tradition. He is best known for his earlier writing, like his novel *Naked Lunch*. But in *The Western Lands* (1987) and *The Place of Dead Roads* (1984) Burroughs explores a surreal, nightmarish world populated by demons, a world he describes in part by way of a magical interpretation of ancient Egyptian religion. There is, of course, a long-standing Western esoteric tradition based on Egyptian religion and magic, of which Burroughs is only one exemplar. His work was popularized not only through film versions of his novels, but also through his spoken word appearances on musical works. Bill Laswell's band Material produced an album featuring as lyrics Burroughs reading from *The Western Lands*, thus widening Burroughs's audience for some of his most "occult" work.

Philip K. Dick's uses of Western esotericism also become most evident in his later work, which he saw not as science fiction, but as secret Gnostic truth.

He believed that he was a Gnostic in the period of the Roman Empire. Dick also claimed that he had encountered what he termed a Vast Active Living Intelligence System, or VALIS, about which he wrote at great length not only in such published works as *Valis* (1981), but also in voluminous journals. Dick inspired a kind of posthumous cult following whose interest turns especially on the Gnostic themes of his later works.[30]

We also see esoteric themes emerging prominently in the works of a variety of other authors, including such highly regarded ones as Argentinean author Jorge Luis Borges (1899–1986) and British poet Kathleen Raine (1908–2003), as well as in more popular fiction with magical, mystical, or "occult" themes. Esoteric themes figure prominently in the works of some significant artists, like British painter Cecil Collins (1908–1989), who worked in the tradition of William Blake. In fact, one could make the case that esoteric traditions were (and continue to be) transmitted in the West primarily via literature and art—precisely the argument of the book *Restoring Paradise* (2004). In truth, we hardly should be surprised when literary works turn out to have hidden esoteric dimensions and many layers of meaning.

NEW RELIGIOUS MOVEMENTS

Among the most important developments in the history of contemporary religions is the emergence of new religious movements. New religious movements began to emerge in the late nineteenth century, manifesting in such diverse ways as Blavatsky's Theosophical Society, Mary Baker Eddy's Christian Science, and various New Thought groups and figures. But it was in the twentieth century that the phenomenon of new religious movements came into its own, particularly from the 1950s onward. New religious movements constitute so diverse a field that we certainly could not outline it fully here, but we must include at least a short section because so many new religious movements represent a complex intermingling of our twin esoteric currents of magic and mysticism.

While perhaps not all new religious movements have clearly esoteric dimensions, many do, often drawing on much earlier esoteric currents or traditions. Sociologically, such groups by and large can be seen as having esoteric dimensions when they emphasize the secret or semisecret nature of their teachings. Thus, for instance, Ramtha's School of Enlightenment—whose center (like that of so many others) is in California—began with J. Z. Knight's "channeling" of a discarnate spirit named Ramtha, starting in 1964. There is a long history of "channeling" in Western history, part of which includes the nineteenth-century phenomenon of spiritualism. What differentiates Knight's group, among other things, is that it developed into an institutionalized kind of modern "Gnosticism," so that Ramtha generated a kind of late twentieth century semi-Gnostic initiatory line. Such a group is esoteric both in terms of claiming secret teachings and of claiming connections to esotericism in antiquity. The list of new religious groups and individuals that do both of these is so long that one could not begin to list them all here.

Many, perhaps nearly all new religious movements are synthetic in nature—they draw on a wide variety of earlier traditions, Eastern, Western, and indigenous. Thus, for example, one finds A. H. Almaas [A. Hameed Ali] (1944–), founder of the "Ridhwan School," an esoteric group that draws to a considerable degree on Buddhism, particularly Tibetan Buddhism, but also on Sufism, combining various religious teachings with an emphasis on contemporary psychological theory and praxis. In Almaas one sees a kind of practical universalism that corresponds in some respects to the intellectual universalism that we saw earlier in Traditionalism. But Almaas emphasizes dialogic practice and personal transformation, in effect adapting some aspects of Buddhism, but maintaining an emphasis on the self and on psychology. Similar or related teachings drawn in part or primarily from Buddhism are to be found in the work of Ken Wilber (1949–), David R. Hawkins (1927–), Stephen Batchelor (1953–), and Peter Fenner, among others.

Then there are groups like the Raelians, or Scientology, whose inner teachings are closely tied to secret or semisecret parahistories involving extraterrestrials. Such groups have interesting connections to science fiction, especially Scientology, since its founder L. Ron Hubbard (1911–1986) was a well-known science fiction author before he turned his attention to developing the technology, mythology, and other dimensions of that new religion. But is a group like Scientology esoteric? Certainly it fiercely defends its secret teachings through lawsuits and other means, and its teachings are organized into initiatory stages or levels. It points adherents toward a state it terms "clear," and toward higher states of consciousness, and it also apparently claims some magical abilities also are awakened in adherents, including telepathy, clairvoyance, even the handy ability to repair small appliances by way of rearranging molecules.[31] Hence Scientology evidently does include aspects of both mysticism and magic, and both sociologically and historically one must recognize that it and movements like it do belong more broadly to the category "esoteric."

To say that a group has esoteric teachings is, of course, neither to endorse nor to attack it. One might say that by the fruit of their actions do we know them. Aum Shinrikyo, the Japanese new religious group founded by Shoko Asahara (1955–), certainly had esoteric teachings and technologies drawn from a wide variety of sources, including Buddhism, Hinduism, and Christian millennialism, but it also turned into an increasingly paranoid and apocalyptic cult that eventually sought nuclear weapons and released the poison gas Sarin on a Tokyo subway, killing a dozen people and maiming many hundreds more.[32] The Swiss Order of the Solar Temple headed by Luc Jouret (1947–1994), indeed derived from Western esoteric origins, but it became notorious when a number of its members were killed or committed ritual suicide in 1994. To mention these spectacular cases is obligatory, because even though they are not characteristic of new religious movements generally, they do offer instructive instances of what nasty things can happen when secrecy, power, money, and religion meet and mingle in an atmosphere of apocalypticism.

Nonetheless (and perhaps also because of such unfortunate developments) new religious movements represent one of the liveliest and most interesting areas for study today. Groups emerge, flourish, join, and mutate into new variants with dizzying speed; new charismatic figures emerge, drawing on new syncretic mixes of teachings, and sometimes on hitherto overlooked areas of religious history. Gnostic groups and institutions, magical groups, all manner of religious innovations take place, particularly in the fertile crescent of California, but also around the world. New religious movements often are drawing on much older esoteric traditions, and one can be sure that these two areas of study, which often overlap, will continue to be mutually illuminating.

INDEPENDENT SPIRITS

If the most visible twentieth-century religious phenomena from a sociological perspective are the "New Age" and new religious movements on the one hand and the emergence of fundamentalist religious movements on the other, still there are other figures who remain stubbornly independent from these various social movements and follow their own paths toward transcendence. We have traced already the various magical groups or movements that derive from the mid-nineteenth century; we have looked at the emergence of intellectual esotericism in Traditionalism; we have seen the emergence of the New Age movement as a secularized esotericism. But we have not yet looked at the twentieth- and twenty-first-century appearance of esoteric figures whose work belongs to the lineage, in the West at least, of the *Cloud of Unknowing* or the works of Dionysius the Areopagite. This, too, is an esoteric tradition, perhaps the most esoteric of all, and we would be remiss if we did not include its most striking and representative figures in our survey of esotericism.

In his *The Book of Enlightened Masters: Western Teachers in Eastern Traditions* (1997), Andrew Rawlinson includes entries on hundreds of Westerners who have taken on the role of spiritual teacher, often but by no means always within various Asian religious traditions. Hence one finds entries on Robert Aitken (b. 1917), Philip Kapleau (b. 1912), John Daido Loori (b. ca. 1945), or Jiyu Kennett (b. 1924), all of whom underwent traditional Zen Buddhist training and became recognized as teachers in their respective schools of Zen Buddhism. Or one might look up Pema Chödron (b. ca. 1938), a female teacher in the Tibetan Buddhist tradition of Chögyam Trungpa, Rinpoche. Such figures, while culturally very important as they represent a wholly new religious phenomenon, do not fall into the category of Western esotericism proper. On the other hand, there are numerous independent spiritual teachers in the West who have been more or less strongly influenced by Asian religious traditions, but who have remained largely or totally independent of formal affiliation, and often these independent spirits can be seen as part of a larger Western esoteric current.

One such case is that of G. Ivanovich Gurdjieff (1866–1949), a controversial figure who may have spent several years [perhaps 1905–1907] studying in a "dervish [Sufi] monastery in central Asia"[33] or, by another account, with a secret group called the Sarmoun[g] Brotherhood somewhere in central Asia. Whatever the truth about his contacts with some hidden Asian spiritual tradition, as is well known, Gurdjieff came to live in Western Europe and established there a center for spiritual training. He also wrote a number of long and seemingly impenetrable books, and attracted a number of prominent disciples, among them J. G. Bennett (1897–1974), Jeanne de Salzmann (1889–1990), and P. D. Ouspensky (1878–1947), each of whom established their own spiritual centers and traditions, Salzmann's being the one most generally regarded as the "orthodox" Gurdjieffian line.

It is rather difficult to outline Gurdjieff's teachings as a whole, not least because he himself was not exactly systematic as a teacher, but also because he was something of a trickster and raconteur who was entirely capable of salting truth with what we may charitably call jokes. But at heart is the idea, common to many esoteric traditions, that humanity is for the most part "asleep" and needs to be awakened. This awakening of others is best encouraged by someone who himself is already "awake," and Gurdjieff and his disciples certainly saw him as having precisely that function of awakening. He is notorious for his confrontational style, for his ordering disciples to do humiliating or painful work, for his sometimes apparently erratic behavior—in short, for his playing the role of the peremptory and all-knowing guru. He did leave a real legacy in the West, no doubt of that, one with a powerful impact on the arts, not only in the dances supervised by Jeanne de Salzmann, his official successor, but also in popular music and the other fine arts.[34] Yet Gurdjieff's influence often remains hidden, for the groups he inspired do not operate publicly—they remain, in the strictest sense of the word, esoteric. One lesser-known example of Gurdjieff's influence is to be found in Taliesin, the school of architecture founded by Frank Lloyd Wright—whose third wife, Olgivanna, had been a dancer at Gurdjieff's school in Paris. Gurdjieff himself visited Wright at Taliesin in 1934.[35]

If Gurdjieff represents one pole of what I am calling independent spirits, that of independent guru-figures with an enduring social and cultural influence, of another kind entirely is that pole represented by Franklin Merrell-Wolff (1887–1985)—an American who although he chronicled his own awakening experience at great length, never established any school or sociocultural forms at all—and Bernadette Roberts (b. 1931), a surprisingly little-known American Christian gnostic. Merrell-Wolff and Roberts each underwent a profound spiritual awakening, which they detailed in lengthy autobiographical analysis in their respective books. They are, in my view, extremely important figures because they represent what we might call the austere and individual path toward spiritual awakening or transcendence, a path without flamboyant teachers like Gurdjieff, without institutional support of any kind, but rather the straight and steep path toward sheer self-transcendence.

Merrell-Wolff's primary account of his spiritual awakening is to be found in his book *Pathways Through to Space* (1944/rpt. 1994), which he describes as "a record of transformation in consciousness written down during the actual process itself."[36] The book begins with the chapter "The Light Breaks Forth" and with the sentence "The ineffable transition came, about ten days ago." Merrell-Wolff had been reading *The System of the Vedanta* by Paul Deussen, an exposition of Shankaracarya's metaphysics, while prospecting for gold in California. Then, sitting on a porch swing, he had what he called a "Recognition," after which he wrote, "I have been repeatedly in the Current of Ambrosia. Often I turn to It with the ease of a subtle movement of thought. Sometimes it breaks out spontaneously."[37] He discovered subsequently that this "Current" could be perceived and experienced by others, including his wife. The essence of this Current was the realization of transcendence of self, and Merrell-Wolff describes it in traditional alchemical terms: "Emptiness is thus the real Philosopher's Stone which transfers all things to new richnesses; it is the Alkahest that transmutes the base metal of inferior consciousness into the Gold of Higher Consciousness."[38]

Perhaps the most striking aspect of Merrell-Wolff's writing is his unusual combination of direct personal spiritual experience on the one hand, and intense scholarly study on the other. His writings are full of first-person narrative about his spiritual awakening, from which it is clear that he did indeed undergo a series of illuminations. But in order to understand, develop, and explain these illuminations, he then intensively studied a wide range of philosophers and religious works, eventually coming to the conclusion that while Shankara was a great exemplar of Hindu religious inclination (inward or subjective), and while Jesus Christ was the great exemplar of Christian religious inclination (outward or objective), Shakyamuni Buddha was the one great exemplar of a synthetic "World Teacher" who transcended both objective and subjective inclinations, and who was most aligned with Merrell-Wolff's own experiences. It is possible that Merrell-Wolff is the only major author of this kind also to have outlined his spiritual illuminations in mathematical formulae.[39]

Merrell-Wolff is without doubt among the most fascinating people of the twentieth century, and his work certainly fits into the category of esoteric in the strict sense of the word—but it not the kind of work one would expect to be read by the masses. On the other hand, it is very lucidly written and because of its autobiographical nature, it is for the most part easily followed. Merrell-Wolff did draw upon the language and symbolism of alchemy, but he also represents the influx of Asian religious thought into the American intellectual current of the twentieth century. He is a synthetic writer, whose work uniquely in the twentieth century conjoins the American philosophical current of William James with Buddhist and Hindu perspectives. In sum, Merrell-Wolff in many respects can be seen as an extension of the American Emersonian tradition of the independent sage, one who does not seek to ascend by degrees, but who leaps at once into the throne, as Emerson put it in his first book, *Nature*. Merrell-Wolff is very much an Emersonian sage.

Quite a different character is Bernadette Roberts, a Christian contemplative more or less in the lineage of Dionysius the Areopagite, Meister Eckhart, and the author of the *Cloud of Unknowing*. I write that she is "more or less" in that lineage because she does not readily see herself as having these direct antecedents but rather as "outside the traditional frame of reference—or the beaten path of mystical theology so well travelled by Christian contemplatives."[40] Of course, when one looks closely at her work, and in particular its central theme of realizing one's absence of any substantive self, one has to think of Buddhism, and indeed, she did spend at least a week with Zen Buddhist contemplatives.[41] But unlike Merrell-Wolff, she insists that Buddhism and Vedanta are not central influences for her; she is indeed a Christian contemplative. What she does not acknowledge so readily is that her antecedents in the Christian tradition are figures like Dionysius, Eckhart, and the author of the *Cloud*, or that she belongs to the long-standing tradition of the *via negativa*. She even writes early on (rather unbelievably) that "In the Christian tradition, the falling away of self (not the ego) has never been addressed!"[42] Still, late in her book *The Experience of No-Self*, she does recognize her deep affinity with Eckhart as "one who has made the journey [to no-self] and crossed over," and it is to his tradition that she certainly belongs.[43]

The heart of Roberts's work, has one can quickly see, lies in her journey to and progressive realization of what she calls no-self. She outlines this journey in her book *The Experience of No-Self* (1982/1993), and its culmination in her subsequent book *The Path to No-Self* (1985/1991). *The Experience of No-Self* is, Roberts writes, "the personal account of a two-year journey in which I experienced the falling away of everything I can call a self. It was a journey through an unknown passageway that led to a life so new and different that, despite nearly forty years of varied contemplative experiences, I never suspected its existence."[44] In this book, her journey begins in earnest when she gazes into her empty self and discovers that she can find no self, whereupon she experiences a sensation like an elevator falling hundreds of floors. After this stunning experience, she realizes that "When there is no personal self, there is no personal God." She saw clearly that these two go together—"and where they went, I have never found out."[45]

No personal self, no personal God—by the strictest definition, Roberts's work belongs to the *via negativa*. What we found in the writings of Dionysius the Areopagite, we find also in the work of Roberts—in the works of both, we encounter sheer transcendence. The difference, and this may be a particularly modern difference, is that Roberts's work is strikingly autobiographic in nature; she takes us along with her on her journey to no-self. And this too she shares with Merrell-Wolff, who also offers us the kind of contemplation he undertakes, and a detailed account of his experiences along the way. Roberts is not interested in her antecedents and even goes as far as to suggest that to read the works of prior mystics is misguided, whereas Merrell-Wolff was exceedingly interested in them.

But both Roberts and Merrell-Wolff offer extended, multivolume commentaries on their spiritual experiences, and both of them see themselves as pioneers, individuals striking out into new territory on their own, their books as the chronicles of their inner experiences. It is, I think, no accident that both are American, and both resided in California. They represent very American tendencies—above all, the willingness to strike out on one's own, the refusal to accept received ways of thinking, and the insistence on one's own direct experience as the arbiter of what is true. All of these are Emersonian characteristics that remain deeply ingrained in the American character. And both figures represent the very American notion of an individualized esotericism, an esotericism not of lodges or ancient societies, but an esotericism of one. While neither Merrell-Wolff nor Roberts are at present very well-known, they will without doubt be remembered and studied by historians of religion, for both are historic figures who represent above all the face of esoteric mysticism in an age of individualism.

NOTES

1. See Bradford Verter, "Dark Star Rising: The Emergence of Modern Occultism 1800–1950," Ph.D. diss. (Ann Arbor: UMI, 1998). Verter's argument about magic corresponds to the broader argument about textual transmission in Western esotericism in Versluis, *Restoring Paradise* (Albany: SUNY Press, 2004).

2. See, for some background on the tangled skein of the Golden Dawn's contemporary and predecessor groups, Joscelyn Godwin, *The Theosophical Enlightenment* (Albany: SUNY Press, 1994), especially chapter 11: "From the Orphic Circle to the Golden Dawn."

3. See Patrick Deveney, *Paschal Beverly Randolph: A Nineteenth-century Black American Spiritualist, Rosicrucian, and Sex Magician* (Albany: SUNY Press, 1997), the major work on Randolph. See also Hugh Urban, *Magia Sexualis* (Berkeley: University of California Press, 2006).

4. See J. Godwin, C. Chanel, and P. Deveney, eds., *The Hermetic Brotherhood of Luxor* (York Beach: Weiser, 1995), 68–77, "The Practical Magic of the H. B. of L.," chiefly based on sexuality and including the development of clairvoyance.

5. A major subsequent figure in the Hermetic Brotherhood of Luxor was none other than Thomas Johnson (1851–1919), the American Platonist, who was in fact president of the American Central Council of the HBL! See on this point for documentation, *The Hermetic Brotherhood of Luxor*, 380.

6. See Stephen Flowers, *Fire and Ice: The History, Structure, and Rituals of Germany's Most Influential Modern Magical Order: The Brotherhood of Saturn* (St. Paul, MN: Llewellyn, 1990). See also the website of Peter Koenig, which includes a vast store of archival information on the OTO and the FS and, for related writings, see Frater U.D., *Secrets of Sex Magic* (St. Paul, MN: Llewellyn, 1991).

7. See Stephen Flowers, *Fire and Ice: The History, Structure, and Rituals of Germany's Most Influential Magical Order, the Brotherhood of Saturn* (St. Paul, MN: Llewellyn, 1994).

8. See John Richards, "Folk Magic and Protestant Christianity in Appalachia," *Esoterica* VIII (2006): 7–57; and David Kriebel, "Powwowing: A Persistent American Esoteric Tradition," *Esoterica* IV (2002): 16–28. See also the Foxfire series edited by Eliot Wigginton, beginning with *The Foxfire Book* (New York: Anchor, 1972), and such works as Anthony Cavender's *Folk Medicine in Southern Appalachia* (Durham: University of North Carolina Press, 2003), or for a different set of traditions, Robert Trotter and Juan Antonio Chavira, *Curanderismo: Mexican American Folk Healing* (Atlanta: University of Georgia Press, 1997).

9. Peter J. Carroll, *Liber Null and Psychonaut* (York Beach: Weiser, 1987), 7.

10. Phil Hine, *Condensed Chaos: An Introduction to Chaos Magic* (Tempe, AZ: New Falcon, 1995), 17.

11. Burroughs quotation from cover of Phil Hine, *Condensed Chaos*.

12. See Peter J. Carroll, *PsyberMagick: Advanced Ideas in Chaos Magick* (Tempe, AZ: New Falcon, 2000), 70–71.

13. See Paul Chacornac, *La vie simple de René Guénon* (Paris: Editions Traditionelles, 1958); see also Jean-Pierre Laurant, *Le sens caché dans l'oeuvre de René*

Guénon (Paris: Editions L'Age d'Homme, 1975); in English the books on Guénon are few but include Robin Waterfield, *René Guénon and the Future of the West* (London: Crucible, 1987). For a good if uncritical overview of Traditionalism see Jean Borella, "René Guénon and the Traditionalist School," in A. Faivre and J. Needleman, eds., *Modern Esoteric Spirituality* (New York: Crossroad, 1992), 330–58.

14. The works of Guenon have been made available in English translation by Sophia Perennis. For more information, see www.sophiaperennis.com/guenon.html.

15. Faivre, *Access to Western Esotericism* (Albany: SUNY Press, 1994), 102.

16. See H. T. Hansen, "A Short Introduction to Julius Evola," in G. Stucco, trs., *Revolt Against the Modern World* (Rochester, VT.: Inner Traditions, 1995).

17. Julius Evola, *Revolt Against the Modern World,* G. Stucco, trs. (Rochester, VT: Inner Traditions, 1995), xxxiii.

18. Evola, *Revolt Against the Modern World,* xxxiii.

19. An extensive scholarly study of Traditionalism is Mark Sedgwick's *Against the Modern World: Traditionalism and the Secret Intellectual History of the Twentieth Century* (New York: Oxford University Press, 2004). Sedgwick recounts in detail the lives, if not so much the works, of the various major Traditionalists, and offers an analysis of their significance as a distinctively modern current of thought.

20. Wouter Hanegraaff, *New Age Religion and Western Culture: Esotericism in the Mirror of Secular Thought* (Leiden: Brill, 1996; Albany: SUNY Press, 1998), 521.

21. See Arthur Versluis, ed., *The Hermetic Book of Nature* (St. Paul, MN: Grail, 1996), for the full text of Emerson's *Nature* along with extensive essays demonstrating the relationships between Emerson's work and Hermeticism, Christian theosophy, and other esoteric traditions. See also Emerson's essay "The American Scholar" (1837), which demarcates what he sees as the "signs of the times."

22. For more on Davis and Harris, see Versluis, *The Esoteric Origins of the American Renaissance* (New York: Oxford University Press, 2001).

23. Hanegraaff, *New Age Religion,* 437.

24. See David Spangler, *Revelation: The Birth of a New Age* (Findhorn, Scotland: Findhorn, 1977), 91.

25. Christoph Bochinger, *"New Age" and Moderne Religion: Religionwissenschaftliche Untersuchungen* (Gütersloh: Chr. Kaiser, 1994).

26. This was precisely the critique of James Redfield's "New Age" novels by those familiar with the actual traditions that he purportedly was drawing on in his fiction. His depiction of Tibetan Buddhism so annoyed and disappointed some American practitioners that the magazine *Shambhala Sun,* usually loathe to criticize, devoted a lengthy review to pointing out how Redfield distorted and confused elements of Tibetan Buddhism in his novel. The primary argument of the reviewer was that Redfield's work did not encourage self-transcendence but rather seemed a monumental bloating of authorial self-importance in a nominally Buddhist setting. See Robin Kornman, "Comforting Myths," in *The Shambhala Sun* VIII (March 2000) 4:79–84. Kornman writes that the book represents a "New Age dreaminess—projecting a fantasy and living it, and calling that spirituality. The result is a sort of fantasy religion, dreamed up in the pasteboard world of Redfield's novels" (82). And "to me the most interesting thing about this book is its intense narcissism. The writing is tasteless, col-

orless and characterless, but it does convey one clear feeling: a sense of self-centeredness on the part of the author. He is really the star of his own fantasy" (84).

27. See Versluis, *Esoteric Origins*, 233.

28. The esoteric aspects of all these authors' works (and a number of others) are discussed in Versluis's *The Esoteric Origins of the American Renaissance*. Dickinson's autobiographical record in her poems is comparable to the spiritual autobiographies of women like the seventeenth-century Ann Bathurst, part of whose spiritual diary is to be found in Versluis, ed., *Wisdom's Book: The Sophia Anthology* (St. Paul, MN: Paragon House, 2000).

29. Susan Friedman, *Psyche Reborn* (Bloomington: Indiana University Press, 1981), 157–206.

30. See Lawrence Sutin, *Divine Invasions: A Life of Philip K. Dick* (New York: Carroll and Graf, 2005), as well as various websites. Good collections of links can be found via the "Scriptorium" on www.modernword.com or via www.philipkdick.com

31. See Hugh Urban, "Fair Game: Secrecy, Security, and the Church of Scientology in Cold War America," *Journal of the AAR* 74 (2006) 2: 365. See also Roy Wallis, *The Road to Total Freedom: A Sociological Analysis of Scientology* (New York: Columbia University Press, 1976), 121.

32. See Robert J. Lifton, *Destroying the World to Save It* (New York: Metropolitan, 1999); for first-hand accounts, see Haruki Murakami, *Underground: The Tokyo Gas Attack and the Japanese Psyche* (New York: Vintage, 2001).

33. See Gurdjieff, *Meetings with Remarkable Men* (New York: Dutton 1963), 161; *Herald of Coming Good* (Paris: La Société Anonyme, 1933), 19; Andrew Rawlinson, *The Book of Enlightened Masters* (Chicago: Open Court, 1997), 282–91.

34. Among the popular musicians influenced by Gurdjieff is rock musician Peter Gabriel, whose lyrics often reflect characteristically Gurdjieffian themes and symbols, but who has not to my knowledge openly written or spoken about this connection. Thus Gurdjieff's influence remains esoteric even when it penetrates into the public sphere of popular music or film. For an example, in prose, see Jacob Needleman, *Why Can't We Be Good?* (New York: Tarcher, 2007).

35. See Roger Friedland and Harold Zellman, *The Fellowship* (New York: Regan, 2006).

36. Franklin Merrell-Wolff, *Experience and Philosophy* (Albany: SUNY Press, 1994), x.

37. Merrell-Wolff, *Experience and Philosophy*, 7.

38. Merrell-Wolff, *Experience and Philosophy*, 15.

39. See Franklin Merrell-Wolff, "A Mathematical Model of Ego Metaphysics," in *Transformations in Consciousness: The Metaphysics and Epistemology* (Albany: SUNY Press, 1995), 261–70.

40. See Bernadette Roberts, *The Experience of No-Self: A Contemplative Journey* (Boston: Shambhala, 1982), 114.

41. Roberts, *The Experience of No-Self*, 108.

42. Bernadette Roberts, *The Path to No-Self: Life at the Center* (Albany: SUNY Press, 1991), xv. See Arthur Versluis, "The Gnostic Narratives of Bernadette Roberts," *Studies in Spirituality* 16 (2006): 1–8.

43. Roberts, *The Path to No-Self,* 199. After acknowledging Eckhart as an antecedent figure for her, Roberts then holds that "he is unique and unlike any other Christian mystic" (203). This is true, but it begs the question of whether he nonetheless himself belongs to a larger current in the Christian tradition, that of the *via negativa,* to which Roberts herself also belongs.

44. Roberts, *The Experience of No-Self,* 9.

45. Roberts, *The Experience of No-Self,* 25.

Chapter Nine

Conclusion

Until comparatively recently, there was very little scholarship on Western esotericism as a field. There were, of course, various articles and books on aspects of Western esotericism like alchemy or Rosicrucianism, but there was virtually no sense in the scholarly world that these disparate tributaries of thought formed a larger current of Western esotericism as such. Landmark studies in the mid-twentieth century by Frances Yates began to demarcate "Western esotericism" as a field for interdisciplinary or transdisciplinary study. More than anyone else, though, it was Antoine Faivre (1934–) who, in the last quarter of the twentieth century, with numerous major books and articles defined the field as an academic area.

Faivre's typology describes well what we may call the cosmological domain to which many currents of Western esotericism do belong, incorporating as it does such disciplines as practical alchemy, astrology, geomancy, and other forms of divination, as well as secret or semisecret societies as found in Rosicrucianism, Freemasonry, various magical lodges or orders, and so forth. All of these draw on the doctrine of correspondences. What is more, a significant part of Böhmean theosophy belongs to the cosmological domain—one thinks of the doctrine of signatures, the triadic nature of the Böhmean cosmos, and so forth. Böhme too offers a profoundly esoteric view of nature. But to acknowledge the primacy of the cosmological dimension in what has come to be known as Western esotericism must not entail denying the presence of a metaphysical gnostic dimension at least in some of the same currents of thought. This said, the basic principle behind Faivre's methodology— a strictly historicist approach seeking primary definitive characteristics of esotericism—is a necessary one. We need definitions of terminology and of primary concepts, and the conceptual and historicist framework informing Faivre's perspective is of great value in construing the new field.

Wouter Hanegraaff seeks to broaden approaches to the field, observing "a fully developed academic study of esotericism should give attention to all the dimensions which may be distinguished in religious traditions generally (social, ritual, experiential, doctrinal, mythic, ethical, and symbolic)."[1] He emphasizes an "empirical" approach, meaning among other things that a scholar seeks as much as possible not to apply a priori ideological constructs to esoteric subjects, but rather to approach his or her subject with an informed, open, and, so much as possible, neutral mind.[2] And he adds that "A continuing and (self-) critical dialectics of *emic* [insider] material and *etic* [academic] interpretation, in contrast, is the indispensable foundation for an empirical study of esotericism which wishes to go beyond mere description."

The way is now open for the academic study of what German scholar Kocku von Stuckrad terms the claims of higher knowledge and of paths to such knowledge that define Western esotericism.

GNOSIS

As we look over Western esotericism from antiquity to the present, we can discern one characteristic that emerges as central throughout the entire period: gnosis. The word *gnosis* here refers to assertions of direct spiritual insight into the nature of the cosmos and of oneself, and thus may be taken as having both a cosmological and a metaphysical import. Indeed, one may speak of these as two fundamental but related kinds of gnosis: under the heading of *cosmological gnosis* we may list such traditions as astrology and the various forms of -mancies such as geomancy, cartomancy, and so forth, as well as numeric, geometric, and alphabetic traditions of correspondences and analogical interpretations, traditions of natural magic based on these correspondences, and so forth. Cosmological gnosis illuminates the hidden patterns of nature as expressing spiritual or magical truths; it corresponds, more or less, to the *via positiva* of Dionysius the Areopagite. *Metaphysical gnosis,* on the other hand, represents assertions of direct insight into the transcendent; it corresponds, more or less, to the *via negativa* of Dionysius the Areopagite and is represented by gnostic figures like Meister Eckhart and Franklin Merrell-Wolff, to offer two historically disparate examples.

I choose to define esotericism primarily in terms of gnosis because gnosis, of whatever kind, is precisely what is esoteric within esotericism. *Esotericism* describes the historical phenomena to be studied; *gnosis* describes that which is esoteric, hidden, protected, and transmitted within these historical phenomena. Without hidden (or semihidden) knowledge to be transmitted in one fashion or another, one does not have esotericism. Alchemy, astrology, various kinds of magical traditions, Hermeticism, Kabbalah, Jewish or Christian visionary or apophatic gnosis—under the rubric of *Western esotericism* are a whole range of disparate phenomena connected primarily by one thing: that to enter into the particular arcane discipline is to come to realize for oneself secret knowledge about the cosmos and its transcendence. This secret or hidden knowledge is not a product of reason alone, but of gnosis—it is held to derive from a suprarational source.

Gilles Quispel, the scholar of ancient Gnosticism, has argued that European tradition may be demarcated into a triad of faith, reason, and gnosis, with gnosis being the third and hidden current of Western thought. While I do not agree with some of Quispel's Jungian premises, I do think that he is fundamentally right in proposing this triad, and further think that we cannot investigate European, American, or other categories of comparatively recent esotericisms without reference to their historical antecedents at least as far back as late antiquity. One cannot fully understand the triad of faith, reason, and gnosis without considering the full range of European history in which it manifests itself. What is more, we cannot adequately investigate, singly or comparatively, variants of esotericism without an awareness from the outset that we are entering into unfamiliar territory for the strictly rationalist or scientific mind, and that in order to understand it in any genuine way, we will have to learn at least imaginatively to enter into it.

There have already been some limited or preliminary efforts by a few scholars to begin a comparison of Gnosticism in late antiquity with Vajrayana Buddhism, with Böhmean theosophy, or with Persian Sufism, to give several examples.[3] And such efforts are bound to suggest new insights into these disparate but sometimes apparently parallel traditions or spiritual currents. But what we are discussing here is no simple matter. For while the conventional historian must work with rather straightforward historical data—dates, events, major figures—to this the historian of esotericism must also confront an entirely new additional dimension that we may as well describe from the outset as gnosis. This dimension cannot be addressed by conventional history alone, precisely because gnosis represents insight into that which is held to transcend history. A visionary revelation, for instance, occurs in time, but according to the visionary that which is revealed does not belong to time alone. As eighteenth-century visionary Jane Leade wrote, to enter into the visionary realm, one must cast off from the "shoar of time." So must the historian of esotericism attempt to do, at least imaginatively if not in fact, or his or her history may well devolve into mere reductionism and even denigration due to a failure of understanding. And this imaginative effort is all the more difficult if one is attempting to deal with not one but two culturally disparate forms of esotericism.

But this imaginative effort is critical if one is to truly begin to understand one's esoteric subject from within as well as from without. It is here that the work of Henry Corbin reveals its importance. Here I am not referring to the accuracy or lack thereof of Corbin's work—I am not a scholar of Persian spirituality—but to the effort to enter into the perspective one is studying.[4] This is the adventure the study of esotericism offers the scholar that few other fields can present. In the future, comparative esotericism will take its place as a subspecialty, but for now the field as a whole is in its infancy, with vast primary research yet to be done, whole histories yet to be written. Before we can compare European alchemy with that of South India, we must first have a firm grasp of European alchemy itself! And that is a goal as yet not attained, one that will require not only a wide range of knowledge, but also the imaginative capacity to interpret it.

While it may not always be easy to chart a course between the extremes of wholly embracing and wholly rejecting esotericism, this is what is necessary if we are to come to understand this complex and subtle field. An investigator must attempt to understand the world in almost certainly unfamiliar ways, and this requires a sympathetic approach to various figures, writings, and works of art, open to the unexpected, yet also retaining some sense of critical distance. Western esotericism as it is outlined in this book is a vast and profound area for research, one that could perhaps best be characterized as a long series of different investigations into the nature of consciousness itself. It is entirely possible that an investigation into it will discover in its various forms of cosmological or metaphysical gnoses unexpected insights into hidden aspects of nature, of humanity, and of spirituality.

Central to these insights is the relationship between self and other, or subject and object. In an article published in the *Journal of Consciousness Studies*, I argue that

> Western esotericism tends to see and use language in a fundamentally different way than many of us are familiar with—here, language is used not for conventional designation in a subject-object relationship, but in order to transmute consciousness or to point toward the transmutation of consciousness through what we may term hieroeidetic knowledge. Be it Kabbalism or alchemy, troubadours and chivalry, the Lullian art, magic or theosophy, pansophy or esoteric Rosicrucianism or Freemasonry, one finds a consistently recurrent theme of transmuting consciousness, which is to say, of awakening latent, profound connections between humanity, nature, and the divine, and of restoring a paradisal union between them. Hieroeidetic knowledge can be understood in terms of a shift from an objectifying view of language based on self and other to a view of language as revelatory, as a *via positiva* leading toward transcendence of self-other divisions. It is here, in their emphasis on the initiatory, hieroeidetic power of lan-

guage to reveal what transcends language, that the unique contribution of Western esoteric traditions to consciousness studies may well be found.

Near the end of this article, I remark that

> The massive edifice of the modern technological, consumerist state was built from a materialist, secular, and objectified worldview, and the participatory, transformative, and gnostic perspectives characterizing Western esotericism seem far removed from and incompatible with that edifice. Still, for the first time now there are numerous scholars examining both Western esotericism as a general concept, and particular currents within esotericism, and it may well be that such studies will eventually offer unexpected insights into the historical origins of the modern era, as well as further insight into the relationships between Western esoteric traditions and consciousness.[5]

It is important to recognize how different are the premises of Western esoteric traditions from modern ways of thinking and understanding, and how by entering into these currents of thought we may indeed see our own world in new ways.

If Western esotericism is to fully develop as a field of scholarly inquiry, its unique nature must be recognized. Most unique about it is not its transdisciplinary nature alone, but the fact that its manifold currents are each concerned with new ways of knowing, with the transcendence of the self-other dichotomy, be it through initiatory literature, alchemical or magical work, visionary experience, or apophatic gnosis.[6] While purely historical research obviously has its place in this field, the most important works may be those that suggest new ways of seeing and knowing. Perhaps some of the most vital and profound contributions of this fascinating field will be in areas like consciousness studies, but in any case, we can be sure that there is much more yet to be discovered.

SUGGESTED READING

There are many works cited in the notes, and it would be superfluous to repeat them here. Rather, it may be more useful to suggest some books and sources for further investigation in this area. In particular, readers interested in Western esotericism as a field of inquiry should consult the numerous works of Antoine Faivre, among them *Access to Western Esotericism* (Albany: SUNY Press, 1994) and its sequel, *Theosophy, Imagination, Tradition* (Albany: SUNY Press, 2000). Readers are certainly encouraged to consult the monumental reference work presided over by Wouter Hanegraaff, Antoine

Faivre, Roelof van den Broek, and Jean-Pierre Brach: the two-volume *Dictionary of Gnosis and Western Esotericism* (Leiden: Brill, 2005).

A general introduction to the field is Kocku von Stuckrad's *Western Esotericism: A Brief History of Secret Knowledge* (London: Equinox, 2005), and for a more popular approach, readers may consider Richard Smoley and Jay Kinney, *Hidden Wisdom: A Guide to the Western Inner Traditions* (Wheaton, IL: Quest, 2006). Readers interested in literature, art, and esotericism may be interested in Arthur Versluis, *Restoring Paradise* (Albany: SUNY Press, 2004). A wide variety of related topics are covered in the academic journal ARIES and in *Esoterica* (www.esoteric.msu.edu), and there are annual conferences sponsored by two affiliated organizations: the North American ASE (Association for the Study of Esotericism) and the European ESSWE (European Society for the Study of Western Esotericism). As to the study of magic, there is an important book series published by Pennsylvania State University Press, and a journal, *Magic, Ritual, and Witchcraft*. Prominent scholars in this field include Richard Kiekhefer and Claire Fanger, the latter also being instrumental in the scholarly organization Societas Magica. Jewish mysticism and Kabbalah is a field of its own, to a considerable extent founded by Gershom Scholem, and continued by well-known and prolific scholars like Moshe Idel and Elliot Wolfson. The study of Christian mysticism has perhaps lagged somewhat by comparison to the academic study of magic or of Jewish mysticism, but some areas have been mapped. Bernard McGinn's series *Presence of God: A History of Western Christian Mysticism*, beginning with *The Foundations of Mysticism* (New York: Herder, 1994), is an excellent historical survey. An interesting alternative approach is that of consciousness studies, as represented by scholars like Robert Forman and by the *Journal of Consciousness Studies*. Scholarly investigation into all of these areas continues—we can anticipate much more will emerge in coming years.

NOTES

1. See Wouter Hanegraaff, "On the Construction of 'Esoteric Traditions,'" in *Western Esotericism and the Science of Religion* (Leuven: Peeters, 1999): 42–43.

2. Hanegraaff, "On the Construction of 'Esoteric Traditions,'" 13.

3. See Versluis, "Christian Theosophy and Gnosticism," *Studies in Spirituality* 7 (1997): 228–41. John Reynolds and Keith Dowman, both pioneering translators and interpreters of Tibetan Buddhism, have employed the term *gnosis* in their analyses of Dzogchen and other advanced Buddhist practices. Reynolds has even indicated, in private correspondence, that he is interested in publishing a book comparing Gnosticism in antiquity with Vajrayana Buddhism, which he thinks may be historically linked. See John Myrdhin Reynolds, *The Golden Letters: The Three Statements of*

Garab Dorje (Ithaca, NY: Snow Lion, 1996): 110, 122, 205, 270; and see Keith Dowman, *Sky Dancer: The Secret Life and Songs of the Lady Yeshe Tsogyal* (London: Arkana, 1984), 333, for examples of his use of the term *gnosis* in translating a Buddhist concept.

4. The comparative work of Henry Corbin includes such titles as *L'Imagination créatrice dans le soufisme d'Ibn 'Arabi* (1958) *[Creative Imagination in the Sufism of Ibn Arabi]* (Princeton, NJ: Princeton University Press, 1969); *Terre céleste et corps de résurrection* (1960) *[Spiritual Body and Celestial Earth]* (Princeton, NJ: Princeton University Press, 1977); and *Temple et contemplation* (Paris: Flammarion, 1980). Corbin's work goes beyond what we might usually think of as the domain of scholarship into new terrain. Corbin's work has been quite influential for a number of poets, artists, and authors, as witness the Temenos Academy and the journal *Temenos*, founded by British poet and scholar Kathleen Raine, and the writings of psychologists such as James Hillman or Robert Sardello.

5. See Arthur Versluis, "Western Esotericism and Consciousness," *Journal of Consciousness Studies* 7 (2000) 6: 20–33.

6. On the initiatory functions of literature, see Arthur Versluis, *Restoring Paradise: Western Esotericism, Literature, Art and Consciousness* (Albany: SUNY Press, 2004), esp. 1–15.

Index

About the Author

Arthur Versluis is professor of American Studies at Michigan State University, the founding president of the Association for the Study of Esotericism, and the editor in chief of *Esoterica*, an electronic journal devoted to the academic study of esotericism. Among his books are *The New Inquisitions: Heretic-hunting and the Intellectual Origins of Modern Totalitarianism; Restoring Paradise: Esoteric Transmission through Literature and Art; The Esoteric Origins of the American Renaissance; Wisdom's Book: The Sophia Anthology; and Wisdom's Children: A Christian Esoteric Tradition.* He was awarded a Fulbright Fellowship for study and teaching in Germany, and has traveled and researched extensively in England, Europe, and Asia. His website is www.arthurversluis.com.